The Making of Modern Agriculture

The Making of Modern Agriculture

Nelson Rockefeller's American International Association (AIA) in Latin America (1946–1968)

Claiton Marcio da Silva

First published 2023 by
The White Horse Press, The Old Vicarage, Winwick, Cambridgeshire PE28 5PN

Set in 11 point Adobe Garamond Pro

British Library Cataloguing in Publication Data
A catalogue record for this book is available from the British Library

ISBN 978-1-912186-69-3 (HB); e-ISBN 978-1-912186-70-9

CONTENTS

LIST OF ILLUSTRATIONS

LIST OF ABBREVIATIONS

ABCAR: Associação Brasileira de Crédito e Assistência Rural (Brazilian Association of Credit and Rural Assistance)

ACAR: Associação de Crédito e Assistência Rural de Minas Gerais (Association of Credit and Rural Assistance of Minas Gerais)

ACARESC: Associação de Crédito e Assistência Rural de Santa Catarina (Association for Credit and Rural Assistance of Santa Catarina

ACARPA: Associação de Crédito e Assistência Rural do Paraná (Association for Credit and Rural Assistance of Paraná, ACARPA

AIA: American International Association for Economic and Social Development

ANCAR: Associação Nordestina de Crédito e Assistência Rural (Northeastern Association for Credit and Rural Assistance)

ANCARBA: Associação Nordestina de Crédito e Assistência Rural da Bahia (Northeastern Association for Credit and Rural Assistance, State of Bahia)

ANCAR – RN: Associação Nordestina de Crédito e Assistência Rural do Rio Grande do Norte (Northeastern Association for Credit and Rural Assistance, State of Rio Grande do Norte)

ANCARCE: Associação Nordestina de Crédito e Assistência Rural do Ceará (Northeastern Association for Credit and Rural Assistance, State of Ceará)

ANCARPA: Associação Nordestina de Crédito e Assistência Rural da Paraíba (Northeastern Association for Credit and Rural Assistance, State of Paraíba)

ANCARPE: Associação Nordestina de Crédito e Assistência Rural de Pernambuco (Northeastern Association for Credit and Rural Assistance, State of Pernambuco)

ANCARSE: Associação Nordestina de Crédito e Assistência Rural do Sergipe (Northeastern Association for Credit and Rural Assistance, State of Sergipe)

APCAR: Associação Paulista de Assistência e Crédito Rural (São Paulo Association for Credit and Rural Assistance)

ASCAR: Associação Sulina de Crédito e Assistência Rural (Southern Association for Credit and Rural Assistance)

CBR: Consejo de Bienestar Rural (Rural Welfare Council)

CIDEA: Consejo Interamericano de Educación Alimenticia (Inter-American Council of Nutrition Education)

CVF: Corporación Venezoelana de Fomento (Venezuelan Development Corporation)

DNPEA: Departamento Nacional de Pesquisa Agrícola (National Department of Agricultural Research)

ECA: Economic Cooperation Administration

EMA: Empresa de Mecanização Agrícola (Agricultural Mechanization Company)

ESALQ: Escola Superior de Agricultura Luiz de Queiroz (Luiz de Queiroz College of Agriculture)

ESAV: Escola Superior de Agricultura e Veterinária de Viçosa (Viçosa College of Agriculture)

ETA: Escritório Técnico de Agricultura Brasil-Estados Unidos (Brazil/U.S. Technical Agriculture Office)

FAO: United Nations Food and Agriculture Organization

FIEMG: Federação das Indústrias do Estado de Minas Gerais (Federation of State Industries of Minas Gerais)

FmHA: Farmers Home Administration

FSA: Farm Security Administration

FSD: Food Supply Division

IAC: Instituto Agronômico de Campinas (Agronomic Institute of Campinas)

IAIAS: Inter-American Institute of Agricultural Sciences

IBEC: International Basic Economy Corporation

IIAA: Institute of Inter-American Affairs

IRI: IBEC Research Inc. or IRI Research Institute

ITIC: Instituto Técnico de Imigración y Colonización (Technical Institute of Immigration and Colonization)

JICA: Japan International Cooperation Agency

NCRSP: National Committee on Rural Social Planning

OIAA: Office of the Coordinator of Inter-American Affairs

PSD: Partido Social Democrático (Social Democratic Party)

PTB: Partido Trabalhista Brasileiro (Brazilian Labor Party)

RA: Ressetlement Administration

RBF: Rockefeller Brothers Fund

SAPS: Serviço de Alimentação da Previdência Social (Social Welfare Food Service)

SASA: Sementes Agroceres S/A (Sementes Agroceres Limited Liability Corporation)

SESP: Serviço Especial de Saúde Pública (Special Service on Public Health)

SBF: Simon Bolivar Foundation or Bolivar Foundation

SVA: Setor de Visitação Alimentar (Food Visitation Sector)

UDN: União Democrática Nacional (National Democratic Union Party)

USAID: United States Agency for International Development

USDA: United States Department of Agriculture

VBEC: Venezuelan Basic Economy Corporation

ACKNOWLEDGEMENTS

This book is both a direct and an indirect result of almost two decades of research, with sporadic hiatuses, although I have kept the subject close at hand – at least in my imagination. After having written a regional history study about the emergence of 4-S Clubs – an adaptation of the US 4-H Clubs – during the Brazilian civil-military dictatorship, I received a valid suggestion from Professor Robert Wegner about the importance of studying international agencies in the consolidation of agriculture and sanitation policies in Latin America. In 2005 I started my Ph.D. at the Oswaldo Cruz University in Rio de Janeiro, diving into a transnational history of Brazil and the United States through the influence of the American International Association for Economic and International Development – Nelson Rockefeller's AIA. During an intense winter in 2007–2008, I had the pleasure of developing a doctoral internship at the University of Guelph, Canada, under the supervision of Professor Stuart McCook. During my first stay in North America, I also had the opportunity to visit archives such as the Rockefeller Archive Center and, back in Brazil, I wrote my Ph.D. dissertation, defended in 2009. In this first phase, professors Robert Wegner and Stuart McCook played a fundamental role in the elaboration of my arguments. I am very grateful to both of them, as well as to other colleagues at COC/Fiocruz with whom I had the opportunity of sharing my training process: professors Dominichi Miranda de Sá, Magali Romero de Sá, Gilberto Hochman and Nísia Trindade Lima, as well as students such as Vanderlei Sebastião de Souza, André Felipe Cândido da Silva and Rômulo de Paula Andrade. Eventually, a shortened version of my Ph.D. dissertation was published in Portuguese in 2015.

But the work I present here for the first time in English is completely rewritten, adding new arguments and updated literature and, finally, expanding the regions studied. *The Making of Modern Agriculture* remains an AIA study, but now including several countries in Latin America and, to a lesser extent, Asia, pursuing the relationships between science, politics and socio-environmental change. My thanks for this 'second phase' of AIA research must mention the constant academic exchanges with my colleagues Jó Klanovicz (Unicentro), Samira Moretto, Marlon Brandt, Delmir Valentini, and José Radin (all from UFFS, who also stood in for me at various times to enable my work to progress), as well as my Master's students who embarked on the topic of agricultural modernisation and environmental history. During this period, I also had the pleasure of meeting new colleagues interested in the Rockefellers' work, such as Antônio Pedro Tota, Maria Gabriela Marinho, Ryan Nehring, Cliff Welch, João Márcio Mendes Pereira, Sandro Dutra, Shane Hamilton and Ursula Prutsch, among many others. I also thank Professor Deborah Fitzgerald and colleague Willian San Martin for the excellent suggestions about the progress of my work during my stay at MIT. I express special thanks to the Rachel Carson Center for Environment and Society at the Ludwig-Maximilian University of Munich, where I found a very favourable environment for the advancement of my readings on Latin America. In particular, colleagues like Roberta Biasillo and Serenella Iovino opened many theoretical perspectives that are, even if briefly, inserted here. Also, special thanks to my friend Claudio de Majo, with whom I wrote a number of articles and co-edited a book during this period. Finally, after the defence of my Ph.D. dissertation, I returned to the Rockefeller Archive Center, as well as researching in the library and database of MIT, the Rachel Carson Center, the Emater libraries (Minas Gerais) and the Epagri collection (Santa Catarina), where I was always well received and to all of whom I express my sincere thanks! I also acknowledge the Coordination of Superior Level Staff Improvement, the Conselho Nacional de Desenvolvimento Científico e Tecnológico (CNPq), the Universidade Federal da Fronteira Sul (UFFS) and the Rockefeller Archive Center for providing the fellowships and grants that enabled me to conduct this research. Fortunately, I was able to count on the reading of the original by several readers and translators, whom I thank: Claire Lagier, Earl Richard Downes and, most recently, my dedicated editor Sarah Johnson. Thank you for your patience and suggestive reading!

None of this would be possible without the support of Marina Andrioli, and more recently, our beloved Martina Luísa, to whom I dedicate this work.

PREFACE

It is an honour to write the foreword to *The Making of Modern Agriculture*. This is the third iteration of Claiton da Silva's work exploring the development work of Nelson Rockefeller's AIA. The initial project was his doctoral dissertation for the Fundação Oswaldo Cruz; this version focused on the AIA's work in Brazil. In 2015, he published a revised and expanded version of the dissertation as *De agricultor a farmer: Nelson Rockefeller e a modernização da agricultura no Brasil*. Since then, he has been researching and writing prolifically – in both Portuguese and English – on a wide range of themes and topics, most of which explore the often contentious process of agricultural modernisation in Brazil, and in the Global South more generally. *The Making of Modern Agriculture* is much more than an English-language translation of *De agricultor a farmer*. It is a larger, more ambitious, book that situates the AIA's work in Brazil in a global framework, and engages in larger scholarly conversations. It makes one of da Silva's most important contributions accessible to English-speaking audiences.

The Making of Modern Agriculture joins the recent surge of historical writing on post World War II agricultural modernisation programmes. Much of this writing focuses on the green revolution, a Cold War programme of technological modernisation focused on increasing the productivity of key food crops. American foundations, especially the Rockefeller and Ford Foundations, played key roles in this 'diplomacy of private enterprise'. The Rockefeller and Ford Foundations, in particular, emphasised scientific and technological improvements in agricultural productivity. They promoted and implemented green revolution technologies around the globe, especially in Asia and the Pacific.

The Making of Modern Agriculture focuses on a different model of agricultural development, promoted by Nelson A. Rockefeller's American International Association for Economic and Social Development (AIA). The AIA's projects focused primarily on promoting the health of rural workers, and providing agricultural credit. While *The Making of Modern Agriculture* is rooted in the AIA's work in Brazil, da Silva situates these events in global, regional and local contexts. He shows how the AIA's work in Brazil was informed by its experiences elsewhere, especially in Venezuela, and later in China and India – as well as the prior experience of the AIA staff in the United States during the Great Depression and World War II. As such, *The Making of Modern Agriculture* is an important contribution on the role of science, technology and expertise in the global Cold War.

Like many other technical assistance organisations in these years, the AIA presented itself as fundamentally apolitical. This technocratic vision of agricultural modernisation preceded the Cold War. But Truman's Point Four programmes made this vision a core part of US foreign policy during the Cold War, a move that was *inherently* political. In compelling small vignettes, da Silva shows us how different Brazilians interpreted the AIA's technocratic mission. Some inhabitants of the rural municipality of Martins Guimarães apparently thought the officially secular ACAR was a American 'communist' project; in the municipality of Machado, the Catholic priest complained that the local ACAR home economist was a Protestant and asked that she be dismissed. In a different context, however, Juscelino Kubitschek and some political leaders in Brazil wanted American officials to continue leading ACAR, since that way the organisation would 'stay away from [domestic] political issues' and 'provide an atmosphere of neutrality'. The rhetoric of technocratic neutrality was, and remains, politically loaded – in spite of what its advocates say.

Da Silva pays careful attention to political and institutional power at different scales, and moves effortlessly between different levels of analysis. Histories of agricultural modernisation often focus on the nation-state as the unit of analysis. While nation-states matters to this story, his analysis of the AIA's work in Brazil moves seamlessly between the national, state and municipal scales. He shows how actors at each level shaped the development of the AIA's projects. In the Brazilian story, the state governments that stand out as the main actors, especially in the powerful central states of São Paulo and Minas Gerais. Key governors – Milton Campos and Juscelino Kubitschek, among others – played an instrumental role in facilitating and promoting the AIA's work in their home states. These and other powerful governors also influenced the national government to promote and ultimately nationalise the AIA's initiatives – especially when Kubitschek was elected president.

Above all else, *The Making of Modern Agriculture* serves as a compelling exploration of the development agendas of Latin Americans themselves. The landscapes, peoples and institutions of Latin America were not developmental blank slates, upon which agents of the AIA could develop their ideas and programmes. Rather, the work of the AIA succeeded in places to the extent that they could align their vision of development with those of the political and economic leaders in the places they worked. And, as da Silva shows, the lines of influence worked both ways; the AIA had to adapt or abandon plans that did not align smoothly with the local needs or interests. 'Development', he argues in the conclusion, is 'polysemous'. And contested, and constantly evolving.

The Making of Modern Agriculture embraces this complexity and navigates it skilfully, all the while resisting simplistic, reductive answers. In the end, this is much more than a history of the AIA; it is a reflection on the practice and politics of development – then, and now.

Stuart McCook

INTRODUCTION: DRAFTING A NEW WORLD FROM A MANHATTAN OFFICE

In 1974, while attending a second session of the Judiciary Committee of the House of the Representatives, Nelson Rockefeller (1908–1979) evoked his war experience to argue for his nomination as Vice President. 'The Nazi propaganda during the war', he said, was 'our real adversary down there' in South America. Answering more than a hundred questions in the course of ten days, Rockefeller summarised what 'they said' – or the German-Nazi rhetoric against the US: 'This was a nip-and-tuck proposition, their propaganda was the United States [would] drop you like a hot potato as soon as this war is over. They have no real interest in you.' Rockefeller went on to affirm that he felt a personal identification with Latin-American people and governments and that he had therefore taken a different approach from that of typical US official diplomacy. After the war, this self-proclaimed identification with Latin Americans led him to set up two corporations. The first was a nonprofit, the American International Association for Social and Economic Development (AIA), 'to undertake cooperative ventures with governments in agriculture extension, agricultural credit, in education and in other fields of government services'.[1] The other, the International Basic Economy Co. (IBEC), was primarily concerned with the 'development, distribution, and selling foodstuffs, housing, and other things that related to their basic economy'.[2] Answering questions retrospectively about his decades of involvement in Latin America, Rockefeller hinted at his plans to reinvent Latin America after 1945, something he had been, to a certain extent, because of his political influence and economic power, in a position to try.

The focus of this book is the philanthropic work of the AIA in agriculture between 1946 and 1968 in Latin America, primarily in Brazil and Venezuela,

1. Hearings before the Committee on the Judiciary House of the Representatives. Second Session on Nomination of Nelson Rockefeller to be Vice President of the United States. (Washington: US Government Print Office, 1974).

2. Hearings before the Committee on the Judiciary House of the Representatives. Second Session on Nomination of Nelson Rockefeller to be Vice President of the United States. (Washington: US Government Print Office, 1974). For a detailed history of IBEC, see Darlene Rivas, *Missionary Capitalist: Nelson Rockefeller in Venezuela* (Chapel Hill, North Carolina: University of North Carolina Press, 2002); and Shane Hamilton, *Supermarket USA. Food and Power in the Cold War Farms Race* (New Haven and London: Yale University Press, 2018)..

although with programmes also carried out in India and China for a brief period. Throughout the 22 years of its work, the AIA supported supervised rural credit, land reform planning, agricultural extension, rural youth club work and health and vocational education, motivated by the fact that government policymakers and private institutions considered the health of workers to be as precarious as their agricultural techniques. According to the AIA journalist Martha Dalrymple – who published the AIA official history entitled *The AIA Story* in 1968 – the agency 'had an objective that is much simpler than its name. It was set up to do things that needed to be done but that nobody else was doing, and it was set up to be impermanent.' Then, 'its whole method of operation was to encourage self-development, to improve living standards, in general to help make life a little better for people in the less fortunate areas of the world, and then to help them to do it for themselves'.[3]

Due to Latin America's strategic position and its support of the Allies against the Nazis, some Latin American leaders as well as US businessmen and politicians – among them Nelson Rockefeller – understood that US diplomacy should maintain solid relations based on financial aid with the entire continent. With the Truman administration directing more and more of its energies and resources to the recovery of a devastated Europe, foundations like Ford and Rockefeller, and associations like AIA, IBEC and the later IBEC Research Institute (IRI), founded in 1950 and also linked to Nelson Rockefeller, would play an important role in maintaining and expanding international relations between the United States and Latin America – and part of what we now understand as the Global South – through a diplomacy of private enterprise. Even though they were financially supported by some of the most powerful families on the planet at the time, these agencies did not command resources comparable to the Marshall Plan. In the case of the AIA, though, their activities were extremely influential, albeit controversial at times. This is because, although there had been agronomic institutes and colleges in Latin America since the late nineteenth century, the work of the AIA in conjunction with local governments inaugurated a model of agricultural development that expanded throughout the region.[4]

3. Martha Dalrymple, *The AIA Story: Two Decades of International Cooperation* (New York: AIA, 1968), p. 1

4. See Claiton Marcio da Silva, *De agricultor a farmer. Nelson Rockefeller e a modernização da agricultura no Brasil* (Guarapuava/Curitiba: Unicentro/UFPR, 2015). See also Herbert Klein and Francisco Vidal Luna, *Feeding the World. Brazil's Transformation into a Modern Agricultural Economy* (Cambridge: Cambridge University Press), ch. 4.

In a general sense, therefore, this book recounts relations between the United States and Latin America from the 1940s to the 1960s, addressing the work of the AIA in Latin America. As Rockefeller explained, the AIA worked on small-scale technical assistance projects, aiming to nationalise these services in order to support Latin American governments – especially in Venezuela and Brazil.[5] More specifically, this book argues that the AIA's activities were guided by a new form of intervention in Latin America, away from the Big Stick Policy and closer to a benevolent rhetoric. Ideally, the AIA aimed to serve as a bridge by which the successful projects of the Good Neighbor Policy would reach the post-war world, no longer as state policy, but as diplomacy enacted by private groups.

Even though the AIA is contemporary with the dramatic changes in global agriculture of the post-1945 period, it is a mistake to affirm that agencies like the AIA worked simply as propagators of the technical packages of the green revolution. In fact, the AIA had among its technical staff some experienced professionals, who preferred certain technological innovations but sought practical and cheap solutions, sometimes better adapted to the local ecology. Including the point of view of Latin Americans in the analysis, my central argument refutes the literature's portrayal of uncomplicated acceptance of the AIA's programmes within Latin American institutions and rural society. Challenging this one-sided view, my anti- and post-colonial analysis demonstrates that the AIA's projects needed to negotiate and adapt to local and institutional resistance. Based on unpublished primary sources, I demonstrate how the AIA followed non-place based, theoretical paths to put into practice its ideology of development and modernisation. Foregrounding aspects such as the lack of knowledge about the culture of local people and their traditional knowledge, the inconsistencies of bureaucratic political elites, and the stubborn insistence on replicating programmes created in the United States for countries labelled as underdeveloped enable this book to present a different approach from the literature on Nelson Rockefeller and the AIA. Unlike other accounts, it weaves together the relationships between different agents, considering Latin Americans' capacity for historical agency.

Some scholars demonstrate that economic or materialistic arguments have dominated the academic approach to US-Latin American relations since the 1960s. The liberal tradition of studies highlights a missionary calling in the foundation of the AIA: to help peoples then considered underdeveloped to

5. On Brazil, see da Silva, *De agricultor a farmer*. See also Rivas, *Missionary Capitalist* and Hamilton, *Supermarket USA*.

encounter development[6] – an aim best formulated in John Dewey's philosophical pragmatism. Alternatively, from a materialistic or structuralist perspective, this agency would be considered more as an instrument in the complex US imperialist apparatus planning the domination of Latin America than as a missionary agency.[7] In recent decades, with the renewal of studies on relations between the US and Latin America, scholars have added other variables to the discussion, broadening interpretations previously guided by ideological or simply economic realms of international relations. Analytical oppositions such as mission or imperialism, conflict or agreement, domination or resistance, which dominated the debate up to the 1980s, did not explore the full complexity of the power relations involved. Questioning these interpretative limitations, historian Darlene Rivas argues that the historiography of US/Latin American relations incorporated the concept of culture into the discussion in the late 1990s, although mainly in the context of economic development and the emergence of a consumer culture in the twentieth century.[8] Meanwhile, post-colonial studies have provided a new perspective by linking discursive strategies, power relations and material practices to understand the complex interactions between the different governmental and non-governmental actors involved in the post-colonial venture or encounter.[9] More recently, environmental studies have the potential to develop aspects that better assess the impact of foundations such as Rockefeller and AIA in Latin America – although there are still very few studies on the Rockefellers in these terms, though research is well developed in terms of history of sciences and medicine.

The experience of Nelson Rockefeller and the AIA offers an important case study for interpreting not only the classic issues surrounding such encounters – such as relations of domination, imperialism, resistance and mission – but also the importance of Latin Americans themselves in the reconfiguration of relations between the US and Latin America. The first wave of literature (up to the late 1990s) on both the AIA's work and Nelson Rockefeller's experience in Latin America explored, with some exceptions, conceptual binaries such as mission/imperialism, philanthropy/domination. The late 1990s renewal of historical studies on relations between the United States and Latin America provided new approaches that, in turn, demonstrated greater complexity in

6. Darlene Rivas, *Missionary Capitalist.*
7. Ibid.
8. Ibid.
9. Cecília Azevedo, *Em nome da América: os Corpos de Paz no Brasil (1961–1981)* (Rio de Janeiro: Alameda, 2008).

economic, political, social, cultural and environmental relations. From this perspective, by exploring unpublished primary sources, the present volume discusses the complex entanglements between technological modernisation and environmental-cultural change, combining macro and micro-scale analyses. Its core argument is that diverse national and local relations, characterised by a mix of support and resistance, shaped the negotiations that framed the AIA's work in Latin America. As historian Daniel Immerwahr reminds us, modernisation refers to a political vision: 'the desire to achieve a particular social configuration in which institutions are oriented toward industry, governed by urban norms, shaped by bureaucratic practices, and centralized to a significant degree'. In some aspects, the term development 'is often used as a synonym for modernization'; however, Immerwahr refers to development as a way to achieving 'increase of social capacity'.[10] At least before the rise of Walt Whitman Rostow's Modernization Theory in late 1950s, experts entangled words such 'to modernise' and 'to develop' in different programmes, and sometimes obliterated them in rhetoric that preferred to incorporate local concepts. Overall, these concepts carried the desire to break with traditional knowledge; as Immerwahr summarises, 'modernization is one form of development, but it may be possible to improve people's lives without centralizing their institutions'. This need not mean, 'they [want] to return to the past' but rather that 'they [have] mapped out an alternate route forward', summarised as 'development without modernization'.[11] Last but not least, modernisation should, according to Rostow and some of his contemporaries, such as British conservative politician Cyril Black, be placed above democracy. This means that, when the imperatives of modernisation conflict with democratic autonomy, the latter should be sacrificed for the sake of the former.[12]

In this book, I demonstrate how some decisions about how to implement modernisation projects were driven from a luxurious office in Rockefeller Plaza, New York. But, gradually, these decisions were increasingly informed by reports from AIA technicians and directors working in Latin America, showing how the Association's wishes clashed with those of local governments and socioenvironmental actors. Therefore, this book doesn't only discuss the plans of US agents, but how the interests of local governments and actors interfered

10. Daniel Immerwahr, *Thinking Small. The United States and the Lure of Community Development* (Cambridge, Massachusetts; London: Harvard University Press, 2015).

11. Ibid.

12. João Feres Jr. *A história do conceito de Latin America nos Estados Unidos* (Bauru: Edusc, 2005), p. 105.

with and modified the original modernisation projects. We will thus gain an idea of how modernisation and development are concepts that are tested in certain realities: their materialisation carries within it new 'genes' added from the places where the programmes were applied, and possibly incorporated into new conceptions. By this argument, we can think of a hypothetical programme initiated during the Great Depression by the US Farm Security Administration, tested in Brazil by the AIA in the 1950s and, due to application difficulties, having its initial notion reformulated. Later, this 'hybrid' programme might have been developed by the Ford Foundation in India and, according to local needs, have had to undergo new adaptations.

We can question a diffusionist analysis by understanding that certain aspects of the relations between the US and Latin America depend on situational variables; even if at different, unequal levels of power, it is important to discuss how Latin America also influenced the empire. Following this perspective, I ask whether the actions of these agents figured as mission or imperialism, but I also explore how the AIA modified its ideals by establishing relationships that responded to geopolitical stimuli, national issues, regional political arrangements and unique historical characteristics. In summary, in the macro context, the AIA was not only an immovable reflection of the geopolitics of the Cold War, but also an important agent – along with the Ford Foundation, Carnegie, Rockefeller and the World Bank – in consolidating a political agenda for Latin America under the aegis of Point Four and the Alliance for Progress.[13] While a scholar such as Parmar focuses – in his study about the 'Big 3' Ford, Carnegie and Rockefeller Foundations – on the role of private enterprise through philanthropy in constructing the US hegemony,[14] my focus is on the role of agricultural experts in mediating social and cultural transformation through programmes of rural development.

Chronologically, the work of the AIA is part of the Cold War; historically, it resonates with important US ideologies rooted in the nineteenth century, such as Manifest Destiny, the Frontier myth and the Yeomanry; with Theodore

13. The Point Four and Alliance for Progress were programmes that marked the renewal of US foreign policy toward a more internationalist approach, spurring geopolitical hegemony after 1945. See Arturo Escobar, *Encountering Development. The Making and Unmaking of the Third world* (Princeton, New Jersey: Princeton University Press, 1995). See also Felipe Loureiro, *A Aliança para o Progresso e o governo João Goulart (1961–1964). Ajuda econômica norte-americana a estados brasileiros e a desestabilização da democracia no Brasil pós-guerra* (São Paulo: Editora da UNESP, 2020).

14. Interjeet Parmar, *Foundations of the American Century: The Ford, Carnegie, and Rockefeller Foundations in the Rise of American Power* (New York: Columbia, 2012), p. 2.

Roosevelt's progressivism; the ideals of industrialisation of agriculture of the 1920s; and certain characteristics of the New Deal, such as providing land for poor blacks in the South or Mid-West. In this book, I address in general terms these ideologies, which, although different in time and space, have connections mainly as they concern agricultural activities. In the imaginary related to the advance to the West, mythologised by authors such as historian Frederick Jackson Turner, rural life and agriculture played a fundamental role in the construction of civilisation; the socio-political imaginary of the nineteenth-century United States was shaped by the attraction of a 'free land', drawing populations to the lands beyond the Alleghany mountains, the Mississippi valley and above the plateaus and mountains of the far west.

Classic authors such as Henry Nash Smith have understood that the process of constituting the socio-political ideals of the American nation recurrently projected the image of an Empire. One group manifested an interest in controlling the oceans in the manner of the British navy; to another, the notion of success was a numerically populous society occupying the interior of the continent. Although not opposed in their entirety, these ideas were based on different economic policies, the first inspired by the mercantile practices of the British, and the second requiring a demographic increase with the creation of new states to the west resulting from agricultural expansion into an 'empty' and fertile territory. Although both theses required the expansion of territory to the West – the first would aim to reach the Pacific Ocean – the second turned out to be closer to the actual course of history in the nineteenth century: an 'American Empire based on agrarian assumptions'.[15] More specifically, the frontier, in this perspective, is not established as static, but as the result of successive human experimentation, imposed by economic and environmental conditions: first there is a reversion to the primitive, followed by a succession of frontier types that brought high levels of enterprise and complexity. In historiographical terms, the progressivism of Turner, Charles Beard and Vernon Louis Parrington consolidated ideals that were intended to free man from the

15. Henry Nash Smith, *Virgin Land. The American West as Symbol and Myth* (Cambridge: Harvard University Press, 1971), p. 3. The notion of free lands in the West influenced social thought by Benjamin Franklin, Emerson, Lincoln, Whitman and others. But this imaginary was consolidated at the end of the 19th century and lasted until the 1950s through the work of the aforementioned Wisconsin historian, Frederick Jackson Turner. Frederick Jackson Turner, 'The significance of the frontier in American History, 1893', in John Mack Faragher (ed.), *Rereading Frederick Jackson Turner* (New York: Holt, 1994), pp. 31–60. Although there is some question about the permanence of the frontier myth after WWII, we will observe throughout this book how this was a recurring theme for characters like John Camp and Walter Crawford.

past and ensure the qualities of the New World as opposed to the Old. Thus, believing in the fundamental newness of the new land, this movement needed to believe that when something was not going well, injustices and reactionary interests were hindering the natural development of a naturally democratic people and a just society.[16] I do not consider the efforts of international agencies during the Cold War to be a simple echo of the expansionist imaginary; rather, I argue that, in a certain time and space, the ideal of farmers occupying the 'empty lands' of Latin America would be taken up by AIA to justify a liberal and democratic society, sometimes amalgamating with agrarian ideals based on latifundia and with still visible scars of plantation slavery. In countries like Brazil, the notion of 'free lands' to the West and successive comparisons with the myth of the US frontier fomented the debate and legitimised conquering hinterlands: 'the last great frontier of the Western Hemisphere now lies south of Rio Grande',[17] asserted Texas A&M Dean E.J. Kyle during his 1943 visit to Nelson Rockefeller in Latin America; 'fortunately', John Camp would say in the early 1960s, Brazil has a large empty frontier area offering prospects for the development of a new rural economy. According to him, the opening of a new 'West' in Brazil should be conducted in the same manner as the opening of the US West under the Homestead Act after the Civil War.[18]

In addition, programmes such as Point Four and the Alliance for Progress synthesised some of the principles present in nineteenth and early twentiethth century ideologies, incorporating them into larger prescriptive models of development and modernisation – above all, the temporality of programmes like the Alliance for Progress is posited as diachronic, meaning that the United States experiences a different *tempo* from that of Latin America, which in its future will achieve similar progress as long as it adopts the prescriptions of modernisation. Moreover, Americanisation here also means a multiple experience of exchange, liked that addressed by Hodge in his study on the legacies of British colonialism. Hodge's argument may be adapted to this topic to understand, 'the way development as a framework of ideas and practices emerged out of efforts to manage the social, economic, and ecological crises of the late colonial

16. Lucia Lippi de Oliverira, *Americanos: representações de identidade nacional no Brasil e nos Estados Unidos* (Belo Horizonte: Editora da UFMG, 2000), p. 133.

17. Edwin Jackson Kyle, 'The mission of the land-grant colleges in promoting our good neighbor policies among the Latin American republics', *Science, New Series* 97 (2507) (1943): 55.

18. Gerhardt Colby and Charlotte Dennett, *Thy Will Be Done: The Conquest of the Amazon: Nelson Rockefeller and Evangelism in the Age of Oil* (New York: Open Road Media, 2019), p. 289.

world'. According to Hodge, the economic interwar depression and the rising social unrest 'marked a critical turning point in the colonial encounter, setting off a far-reaching process of official rethinking and reform designed to forestall popular discontent and give a new lease on life and legitimacy to the imperial project'.[19] By the end of WWII, conferences such as Bretton Woods indicated an intense exchange of technical experience, in which foundations such as Ford and Rockefeller played a decisive role in the financing and adoption of practices created in colonial encounters. On the other hand, as we shall see, although the tradeoffs do exist, the AIA actually followed a pattern closer to that consolidated through the New Deal.

The renewal of studies on the relationship between the US and Latin America from a anti- or post-colonial perspective does not relativise power structures to the point of denying the asymmetrical relations between the two regions. Although their works seek to identify resistances and unforeseen rearrangements in the hierarchies of power, the authors who have developed this approach have no intention of glossing over the interventionist character, the intention of domination and the civilising perspective embedded in the imperial actions of the US.[20] Shifting the debate's focus to culture, gender, ethnicity, linguistic analysis – and environment – as well as questioning static concepts of modernity, development, state, nation and nature, and demonstrating the role of local actors in the constitution of these power relations, does not mean leaving aside the power asymmetries built up over time. In Venezuela, Rockefeller surrounded himself with similarly minded people who, with their academic and business knowledge and insights as government insiders, were able to implement the desired activities. In the Brazilian experience, it is important to note the importance of Kenneth Kadow, John Benjamin Griffing, Walter Crawford and Santiago Apodaca, among others, in the foundation of the AIA's actions, especially when Rockefeller withdrew from it in the 1950s during his tenure as New York state governor.

Nelson Rockefeller scholars have proposed an inspiring interpretation – since it does not necessarily exclude or oppose philanthropy and profit, capitalism and assistance, mission and domination. In this approach, for Nelson Rockefeller, charity and business did not possess well-defined boundaries, as addressed

19. James Morgan Hodge, *The Trimph of the Expert. Agrarian Doctrines of Development and the Legacies of the British Empire* (Athens: Ohio University Press, 2007), p. 2.

20. Azevedo, *En nome da América*, p. 21.

by the AIA co-founder John E. Lockwood.[21] For instance, the activities of the AIA and IBEC were born, as previously observed, under the same institution. Perhaps the AIA was the 'Sunday' agency, where the millionaire could follow the philanthropic tradition of the Rockefeller family and carry out charitable activities, while IBEC would be the 'Weekday' company, directed towards doing business and consequently obtaining profits – part of which could be reverted to philanthropy.[22] In a way, the renewal of studies on imperialism has prompted different perspectives that can broaden the discussion on Nelson Rockefeller's and the AIA's actions in Brazil and the rest of Latin America. Again, studies on the Rockefeller Foundation have generated novel interpretations. *Missionaries of Science*, a book edited by Peruvian historian Marcos Cueto in 1994, indicates that the concern with the diffusion of scientific knowledge was not simply a form of domination.[23] Moreover, historian Steven Palmer clarifies this perspective: analysing the Rockefeller Foundation's work in Costa Rica in the first decades of the twentieth century, Palmer argues that the bibliography on this agency necessarily adopts an imperialist approach; on the other hand, he raises new questions around scholars' addressing of political and everyday practices in the countries hosting these programmes. In this perspective, once Rockefeller Foundation established a scientific mission to combat hookworm in Costa Rica, the foundation's programmes were subject to new influences from environmental dynamics hitherto unknown to US experts, as well as local experts having impacts on their initial ideals.[24] Palmer states that the Rockefeller Foundation's initial intention in promoting biomedical knowledge faced strong resistance from the population because of the ethnic-cultural diversity found in the British Caribbean. He indicates that, rather than converting the masses to scientific truth and a purely biomedical understanding of hygiene, this early public health apparatus made deep concessions to the cultural differences and medical practices of the target population and ultimately legitimised and promoted medical pluralism.[25] Thus, for Palmer, initiatives in international

21. Cary Reich, *The Life of Nelson A. Rockefeller: Worlds to Conquer (1908–1958)* (New York: Doubleday, 1996), p. 407.

22. Ibid., p. 408.

23. Marcos Cueto (ed.), *Missionaries of Science: the Rockefeller Foundation and Latin America* (Bloomington: Indiana University Press, 1994).

24. Steven Palmer, 'Central American encounters with Rockefeller public health, 1914–1921', in Gilbert Joseph, Catherine Legrand and Ricardo Salvatore (eds), *Close Encounters of Empire: Writing the Cultural History of U.S.-Latin America Relations* (Durham: Duke University Press, 1998), p. 312.

25. Ibid.

public health are not a simple reflection of imperialist imposition. This leads us to the core of an important truth about international public health: its desire for uniformity and biopolitical processing is not easily consistent with the need for active consent by subjects of the action. Thus, to understand its historical impact, Palmer believes that scholars need to combine an analysis of the institutional, in which ideologies and methods may in fact seem very uniform, with a careful study of local manifestations in which the norm is the verification of enormously varied and fundamentally different results.[26]

More recently, historian Antonio Pedro Tota made an interpretative effort in this sense. Nelson was an imperialist, but he was also the philanthropist seeking to redeem the sins of his family and his social class, he states. Above all, Rockefeller considered himself the instrument of transformation and progress in the construction of modern nations in Latin America; he saw bringing the American standard of life to the region as his 'mission'. He was all this together,[27] a multi-faceted actor throughout his performance and, even given his great effort to 'Americanize' Brazil and Latin America, his intentions, projects and actions cannot be considered a mere imposition. Years earlier, Tota put forward a very precise argument that will serve as a complement in our analysis: he claimed that the process of Americanisation in the 1940s happened under certain conditions, since a people only incorporates certain cultural values of another people if it makes sense in the general set of its culture. This means that cultural assimilation is not only imitation, but also a complicated process of recreation.[28] More recently, in a similar attempt, historian Tiago Saraiva explored the modernist notion of anthropophagy as 'part of a continuum of historical practices' able to subsume social, economic and biological spheres of existence.[29] Following these insights, I delineate how the AIA's actions also transcended the initial boundaries of American attempts to establish an informal empire. So, thinking of Palmer's study on Central America, while Costa Rican elites found in the practices of the Foundation a model that could enable the advances of social medicine, the AIA introduced models of agricultural modernisation modified in light of experiences over decades. Later, local governments nationalised these,

26. Ibid.

27. Carlos Haag, 'O capitalista missionário: a aventura brasileira de Nelson Rockefeller', *Pesquisa Fapesp*, São Paulo, n. 157 (2009): 90.

28. Antonio Pedro Tota, *O imperialismo sedutor: a americanização do Brasil na época da Segunda Guerra* (São Paulo: Companhia das Letras, 2000), p. 193.

29. Tiago Saraiva, 'Anthropophagy and sadness: cloning citrus in São Paulo in the Plantationocene era', *History and Technology* 34 (1) (2018): 89–99.

increasingly distancing them from possible philanthropic ideals. In short, the sense of philanthropy changed according to the experiences of negotiation and/or conflict between the different groups involved in the process.

The bibliography on Nelson Rockefeller is unanimous about one element: his anti-communist views. In this regard, the multimillionaire was a man of his time: white, rich and privileged in several aspects, he opposed the rise of Nazism – although its remnants in Argentina did not worry him too much – and, when Hitler and Mussolini were defeated, he directed his fury toward the communists. Obviously, this was expected behaviour for a wealthy Republican in the United States; overwhelmed by Macarthyist hysteria, Rockefeller and other influential men created modernising apparatuses during Point Four as a way to roll back communism. As these instruments became ineffective, they opted for torture and the elimination of left-wing supporters in Latin America, sponsoring coups, strengthening authoritarian governments and informing Central Intelligence Agency agents. Thus, the anti-communist dispute in the 1950s began with the diffusion of educational programmes during Point Four and ended in the 1970s with support for training programmes for torture agents during the Alliance for Progress period. The participation of the US government or figures like Rockefeller in the anti-USSR and Cuba agenda is a canonical subject, but during the 1950s other less-studied enemies joined anti-Communism. In fact, in my research, I have rarely found direct mention of communism; if capitalism and communism divided the hearts and minds of politicians and decision-makers, technicians faced bureaucracy, tradition and patrimonialism in their daily lives. For this reason, if fighting communism was the ultimate goal in the minds of US modernisers and their Latin American allies, other struggles took place on the battlefield of bureaucracy and lack of resources, where technocracy faced political profiling for positions in Latin America.

Instead of understanding the AIA as a *continuum* of Nelson Rockefeller's projects in Venezuela with Creole Petroleum and in Brazil with the Office of the Coordinator of the Inter-American Affairs (OIAA), I suggest the pursuit of other issues left unexplored by the classic historiography of scholars such as Dalrymple. For instance, I explore internal aspects of the American economy around 1945; at the same time, the departure from an isolationist political posture justified the supposed need to shape the world in the image and likeness of the USA, as evidenced by the rise of development and modernisation ideologies. Moreover, I discuss how some of the characters involved in the creation of the AIA had a broad sense of their strength in the making of a new world order. On the other hand, I shed light on how Latin-American elites pursued development on their own basis and how local power often resisted.

This book has three parts: the first, 'New York – Caracas – Rio de Janeiro', explores Nelson Rockefeller's early experiences, travelling from his comfortable office situated in the Rockefeller Plaza to Latin America. In the first chapter, I demonstrate how new programmatic content sought to differentiate itself from imperialism and colonialism to justify its work outside the territory of the United States. Here, I elaborate on the ideological proximity between the emerging ideal of development and modernisation and the AIA's perception about its role in the underdeveloped world. From this assumption, I identify in the second chapter how the coordinator of the Office for Coordination of Commercial and Cultural Relations between the American Republics – later, Coordinator of Inter-American Affairs between 1940 and 1944, and finally Office of Inter-American Affairs – founded a first organised intervention in Latin America that survived the Good Neighbor Policy and stimulated the emergence of agricultural modernisation programmes after World War II. Finally, I demonstrate in chapters 3 and 4 how the resurgence of political nationalism post-1945 hardened negotiations between private US associations and Latin American countries. The rise of *Acción Democrática* in Venezuela (chapter 3) became a key example in two senses: first, Latin Americans were also seeking ways to insert themselves into the industrialised world; second, the difficulties of negotiation led North Americans to invest increasingly in philanthropic rhetoric, as discussed through the *Serviço de Alimentação da Previdência Social* (Social Welfare Food Service, SAPS) case in chapter 4. In summary, the disagreements among US modernisers and Latin American political elites demonstrate how the initial idea of governing and organising Latin America from a distant office in New York encountered local resistance. The modernising intervention intended by white-wealthy-men with degrees from the most renowned universities was not readily accepted – actually, it was challenged.

Part II, entitled 'Over the Hills and Far Away: Dusting off the Boots in Latin America', discusses how North American agricultural experts immersed themselves in the politics and the rural world of Latin America – to promote social change. Starting in chapter 5, I describe how, from the 1950s on, local leaders and government officials engaged in dialogue with and adapted the agricultural development projects in an anthropophagic way. Understanding that the history of Latin America is not only the history of oppression and resistance, I guide my argument via the constant disputes around the creation and control of agencies dedicated to agricultural research and modernisation.

This form of Latin American cultural anthropophagy – according to Saraiva's approach – which appropriates ideas and transforms them into something tangible, figures in the case of São Paulo as a classic piece of extension service work. In chapters 6 and 7, on the other hand, I offer a counterpoint to the São Paulo case, discussing how the ideal of merging agriculture and industry found a favourable environment in Minas Gerais. In this Brazilian state, the most important agricultural development programme of the second half of the twentieth century, the ACAR, developed a supervised credit and technical assistance model, closer to the US Farm Security Administration ideal. Little by little, Brazil served as fertile ground for the AIA's programmes, though Nelson Rockefeller completely separated himself from the venture in 1958, when he became governor of New York.

In the final part of the book, entitled 'Low-Budget Imperialism', I demonstrate in chapter 8 how the AIA gravitated to the orbit of Point Four, failing in its attempt to settle its modernising projects in Asia. On the other hand, between 1957 and 1963, the IRI Research Institute became the experimental research arm within the AIA, offering practical solutions in terms of techniques and technologies. In a sense, IRI ensured the continuity of the ideals forged by AIA even after the philanthropic agency closed in 1968, by associating itself with the nascent green revolution – expanding its territory of operation and promoting the global circulation of technology (chapter 9). Eventually, in the late 1950s and early 1960s, the usual sponsors reduced their funding to every project. On the other hand, I demonstrate in chapter 10 how Brazilian political elites accepted the ACAR model. Together with other national or Point Four-linked institutions, they nationalised the programme initiated by the AIA in 1949. Finally, in chapter 11, I demonstrate how the historical context of the Alliance for Progress was influential in displacing relatively small agencies and institutions such as the AIA because of the governmental programmes and bigger resources available in a new era of technical cooperation – these became possible because of the AIA's and other agencies' work since WWII. In its last seven years, the AIA worked more in connection with Alliance for Progress projects or as a true think tank, spreading its ideals; its 1960s projects, along with their predecessors, were forgotten, merged or adapted at regional and national levels in the years following 1968, when the Association closed its operations. In summary, this book – taking the methodological choice not to follow the chronology of events religiously, but to revisit them according to the needs of the argument – hopes to contribute to a renewed research agenda based on multi-scale and connected studies of agricultural modernisation in the Global South.

PART I – NEW YORK – CARACAS – RIO DE JANEIRO

CHAPTER 1.

NELSON ROCKEFELLER'S BRAVE NEW WORLD: CAPITALISM, PHILANTHROPY AND PRESCRIPTIVE MODELS FOR LATIN AMERICAN AGRICULTURAL DEVELOPMENT

American International Association
for Economic and Social Development
30 ROCKEFELLER PLAZA • NEW YORK 20 • NEW YORK

Figure 1. AIA logo – including its New York office address. Rockefeller Archive Center, Collection 1027 AIA, Series 2, Box 2, Brazil.

John Davison Rockefeller Jr. (1874–1960) and Abigail Greene 'Abby' Aldrich (1874–1948) named Nelson Aldrich Rockefeller in honour of his maternal grandfather, Republican Senator Nelson Aldrich (1841–1915). His siblings included Abigail Aldrich Rockefeller (1903–1976), John Davison Rockefeller III (1906–1979), Laurance Spelman Rockefeller (1910–2004), Winthrop Rockefeller (1912–1973) and David Rockefeller (1915–2017). Over the span of his public life, Nelson – also known as NAR or 'Rocky' – was an executive, a philanthropist, an art collector and a politician. The most remarkable roles he held during his political career were those of Head of the Office for Coordination of Commercial and Cultural Relations between the American Republics (OIAA) during World War II, Under Secretary of Health, Education and Welfare (1953–1954), 49th governor of New York from 1959 to 1973 and, finally, 41st Vice-president of the United States from 1974 to 1977. Intriguingly, for a member of the Republican Party, Nelson had a liberal, progressive and, in many cases, moderate line of action on the role of government in matters such as medical care, environment protection and access to education, among other controversial issues for Republicans. Moreover, he belonged to a family that had amassed a great fortune exploiting natural resources, most notably petroleum. In the late nineteenth and early twentieth centuries, the Rockefeller family had started funding philanthropic activities, and later Nelson himself situated the AIA's work within what he considered to be family tradition – guided by religious concerns.[1]

Sometimes portrayed as a brilliant businessperson, a missionary and one of the greatest symbols of Yankee imperialism, Nelson Rockefeller travelled to Caracas in late 1937, to examine the Venezuelan Museum of Modern Art in preparation for an exchange programme involving Latin American artworks. The same year, he became a member of the Board of Directors of Creole Petroleum Corporation, a Venezuelan subsidiary of Standard Oil Company, a position he kept until 1940. In 1937, he visited the oilfields in the region of Lake Maracaibo to inspect his investments and came across a dramatic social contrast between the standards of living of American engineers and Venezuelan workers. According to Brazilian historian Antônio Pedro Tota, Nelson felt more worried than impressed, finding a 'concentration camp inside out', where the *prisioneros* stood outside Creole's high barbed wire fences, without hospitals, schools or any kind of assistance. Quickly, he started a modification programme, bringing twelve Spanish teachers to teach in schools in the region, ordering the tearing down of Creole's fences, the paving of streets and extensive building. Shortly after, he left Venezuela for Trinidad and Tobago and later visited Brazil for the first time to address oil-related issues. He was behind the building of a luxury hotel in Caracas in the following years.[2]

The reformist impetus of promoting encounters between US technicians and local workers finds its roots in the American political and social context of Nelson Rockefeller's formative years. Entering public life during the early days of the New Deal, Rockefeller came across the programme of recovery for the US economy initiated by Democrats in a perspective compatible with isolationism, since, for the New Dealers, the solution to the economy's problems would be homegrown.[3] If, in the early years of the New Deal, international cooperation was not seen as a solution, with the entry of Americans into World War II in 1941, internationalism would strengthen.[4] Unlike isolationists, a group that advocated maintaining traditional relations with Latin America during the New

1. Dalrymple, *The AIA Story.*

2. Antônio Pedro Tota, *O Amigo Americano. Nelson Rockefeller e o Brasil* (São Paulo: Companhia das Letras, 2014), pp. 65–67.

3. M.J. Heale, *Twentieth-Century America: Politics and Power in the United States, 1900–2000* (London: Arnold-Hodder Headline Group, 2004), p. 131.

4. Michael Adas, *Dominance by Design. Technological Imperatives and America's Civilizing Mission* (Cambridge: Harvard University Press, 2006).

Deal, internationalists proposed another political orientation south of the Rio Grande, since the possibilities for trade would increase significantly. Moreover, Nelson Rockefeller stood as a good example of the internationalised interests of the American economy, since he maintained personal investments in Latin America.[5] While leading the OIAA, he took advantage of the favourable context of political and economic relations created in Latin America. After leaving this office, Rockefeller envisioned some of the programmes developed during World War II continuing, no longer by means of agreement between US and local governments, as had been the case in wartime, but on the initiative of a private philanthropic agency, the AIA. Leading a team from OIAA days – architect Wallace Kirkman Harrison (1895–1981), horticulturist Kenneth John Kadow (1908–1998), 1933 Pulitzer Prize winner Francis Jamieson (1904–1960) and lawyer John E. Lockwood (1907–1996) – Nelson Rockefeller was at the head of the AIA, an agency that developed technical cooperation projects, mainly in the agricultural sphere. From an international perspective, the design and projects developed by the AIA, the Rockefeller Foundation and Ford would help define an agenda for technical cooperation that directly influenced the organisation of President Harry Truman's government programme Point Four, incorporating technical and financial assistance to help countries considered underdeveloped.

Created in 1946 as an agency that initially aimed at raising funds and later at investing in philanthropic activities, the AIA was forced by US legislation to spawn two other agencies. Although the names of these post-war Rockefeller agencies seem to have originated from a Monty Python show, the International Basic Economy Co. (IBEC, in 1947) and the IBEC Research Institute (later IRI Research Institute) wered offspring of the AIA. The first aimed to expand agricultural business in Latin America – such as hybrid corn seeds, supermarkets or agricultural machinery – and the latter focused on techno-scientific research in agriculture.[6] The main territorial area of the AIA's activities was Latin America, especially Brazil and Venezuela, with some more isolated initiatives; and it also acted in other Latin American countries, mainly in the 1960s, as well as in China and in India. In addition, the AIA became an important factor in

5. André Luiz Vieira de Campos, *Políticas internacionais de saúde na Era Vargas: o Serviço Especial de Saúde Pública, 1942–1960* (Rio de Janeiro: Editora Fiocruz, 2006), pp.48–49.

6. On the IBEC, see Hamilton, *Supermarket USA*; about the IRI, see Claiton Marcio da Silva and Claudio de Majo, 'The making of a pastureland biome: American scientists, miracle grasses and the transformation of the Brazilian *Cerrado*', *Environment and History* 29(2): 185–210.

the constitution of this brave new world designed by influential figures such as Nelson Rockefeller and his allies. While the literature on the AIA and the Rockefeller Foundation puts a disproportionate focus on the classical philanthropy approach, one should not lose sight of the links between philanthropy, science and technical assistance. While it is true that AIA was a philanthropic agency, it was a product of its political and cultural background – and, ultimately, its mission was to promote technology-driven social and economic change. Ideals and ideologies reified in the actions of agencies and governments built a new model of action for the period, associating development and modernisation as final objectives for the construction of a liberal, democratic and capitalist West. Science and technology would be the main instruments to achieve these goals, as discussed in the next section.

'New Highways for the March of Science and Technology Over the Obstacles of Language, Race and Customs': Nelson Rockefeller's Beliefs in Development and Modernisation

> *If we, with our technical knowledge and experience, cannot make science pay we had better stay home and let our Latin neighbors solve their own problems as best they can.*
> (Kenneth Kadow, 1945)

In the early 1950s, a few years after the constitution of the AIA, Nelson Rockefeller made this philosophy clear: 'Tomorrow's world, bright with promise of better living, needs new highways for the march of science and technology over the obstacles of language, race and customs.' 'The AIA', he claimed, 'is one way of bridging these gaps between people so that the benefits of science and the new technology can spread more widely over the earth'.[7] Rockefeller's concept of the AIA's mission echoes Enlightenment-era and nineteenth-century Positivist assumptions, considering science and technology as the most appropriate ways to bring progress to different nations – or races, in Rockefeller's words. In a way, these conceptions were in consonance with the views of United Nations experts who took upon themselves the goal of disseminating economic policies, reasoning in 1951 that economic progress would not be possible without undoing old social institutions such as class differences, race and creed.[8]

7. Dalrymple, *The AIA Story*, p.15.

8. Arturo Escobar, *Encountering Development. The Making and Unmaking of the Third World* (Princeton; New Jersey: Princeton University Press, 1995), p. 20.

On the other hand, this unshakeable faith in science and technology as instruments of social change did not foresee any developmental phenomenon dissociated from what Nelson Rockefeller considered the greatest nation ever to exist in human history: the United States. With this line of thought, Rockefeller expressed positions that were similar even for New Deal critics and isolationists like Nebraska Republican Senator Kenneth Wherry (1892–1951). Common ground between these two currents of thought included the notion that the United States represented the highest form of societal evolution. Historian Michael Latham noted how during the war, Wherry 'was hardly the typical proponent of an American campaign to modernize the world in its own image';[9] nevertheless, conservative Wherry was not the only one to maintain that liberalism, capitalism and US-style democracy were human end-stages that other societies must catch up to – nor were these ideals restricted to the upper class of North American politicians. Kenneth John Kadow, professor of horticulture at the University of Delaware and Nelson's partner in the creation of the AIA in 1946, expressed a very similar idea:

> If we in America believe in economic, political, and social philosophies, as well as in the practices that have made us a great nation, it is our task and privilege to do everything we can in a concrete way to work with other peoples of the earth toward similar or equally satisfactory goals.[10]

In other words, it was a duty to develop and modernise other countries in the image of the United States. Where Wherry's emphasis was on China, Nelson Rockefeller, Kenneth Kadow and other AIA agents sought to intervene in Latin America. Before World War II, the term modernisation had rarely been used, except by missionaries, educators and engineers who promoted cultural, political and economic changes in China, the Philippines and Latin America in the interwar period.[11] The end of World War II thus marked a rupture, with the rise of precepts such as development and modernisation; for anthropologist

9. Michael Latham, 'Introduction: modernization, international history, and the Cold War world', in David Engerman, Nils Gilman, Mark Haefele and Michael Latham (eds), *Staging Growth. Modernization, Development, and the Global Cold War* (Amherst: University of Massachusetts Press, 2003), p. 1.

10. The American International Association for Economic and Social Development. An explanation of its objectives and method of operation by Kenneth J. Kadow for Nelson A. Rockefeller. 19 Feb. 1946. Collection: Family. Record Group: III 4 B. Box 01, Folder AIA – Simon Bolivar Foundation. p. 14.

11. Michael Adas, 'Modernization theory and the American revival of the scientific and technological standards of social achievement and human worth', in David Engerman, Nils Gilman, Mark Haefele and Michael Latham (eds), *Staging Growth. Modernization,*

Arturo Escobar, a decisive moment for the construction of an agenda based on these new precepts occurred in US President Henry Truman's inauguration speech on 20 January 1949. Truman's words merged with the notion that the United States should actively facilitate the development and modernisation of other countries. Escobar argues that Point Four's intent was 'quite ambitious', bringing about the 'conditions necessary to replicating the world over the features that characterized "advanced" societies of the times', which would mean 'high levels of industrialization and urbanization, technification of agriculture, rapid growth of material production and living standards'; and finally, 'the widespread adoption of modern education and cultural values'.[12] In sum, in Truman's vision, capital, science and technology were the main ingredients that would make this massive revolution possible.[13] Because of Truman's Point Four and Rostow's Modernization Theory, expressed by the World Bank, the United Nations and foundations such as Ford, Rockefeller and the AIA, IBEC and IRI, a powerful, prescriptive model of analysis had been set up. Historian Michael Latham argues that this ideal became the most influential way of understanding the world and idealising its future until at least the 1970s.[14] Meanwhile, Latin American historians have emphasised how local elites had similar aspirations, making development and modernisation projects not only imperative, but also the subject of intense negotiation and adaptation.[15]

Crucially, the AIA idealised and propelled into the post-war context many practices that were prominent as early as the 1920s and 1930s and actively materialised these ideals, on a private basis, by undertaking systematic technical assistance in accordance with Truman's Point Four principles. This new geopolitical arrangement based on cultural, political and economic change through science and technology marks a fundamental difference from the old geopolitics. Historian Michael Adas states: 'Although modernization theory differs in important ways from its European colonial civilizing-mission predecessors', in most of its more influential formulations 'it shared an emphasis on

---

Development, and the Global Cold War (Amherst: University of Massachusetts Press, 2003), p. 26.

12. Escobar, *Encountering Development*, p. 4.

13. Ibid.

14. Latham, 'Introduction: modernization, international history, and the Cold War World', p. 18.

15. Rômulo de Paula Andrade, 'A TVA to the Amazon Forest? Shaping experts for development'. *Diálogos Latinoamericanos* **30** (2021).

the scientific and technological measures of human worth and achievement that have long been vital components of ideologies of Western dominance.'[16]

The work of international agencies such as the AIA and the Ford and Rockefeller foundations grounded itself in charitable and benevolent ideals. This essential change in ideology, shaped by the post-war context, marked a shift from the legitimised extraction of resources from colonised territories to the ideal of sharing science and technology's benefits 'widely on earth', as Nelson Rockefeller himself put it. The use of these potential benefits as an effective political instrument – an ideology, Latham suggests – would insert development and modernisation ideologies into the post-war debate; the promise was to make use of science and technology to materialise specific visions of social change and progress. This would guarantee a world order in which the United States would leverage processes of decolonisation and development to build hegemony for US-style capitalism, liberalism and democracy in the countries of Latin America.[17]

Another issue is the discreditation that science and technology suffered in Europe during and after World War I. In the early years of the interwar period, major powers such as Britain and France questioned the assumed benefits of technology. Whether technology had led to net social advances or ultimately intensified the war itself, moving humankind backwards, was hotly debated in the Old World.[18] Adas argues that, far from fuelling this unresolved debate, American leaders of the same era hailed technological developments as a way to resolve social contradictions.[19] It is true that Europeans had used technological advances to justify their self-proclaimed superiority over the rest of humanity in the aftermath of the Industrial Revolution, thus establishing new hierarchies and representing themselves as rational, disciplined, punctual, efficient and in possession of a self-proclaimed progressive mentality. However, the Americans involved in colonising efforts between the 1890s and the First World War were the strongest proponents of these ideals in the early twentieth century. In different ways, the proponents of modernisation theories would invoke them once again in the 1920s and 1930s. Most importantly, such ideals would take on special significance during the Cold War.[20] Kenneth Kadow would provide a

16. Adas, 'Modernization theory', p. 37.
17. Latham, 'Introduction: modernization, international history, and the Cold War World', p. 3.
18. Adas, 'Modernization theory', p. 33.
19. Ibid., p. 26.
20. Ibid., pp. 27–29.

practical example of reifying ideologies in institutions, associating technology with superiority. In a letter addressed to Nelson Rockefeller in December 1945 he stated that Latin America did not have enough technically skilled workers to develop its natural resources, and that the AIA would work to fill this gap. An ardent believer in American technical capital, Kadow argued: 'If we, with our technical knowledge and experience, cannot make science pay we had better stay home and let our Latin neighbors solve their own problems as best they can.'[21] Finally, he added: 'the scientific development of a nation's natural and human resources is a necessary supplement to the prosperity of the people'.[22] Kadow thus tacitly reflects a repositioning of discourses and their agents in the formulation of a brave new world.

Michael Adas claims that, after World War II, the paradigm of modernisation replaced the civilising mission as an ideology of Western domination. Unlike eighteenth- and nineteenth-century colonial expansion, the representatives on the ground were no longer European missionaries, travellers and merchants. Instead, social scientists came to formulate a new ideology more systematically and coherently articulated than its predecessor.[23] New hierarchies were rooted in categorising levels of development – first, second, third, and (later) fourth world; postmodern, modern, traditional, primitive; mature and underdeveloped. These categories replaced earlier terms, such as the civilised/barbarian/savage triptych, which served as standards during colonial expansion.[24] In fact, although Rockefeller refers a couple of times to the other nations of the Latin America using the concept of race, the rhetoric used by the AIA and its agents increasingly embraced the semantics of post-1945 constructs. Therefore, in my argument, the elites used technical terms or ethnocentric conceptions of science and technology as a substitute for racism in pursuing the maintenance or expansion of domination.

Despite its obscuring or relativising of classical colonialism and imperial violence, the AIA disseminated an idea of superiority through science and technology produced in American or European universities and experimental stations, mostly by white men. Development and modernisation, in this perspective, were associated with rationality, empiricism, efficiency and progressive change, whereas tradition connoted fatalism and support for obsolete customs,

21. From Kenneth J. Kadow to Nelson A. Rockefeller. 7 Dec. 1945. Collection: Family, Record Group: III 4B, Box: 01, Folder: AIA – Bolivar Foundation. p.01.

22. Ibid.

23. Adas, 'Modernization theory', p. 35.

24. Ibid.

and connected the sacred to ideas of indiscipline and stagnation.[25] During the Cold War, the notions of development and modernisation shaped the dominant conceptions of reality and society in countries labelled as underdeveloped, while their proponents echoed old representations of Western power and used them politically, economically and administratively as a way of shaping a particular trajectory: an evolution defined in terms of progress. Guided by a model built on selected empirical and historical evidence of what they understood as an organic and natural order, social scientists and policymakers of the twentieth century used old representations to define modernisation as a unitary variable of global change. They also claimed the authority to manage it, positioning their own society's model as the apogée of linear progress.[26]

Critical to understanding this process is awareness of how, in the post-World War II period, agencies such as the AIA tried to justify their actions in Latin America through statements connected to the new times, precisely to try to differentiate themselves from old models of political and economic domination. The AIA's approach made it an agent of this new dynamic, casting doubt on the results of colonialism and imperialism: 'Many of the underdeveloped areas of the world were, in the not-too-distant past, part of some great colonial empire', highlighted an AIA report in 1949. In an attempt to analyse past geopolitics, the report stated, 'the essence of colonialism was that a relatively well-developed country exercised political and economic control over an undeveloped country', while 'the colonies were seen as a source of raw materials. The know-how and capital meant the enrichment of the mother country.' Distancing itself from that conception, the AIA then concluded its critical approach: 'If they increased the (social) standards of the colonized, it was generally incidental and reduced to a small class of colonial leaders.'[27]

The next section discusses how the future planned by governments and international organisations for Latin America in the immediate post-war period involved the maintenance of colonialism and imperialism's characteristics, in spite of a discursive rejection of older forms of domination over Africa, Asia, and Latin America.

25. Adas, 'Modernization theory', p. 38.

26. See Michael Latham, *Modernization as Ideology. American Social Sciences and the 'Nation Building' in the Kennedy Era* (Chapel Hill: The University of North Carolina Press, 2000), p. 15.

27. AIA. The first three years. [1949]. Collection: Family, Record Group: II 4B, Box: 01, Folder AIA General 1946-1958, n. 02(a).

Modernization and Development: Rupture from or Continuity with Colonial Imperialism?

Referring to these historical themes and specifically to Kennedy's Alliance for Progress, Adas argues that the Theory of Modernisation differed from imperialist actions mainly in three aspects. The first is that modernising propositions departed from Nazism and its discourse on racial hierarchies. The second aspect is that, in this context – unlike that of nineteenth-century imperialism, wherein Europeans took it upon themselves to civilise those they construed as savages – local elites themselves were trained to oversee the process of transition from traditional to modern. Finally, the transformation of a traditional society into a modern one was not a catchphrase during the colonial era. For the Ideology of Modernisation, for example, the ideal became the constitution of an industrialised world of competitive nations, interacting in a capitalist network of free trade, which, the theory went, would lead to the modernisation of nations that once served only as suppliers of raw materials for countries undergoing industrialisation.[28] The following discusses details of each of these aspects through examples drawn from the Latin American context.

Concerning the first aspect, Adas argues that Nazism and the atrocities perpetrated in the name of racial purity, as well as Asian and African nationalist uprisings against colonisers' supposed racial superiority, shaped the anti-racist premises of this new ideology.[29] Its proponents sought to accelerate the transition from traditional societies considered backward to modern societies, economically and politically similar to the United States – in a teleological sense. A crucial step in this plan was the development of the notion of culture, more flexible than that of race. Out of the social sciences' understanding that culture possessed more explanatory potential than race when it came to interpreting different societies grew a different way of dealing with these societies.[30] Social scientists such as Franz Boas, Ruth Benedict and Margaret Mead conceived a more malleable world made up of different cultures: race became less important than history. In this conception, it would be possible for the different nations to evolve. The fixed idea of an unchanging divide between preconceptions of savagery and civilisation no longer made sense at a time when the traditional

28. Adas, 'Modernization theory', pp. 35–36.

29. Ibid.

30. Latham, 'Introduction: modernization, international history, and the Cold War World', pp. 2–4.

could transform into the modern.[31] Between the end of the First World War and the beginning of the second, Latin American intellectuals linked the backwardness of agricultural techniques to racial issues. However, after 1945 and the fall of Nazism, the concept of culture replaced race – though not exactly racism.

Since the late nineteenth century, scientific racism and agricultural research have moved closer and further apart in the minds of certain groups and in different contexts, especially in the United States. For some groups of eugenicists, for example, the principles of a supposed racial hierarchy should organise rural life, transferring principles of genetic improvement to agricultural research. On the other side of the political spectrum – in principle, non-racist groups – agricultural missionaries, for example, perceived agriculture as a civilising apparatus, transforming wilderness into garden and savages into civilised. Religious missionaries propagated their agricultural technical knowledge in China during the first decades of the twentieth century. Their experiences, supported by the USDA, functioned as an exemplar for neoimperial experiment in the following decades in Latin America and Africa, introducing machineries, seeds and fertilisers as benevolent dominance.[32] Finally, the perception of political progressivism, broadly speaking, understood that the obstacles that prevented the fulfilment of the civilising mission of the United States were not grounded in race but in culture; this conception gave great impetus to ambitious schemes for the development of the newly colonised Philippines, for instance. Evidence of significant accomplishments by these Asian and Latin American peoples in material endeavours served as argument by the agents of American expansion in favour of modifying the racist restrictions pervasive in the United States itself in the pre-World War I era. Local populations, as Adas has addressed, thus overcame racist assumptions in a process of privileging more mutable cultural characteristics, such as a people's past material achievements or their supposed ability to acquire Western knowledge and operate 'modern' machines. Outside the United States, from the mid-nineteenth century through the twentieth century, the willingness to abandon racist scepticism also reinforced the conviction of numerous missionaries and philanthropists that 'decadent' China – and I would also add the Philippines or Cuba – could be rejuvenated with sufficient infusions of Western education, science and technology.[33] During the New Deal, similar social mobility actions were applied to black and indigenous popula-

31. Ibid., p. 5.

32. Randal Stross, *The Stubborn Earth. American Agriculturalists on Chinese Soil, 1898–1937* (Berkeley: California University Press), 1986, p. 40.

33. Adas, *Dominance by Design.*

tions through programmes like the aforementioned Farm Security Administration and the Resettlement Administration, managed by radical liberals and communists like Rexford Tugwell. In sum, intellectuals and politicians of this stamp believed that social change was possible, no longer condemning blacks, indigenous people and people of mixed race to social immobility. Following this rupture, the prescriptive ideals of modernisation gained ground.

In the early post-war years, albeit only moderately, the AIA supported this increasingly strong non-racist, although ethnocentric, prescription to transform cultures and societies in Latin America into a kind of neo-US from the ground up. Through their experience, AIA experts proudly claimed to have developed an empirical method to facilitate the transition from the traditional to the modern, at least according to South Carolinian Robert Watts 'Pete' Hudgens (1896–1973), director of the agency between 1948 and 1953 (see chapter 9).[34] Considered a 'diehard liberal',[35] Hudgens viewed the initial work of AIA in Latin America to be at the level of 'simple things, like you should boil your water', as he recalled later. In his attempt to demonstrate both the alleged superiority of science over tradition and of experts over Latin American farmers, Hudgens posited that the AIA would have the role of demonstrating that 'you can't defecate any longer on the ground here by the kitchen, you have to go up in the hills and make a hole and you've got to cover it and throw lime in there. They didn't know these things.'[36]

34. 'Supervised credit was first used, successfully, in Abbeville County, S.C. (1932–1933), with the assistance of a grant from the American Red Cross, and eventually became the basis of programmes used by the Resettlement Administration and the Farm Security Administration. Hudgens' success in rural development led to 14 years of service in government organisations: the Subsistence Homestead programme (1934–1935); the Resettlement Administration, as Louisiana State Director (1935–1936) and as regional director for the Southeast (1936–1937); and the Farm Security Administration, as regional director for the Southeast, and as assistant and then associate, director of the administration (1937–1946). Hudgens left government service in 1946 and worked for a year as director of field organisations for the American Red Cross (1946–1947). He then became executive director of Nelson Rockefeller's American International Association for Economic and Social Development (1948–1953), where he was able to work with rural development programmes in other countries, especially in Latin America. These same concepts were carried over to International Development Services, Inc., which Hudgens formed in 1953. He served as its president until his retirement to Chapel Hill, N.C., in 1963'. https://archives.lib.duke.edu/catalog/hudgens#contents

35. Paul Keith Conkin, *Tomorrow a New World: The New Deal Community Program* (Ithaca: Cornell University Press, 1959).

36. As quoted by Reich, *The Life of Nelson Rockefeller*, p. 436.

Secondly, Adas claims that even if US capital and technical assistance played a vital role in the implementation of modernisation processes, the affected populations (in his study's case Africans and Asians rather than Latin Americans) themselves played a decisive role. If nineteenth-century colonial expansion had demanded that Europeans themselves take on the violent civilising mission, in the process of decolonisation this notion had become obsolete: local elites, rather than foreign powers had the task of transforming the traditional into the modern. Here, members of these local elites are Latin-American modernisers, culturally anthropophagic. This fact, along with the Cold War anti-communist frenzy, helps explain why the literature dealing with modernisation relies on political aspects of transformation, unlike colonialist rhetoric. Some of modernisation ideology's most influential aspects centred on social mobility, expansion of political participation and democratisation of political institutions.[37] Moreover, one of the AIA's constant concerns was the necessity for local populations in developing countries to play an active role in the implementation of modernisation programmes. A telling example is the AIA chronicler Martha Dalrymple's statement: 'from the beginning AIA's program was catalytic – in an effort to teach and stimulate others [or Latin Americans] to do things better by and for themselves'.[38]

The AIA thus adopted an innovative rhetoric of management for both personnel and material resources. In the wings of Point Four, the concepts of technical assistance and later technical cooperation became paramount; this rhetoric was consistent with what academics proposed at the time. For example, Roscoe C. Martin, professor of Political Science at Syracuse University, stated in 1952: 'technical assistance is a continuing process which properly conceived, concludes only when the proposals made by the experts have been incorporated into normal practice by the government receiving assistance'.[39] Analysing a possible *modus operandi*, Professor Martin understood that 'techniques are transferable, it may be supposed, if they are not wholly foreign to local … ways of life. Complete acquiescence in the limitations imposed by local customs would of course mean no progress at all.' 'If we [the American experts]', wrote Kadow, cannot make science succeed in Latin America, it would be better 'stay home and let our Latin neighbors solve their own problems'. Martin continued to suggest that the process of transferring technical

37. Adas, 'Modernization theory', p. 36.

38. Dalrymple, *The AIA Story*, p. 13.

39. Roscoe Martin, 'Technical assistance: The problem of implementation', *Public Administration Review* 12 (4) (1952): 260.

knowledge would be possible only by establishing nuanced, cordial relationships. This 'emphasizes anew the imperative need on the part of the technical assistance experts to establish cordial local relations with both public and public servants and more especially with those affected by the program.' Finally, social scientists would occupy a central role in the process of implementing technical assistance. Both social scientists and public administrators would 'carry our one best hope that government throughout the world will make increasing use of the experience and skills at hand for its employment'.[40] Thus, both the academic discourse and the leadership of agencies such as the AIA understood that experts should increasingly negotiate those innovations; as a fundamental example, in my argument the term 'technical cooperation', which meant, at least in theory, a less hierarchical concept, replaced 'technical assistance' in the modernisation rhetoric.

The third and final aspect of Adas' theory and the basis of his argument is that the transformation of a traditional into a modern society would have been unthinkable in the Colonial Era. Even in its most benevolent manifestation, the civilising ideology aimed to reshape the economies of the colonies to make them compatible with serving the economy of the metropolis. For the ideology of modernisation, in contrast, industrialisation almost invariably occupies a central role in the full development of traditional societies. Here, the ideal world is made of industrialised, competitive nations interacting in a capitalist and free trade environment.[41] This ideal clearly expresses the AIA's work in Latin America. The association increasingly considered the disparity between developed and underdeveloped countries, created by long-term historical experience: 'thus there developed serious social and economic problems arising out of the disparity between the under-developed nations and the highly industrialized nations', stated a report of 1949. However, 'there developed an even greater disparity within each nation between the top economic group and the lower economic group that created a more volatile problem, socially and economically',[42] as follows:

> New relations among nations are slowly emerging, and with them, a relation of extending greater material benefits to a larger proportion of mankind. There is a growing international recognition that the two disparities must be eliminated. One of the important factors is the growing struggle for self-improvement among

40. Ibid.

41. Adas, 'Modernization theory', p. 37.

42. AIA. The first three years. [1949]. Collection: Family, Record Group: II 4B, Box: 01, Folder AIA General 1946-1958, n. 02(a). p. 2.

> the under-privileged peoples of the world. Through improved communications they have learned of the ways in which both the quality of the life have been expanded, and they have developed a strong desire for the fruits of modern civilization for themselves and their countries.[43]

Finally, the 1949 report entitled 'AIA. The First Three Years' attempts to 'channel this desire into methods and educational techniques whereby their goals may be achieved – through their own initiative'. This would mean a conceptual change whereby 'under-privileged peoples of the world' should come to be able to solve their problems for themselves.[44]

In short, the emergence of philanthropic agencies like the AIA is part of a context of dramatic changes in geopolitics, due mainly to the scars caused by World War II. This new hierarchy, redesigned by international cooperation programmes such as Point Four and the Alliance for Progress, brought together a series of ongoing initiatives. The AIA emerged in 1946, before both US diplomatic programmes. Development was not a purely US project; rather, local elites were also imagining a new territory full of modern machinery, cities and so on, based on the capitalist ideals. Simultaneously, in this process of building a new world after 1945, some kind of dialogue continued with pre-war paradigms. In what follows, I will explore other issues pertaining to the *modus operandi* of expansionism as practised by certain American groups, such as the Rockefellers.

43. Ibid.

44. Ibid.

CHAPTER 2.

OUTLINING GEOPOLITICAL COOPERATION: FROM THE OFFICE OF THE COORDINATOR OF INTER-AMERICAN AFFAIRS TO THE AIA

As noted in the previous chapter, the theory of modernisation did not constitute an absolute break from older ideologies – although it showed significant differences, it still entails a form of domination and maintenance of privilege of some nations over others. Walt Whitman Rostow, for example, asserted in 1961 that modernisation would take the place of colonialism. Obviously, making use of an optimistic and self-centred conception of the term modernisation, Rostow prophesied that this process would be a way to maintain the privileges of a dominant power in an era when the nations of Africa, Asia, the Middle East and Latin America demanded independence and nationalist regimes gained momentum.[1] Years earlier, using rhetoric that carried more benevolent undertones than classic colonialist discourse, Nelson Rockefeller envisioned that American capital should participate in the economic development of the countries it invested in.[2] Anticipating some ideas that would form the basis of later programmes, Rockefeller distinguished himself from entrepreneurs and politicians of his generation by choosing a new arsenal of weapons to maintain asymmetric relations with Latin America. In doing so, he sought to spread development models that would facilitate the circulation of American capital. This would effectively advance the goals set later by figures like Rostow.

Earlier discussion demonstrated how proponents of modernisation legitimised their vision by promoting the diffusion of technical knowledge in general. Now it becomes relevant to explore under what circumstances technical cooperation programmes in agriculture emerged. I suggest that the AIA's creation was a turning point in the consolidation of Nelson Rockefeller's endeavours in Latin America, which began with the implementation of the Office of the Coordinator of Inter-American Affairs. After the end of the war, a neo-Malthusian narrative emerged, proposing that the welfare of rural populations in so-called underdeveloped countries improved through interna-

1. Latham, *Modernization as Ideology*, p. 16.
2. Dalrymple, *The AIA Story*, pp. 3–4.

tional technical cooperation. With its unstable political conditions, bountiful natural resources and seemingly untapped market potential, Latin America was a perfect candidate for Rockefeller generosity through philanthropic initiatives. Before the growth of a wave of mainly Left-wing nationalistic protectionism, however, World War II generated specific interest from government actors and entrepreneurs in Latin America, as we will discuss below.

Health and Agriculture for War: The Food Supply Division and US–Brazil Cooperation Programmes

Unlike isolationists, who advocated for traditional relations with Latin America during the Roosevelt administration, internationalists such as Nelson Rockefeller proposed another political tactic south of Rio Grande, focused on increasing trade opportunities. During the New Deal, international cooperation did not achieve resonance in the political sphere; but with the beginning of American involvement in World War II, in 1941, internationalism started to gather strength.[3] As a representative of this internationalist-liberal republican side, Rockefeller's ties with Roosevelt went deeper, with the inclusion of Latin America into the US international agenda: Rockefeller defended the need to maintain political agreements in the subcontinent, wary of the risk that the European market would be closed by the Germans during the war. This proposition enabled Nelson Rockefeller's political rise[4] in this respect; he coordinated the activities of the OIAA, an agency created on 16 August 1940 with headquarters in Rio de Janeiro. According to Antônio Pedro Tota, OIAA kept alive the idea of the Good Neighbor Policy practised by Roosevelt since the 1930s, as a way of organising political and commercial relations with Latin American countries. The main objectives of the Office were to persuade Latin American nations to follow the leadership of the US in opposition to the Axis, and to integrate the Brazilian economy with that of the US in the same system. Finally, it aimed to prevent revolutions in the Americas, to fight against the agents of the Axis and to increase US trade. To these ends, the office developed several programmes related to the press, cinema, cultural exchange and health, featuring, among others, evolving stars such as Orson Welles, Walt Disney and Carmen Miranda.[5]

3. Dalrymple, *The AIA Story*, p. 134.

4. Antonio Pedro Tota, *O imperialismo sedutor: a americanização do Brasil na época da Segunda Guerra* (São Paulo: Companhia das Letras, 2000), p. 43.

5. See Ursula Prutsch, 'Americanization of Brazil or a pragmatic wartime alliance? The politics of Nelson Rockefeller's Office of Inter-American Affairs in Brazil during World

Rockefeller's wartime endeavours allowed him to strengthen his personal relationship with former US Secretary of Agriculture and then Vice President Henry A. Wallace. The two men both envisioned Latin American agriculture as a crucial strategic sector. Over the years, Wallace suggested the creation of an agricultural research institute located in Latin America; in 1942, the Inter-American Institute of Agricultural Sciences (IAIAS) was created in Turrialba, Costa Rica, with Rafael Oreamuno nominated as its first director. In Rockefeller's perception, if Latin America did not produce enough supplies for its own needs, it would not provide for the allies in times of war.[6] The chance to realise larger-scale projects in agriculture arose soon after the attack on Pearl Harbor, when representatives of the Americas met at the Third Meeting of Consultation of Latin American Ministers of Foreign Affairs, in Rio de Janeiro on 15–28 January 1942. Besides seeking to maintain an alliance against the Axis, the Rio Conference reinforced Latin America's role as a food and rubber producer. As a result, in September of that year, an agreement between the OIAA and the Brazilian Ministry of Agriculture established the Brazilian-American Food Supply Commission – or *Comissão Brasileiro-Americana de Produção de Gêneros Alimentícios* – as a binational project, aiming to 'improve crop production and nutritional standards in the Amazon and northeast in the light of the restricted food supplies caused by disruptions in coastal shipping'.[7] The main goals of this agreement officially foresaw a) technical assistance to increase and improve the production of foodstuffs of animal and vegetable origin; b) provision of means, tools, equipment, insecticides, etc., to increase the production of animal and vegetable foodstuffs; c) amplification of the resources of the Divisions of Promotion of Vegetal and Animal Production, aiming at the implantation of an efficient extension service, in the mould of the modern agricultural techniques executed in Brazil and in the United States; d) elaboration of plans and technical assistance to the execution of irrigation, drainage and soil conservation works; e) collaboration in the resolution of problems of improvement, storage, conservation and distribution of food products; f) technical and financial assistance to agricultural colonisation; g) improvement of the nutritional conditions of

War II', *Passagens. Revista Internacional de História Política e Cultura Jurídica* 2 (4) (2010).

6. Dalrymple, *The AIA Story*.

7. Seth Garfield, 'The environment of wartime migration: Labor transfers from the Brazilian Northeast to the Amazon during World War II', *Journal of Social History* 43 (2010): 71–72.

the population in the areas of implementation of the Agreement.[8] Brazilian agronomist Oscar Guedes and Kenneth Kadow coordinated the programme in Brazil, and it also featured a crucial player for the AIA after the war, John Benjamin Griffing.[9] In practical terms, aiming to bring 1,450,000 acres under cultivation in the whole country, the OIAA and the Food Supply Division, coordinated by James LeCron and locally by Kadow, also launched a propaganda campaign, developing scripts for films on very specific topics, such as food production and shortage, irrigation, soil conservation, farm machinery and tools, and pest control.[10]

With a constellation of cooperative projects between Brazil and the United States initiated before and especially as a result of the war, Seth Garfield asserts that bilateral projects such as the Board of Economic Warfare, among others, were intended to be a true 'New Deal' for the Amazon. Because Japan had taken control of the rubber producing colonies and the United States consequently lost access to 97 per cent of its traditional sources, the Roosevelt administration's actions on this front were contemporaneous with those of the Food Supply Division, with the creation of the Rubber Survey Committee in August 1942. Faced with the immediate need for increased sources of raw rubber, the US

8. DECRETO-LEI Nº 5.246, DE 12 DE FEVEREIRO DE 1943. Digitally available in https://www2.camara.leg.br/legin/fed/declei/1940-1949/decreto-lei-5246-12-fevereiro-1943-415396-publicacaooriginal-1-pe.html. Accessed 9 Sept. 2022.

9. 'Technicians from the United States with experience in poultry development and livestock began arriving in December 1942, followed by mid-1943 by engineers, and specialists in irrigation, general farming, nutrition, grass and forage crops, and training and extension as well as an entomologist. Especially valuable for the commission's work was John B. Griffing, a Kansan with extensive experience in Brazilian agriculture. Griffing had graduated from Kansas State College with a degree in agronomy in 1904 and became an agricultural missionary, serving in Nanking, China, from 1919 to 1927. He succeeded Peter Rolfs as director of the Escola Superior da Agricultura e Veterinária in Viçosa, Minas Gerais from 1936 to 1939 when Rolfs' collaborator João Carlos Belo Lisboa fell out of favor with the state government. Praised in the Vargas-friendly *A Manhã* newspaper as 'a renowned technician to whom Brazilian agriculture owes much,' Griffing became the CIAA's representative for its Division V, encompassing four key northeastern states. He also served as a personal link to Oscar Guedes. Griffing interacted with several of his former agricultural school's graduates who, by 1943, had attained important positions in various agricultural entities in the Northeast'. Earl Richard Downes, 'Transforming Brazilian Agriculture. The experience of the Brazilian-American commission for the production of foodstuffs, 1942–1945', *Diálogos Latinoamericanos* **30** (2021): 10.

10. Frank D. McCann, Jr., *The Brazilian-American Alliance, 1937–1945* (Princeton University Press, 1973), p. 400.

government became directly involved in the development of projects to meet this objective; connected to the bilateral agreements signed in March 1942, along with rubber research would also come sanitation and health programmes to acclimate the thousands of northeastern migrants encouraged to work in the rubber plantations.[11] Also referring to the Amazon, the OIAA conceived subsidiary corporations such as the Institute of Inter-American Affairs (IAIA) which, in Brazil, created a cooperative agency, the Special Public Health Service (SESP). The basic agreement was signed in July 1942, foreseeing actions such as sanitation for the Amazon Valley, with the objective of controlling the advance of malaria in the rubber producing areas.[12] In practical terms, the health programmes tried to emulate Farm Security Administration experiments such as the migrant health programmes, aiming not only at providing 'acute medical services, but [having] an abiding focus on preventive medicine and health education'[13]. About 1943, the FSA and its medical programmes were disintegrating in the United States due to both domestic issues and concerns about international affairs; moreover, this shift in focus from rural rehabilitation to the war effort led to a decrease in the number of physicians and other health personnel.[14] But in a way, this was the export moment for FSA-influenced actions: after all the troubles faced by the FSA that year, their agricultural programmes at last became suitable to 'export' abroad.

In Brazil, the Food Supply Division was furthermore interested in incorporating a fisheries programme into the plan to increase agriculture in Latin American countries – as it had already done in Venezuela. The Fishery Mission to

11. Seth Garfield. 'A Amazônia no imaginário norte-americano em tempo de guerra', in Magali Romero Sá, Dominichi Miranda de Sá and André Felipe Cândido da Silva (eds), *As Ciências na História das Relações Brasil-EUA* (Rio de Janeiro: Mauad X; FAPERJ, 2020), p. 79.

12. André Luiz Vieira Campos, 'O Instituto de Assuntos Interamericanos e a cooperação em saúde pública entre Estados Unidos e Brasil', in Sá, de Sá and da Silva (eds), *As Ciências na História das Relações Brasil-EUA*, pp. 105–06. Soon after, IAIA was active in 18 countries employing 181 technicians and more than 13,000 civilians involved in environmental sanitation, malaria control, hospital construction and organization, staff training and health education projects. André Luiz Vieira Campos, *Políticas internacionais de saúde na Era Vargas. O Serviço Especial de Saúde Pública, 1942–1960* (Rio de Janeiro: Editora Fiocruz, 2006), p. 36.

13. Michael R. Grey, 'Dustbowls, disease, and the New Deal: The Farm Security Administration migrant health programs, 1935–1947', *Journal of the History of Medicine and Allied Sciences* **48** (1993): 3.

14. Michael R. Grey, *New Deal Medicine. The Rural Health Programs of the Farm Security Administration* (Baltimore and London: John Hopkins University Press, 1999), p. 130.

the Amazon Basin did not succeed, but it opened new perspectives of scientific collaboration to add to the *Instituto Agronômico do Norte* (Agronomic Institute of the North, IAN), created in 1939 and affiliated to the Brazilian Ministry of Agriculture. During and after the war, this institute promoted several studies on artificial selection, genetic improvement and acclimatisation of plant species such as rubber, rice and corn.[15]

Within these war programmes, Kenneth Kadow developed some projects that resonated strongly during and after the Office's closure. He graduated from Washington State College in 1932 and completed his doctorate from the University of Illinois in 1934. From this period, Kadow put his name to numerous technical bulletins deriving from his research at the UI Department of Horticulture, moving to head the Department of Horticulture at the University of Delaware around 1940. In November of that same year, the US and Brazilian governments began a collaboration aimed at building a military operations base called Parnamirim aviation camp, which was split into two areas: one for the Brazilian military and the other for the Americans, located in Rio Grande do Norte. Not far from there, in the metropolitan region of Recife, state of Pernambuco, Admiral Ingram Camp sheltered North American sailors. The OIAA, according to historian Ursula Prutsch, tried to resolve problems of food quality 'by establishing model farms, providing loans to small farmers, organizing agricultural training, and by introducing new hybrid seeds and artificial fertilizers'.[16] So, 'safeguarding the food supply chain in wartime and ensuring troops their nutritional requirements in a tropical environment represented a challenge for both Brazilian and U.S. technicians and governments'.[17] For this

15. Magali Romero Sá and Dominichi Miranda de Sá, 'Ciências, peixes e bois na floresta: a Amazônia nas relações científicas Brasil e Estados Unidos (1940–1950)', in Sá, De Sá and da Silva (eds), *As Ciências na História das Relações Brasil-EUA*, pp. 127–35.

16. Prutsch, 'Americanization of Brazil or a pragmatic wartime alliance?'. Prutsch states: 'As in other policy areas, the OIAA's Food Supply Division relied on the cooperation by Brazilian agencies, and in 1942, the Brazilian-American Commission of Food Production (CBA) was established. The net effect of such efforts is impossible to gauge with any precision, but it is remarkable that the OIAA at least in one region came under harsh criticism. The OIAA boosted meat and vegetable production in the vicinity of military bases, since Brazilian foodstuff did not meet the quality criteria of U.S. soldiers. As the surplus products were dumped on the local market, they actually decreased prices and provoked local producers to protest' (p. 193).

17. Roberta Biasillo and Claiton Marcio da Silva, 'Cultivating arid soils in Lybia and Brazil during World War II: The two-fold war between colonial and neo-colonial experiences', *Global Environment* 12 (1) (2019): 174.

reason, the Food Supply Division quickly adapted to the demands of the war and Kadow joined the programme, around 1942.

In a retrospective analysis, Kadow highlighted the cooperation of the Brazilian Ministry of Agriculture in providing Extension Service seeds of corn, beans and rice, distributed in increased quantities for the 1943 production season, with the aim of cultivating over 500,000 acres. However,

> because of localized drought and other uncontrollable factors, nearly 187,000 acres were lost, resulting in a net production of 313,000 acres. The majority of this was confined to the northeastern States, although some 35,000 or 40,000 acres were produced in the Amazon Valley. Similar results were achieved in 1944 with a small expenditure of funds, since farmers who received the initial distribution of seeds returned, for the most part, twice the original quantity at harvest time for redistribution.[18]

As part of the overall project, additional farms were operated through the cooperation programme, with 'improved seeds, tools, tractors and other equipment furnished either on a rental basis or at cost to private farmers who have the resources and abilities for producing quality seed on a commercial scale'. Moreover, the Food Supply Division arranged small tools and equipment traditional to the local pattern of agriculture: '103,480 hoes, 11,200 axes, and 20,000 *machados* (long knives)', aiming to relieve shortages due to the lack of shipping and manufacturing facilities. Moreover, 730 animal-drawn ploughs were loaned for use by farmer cooperators under the supervision of trained technicians, and ten rice mills were made available; the technicians were also able to combat 'the major' Brazilian insect enemy, the *saúva* ant, providing about 1,300 hand-operated ant exterminators and 173 tons of arsenic and sulphur.[19] Finally, cash loans and technical assistance were made available for small farmers. On this subject, Kadow believed:

> One of the most effective methods of increasing food production was through direct technical assistance by staff of Brazilian and North American Technicians to large private producers. Whenever a farmer was interested in increasing his acreage substantially and at the same time improving his methods and varieties of crops, full cooperation was given him. Plans were drawn up, new varieties introduced, heavy equipment, such as tractors, plows, cultivators, or other animal-drawn equipment, was rented to him on an operation-cost basis, and *agrônomos* were sent to supervise the work. This type of cooperation served the

18. Kenneth John Kadow, 'Attacking Brazil's food problems', *Agriculture in the Americas* V (3) (March 1945): 53–54.

19. Ibid., p. 54.

dual purpose of getting emergency production in those crops most difficult to increase, such as vegetables, and of teaching new methods to those farmers with funds, training, and initiative to continue on their own after they were well started. This was the method used for the production of high-quality seeds of such staple crops as rice, corn, and beans. In this program slightly over 100,000 acres resulted, several thousands of which were in vegetables.[20]

Figure 2. Map of North-Eastern Brazil. During World War II, an alliance between Brazil and the US created two American bases, one in Rio Grande do Norte and another in Pernambuco. The Zona da Mata is overlaid with dots, the Caatinga with horizontal lines.

In an area of transition between the originally fertile Zona da Mata – devastated by centuries of sugar cane plantations introduced by the Portuguese – and the arid Caatinga, Kadow organised the 'Nelson Rockefeller Farm' to supply Parnamirim Field. The group replicated the experiments by other US bases in the region, with a similar formula: loans to small farmers, fertilisers and seeds. According to historian Elisabeth Cobbs, the experiment was surprising

20. Ibid.

because almost all the value of the loans made to small farmers returned to the Office coffers. This was an incentive to cultivate small and honest Brazilian poor farmers, since the loans made to medium and large landowners took more time to be paid back.[21] Cobbs also recounts, in the context of a correspondence between Kadow and Rockefeller, that it would be possible to bring to birth in Brazil a true ideal of the yeoman, a small independent owner with political rights.[22] These ideals were part of the repertoire of dreams fed by rural rehabilitation programmes during the New Deal.

Meanwhile, scholars have been in agreement about US and Brazil ideals on resources development. As synthesised by Richard Downes, 'Rockefeller's concern for raising food production for the rubber-gathering effort coincided with the Vargas government's efforts to improve the standard of living, not only in Amazonia but also the Northeast.'[23] This topic is also emphasised by André Luiz Vieira de Campos regarding the SESP; Magali Romero de Sá and Dominichi Miranda de Sá on the IAN; and Rômulo de Paula Andrade discussing the *Superintendência de Valorização Econômica da Amazônia* (SPVEA), the government agency responsible for development projects in the Brazilian Amazon in the 1950s, using a Tennessee Valley Authority model. In general, post-war institutes or divisions adapted ideas that circulated in the country during the war.[24] In sum, the regional planning experimented with during the war expanded New Deal ideas to South America as they were anthropophagically swallowed by local governments and agricultural experts.

'Help People to Help Themselves': The Bolivar Foundation Project

With the end of the war imminent, Nelson Rockefeller enthusiastically evaluated the FSD experience as a replicable model for Latin America, starting with the creation of a new non-governmental agency, the Simon Bolivar Foundation (SBF or Bolivar Foundation). Aiming to bring together several individuals influential in political and economic circles in the United States and Latin America, Nelson Rockefeller worked with Kadow to put the idea of a new agency, based on FSD's experiences, on paper. On 6 December 1945, Kenneth Kadow answered Rockefeller's suggestions and questions, on an A4-size sheet

21. Elizabeth Cobbs, *Good Work at a Profit. Private Development and United States – Brazil Relation (1945–1960)* (Stanford, 1988, Ph.D. Diss. in History), p. 115.

22. Cobbs, *Good Work at a Profit*, p. 115.

23. Downes, 'Transforming Brazilian agriculture', 8.

24. de Paula Andrade, 'A TVA to the Amazon forest?'

printed with the official information of the Office of the Coordinator of Inter-American Affairs.[25] As can be seen from Figure 3, the words 'of the coordinator' had been officially erased from the original letterhead of the document (a change made on 23 March 1945), which led readers to extrapolate the new name of the agency: 'Office of Inter-American Affairs'. Apparently trivial, this issue reflects Nelson Rockefeller's loss of influence over the agency at the time. With Roosevelt's death in April 1945, the State Department incorporated the Office on 31 August– and Truman then fired Rockefeller before completely shutting it down in 1946.[26]

In the meantime, the first negotiations towards the creation of the Bolivar Foundation were already taking place; on 21 November 1944, while Nelson was still in charge of OIAA, it had been planned that the new foundation would officially continue the Office's activities in enacting state policy. With the end of the war approaching and an initial lack of interest, the group shelved the project; after Roosevelt's death, however, Rockefeller took up the idea again and assigned to Kadow the responsibility of preparing a project for the foundation.

Inspiring himself with experience developed in times of war, Nelson Rockefeller drafted the foundational ideas for an agency dedicated to bringing technical support to countries primarily characterised, in his perception, by poverty, illiteracy and disease. His messy notes, scribbled in pencil, show that these were the three initial words of the project; they referred to the main problems Rockefeller planned to address with technical knowledge. The word international set the tone for the post-war period.[27] This sketch resulted in the creation of the Bolivar Foundation – in honour of Simon Bolivar, widely considered the liberator of Spanish America. As economist and early Bolivar Foundation official James G. Maddox declared, the Foundation acted at a historical moment of uncertainty when it came to the technical cooperation agenda for countries considered underdeveloped, since emergency alliances cast

25. The Bolivar Foundation. Attached to From Kenneth J. Kadow to Nelson A. Rockefeller. 7 Dec. 1945. Collection: Family, Record Group: III 4B, Box: 01, Folder: AIA – Bolivar Foundation.

26. Initially named 'Office for Coordination of Commercial and Cultural Relations between the Americas', the office later changed its name to 'Office of the Coordinator of Inter-American Affairs' (OIAA), reflecting, according to historian Antonio Pedro Tota, Nelson's increasing authority. At the end of the war, changing its name to just 'Office of Inter-American Affairs' perhaps signalled a decline in Rockefeller's influence over the agency. See Tota, *O imperialismo sedutor*, p. 50.

27. Nelson Rockefeller papers. Bolivar Foundation papers. AIA-IBEC Box 1 RAC.

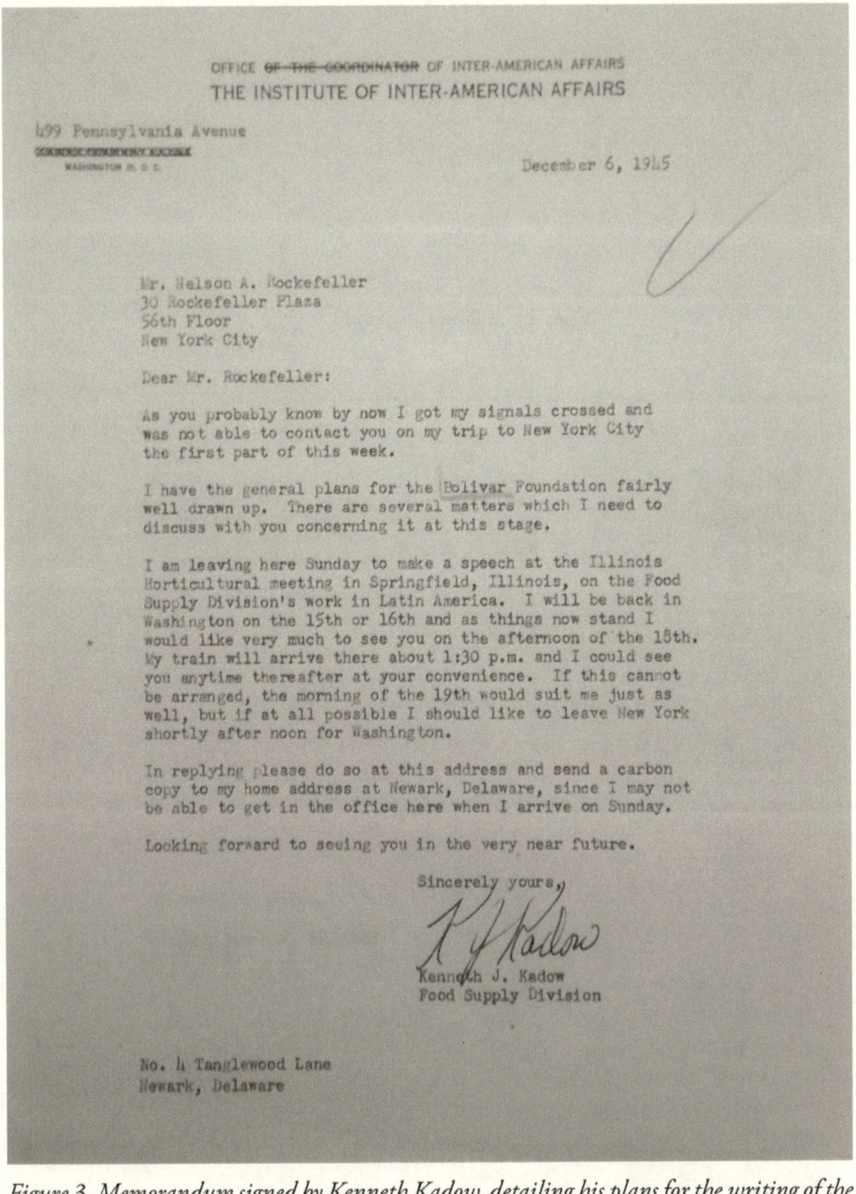

OFFICE ~~OF THE COORDINATOR~~ OF INTER-AMERICAN AFFAIRS
THE INSTITUTE OF INTER-AMERICAN AFFAIRS

499 Pennsylvania Avenue
WASHINGTON 25, D. C.

December 6, 1945

Mr. Nelson A. Rockefeller
30 Rockefeller Plaza
56th Floor
New York City

Dear Mr. Rockefeller:

As you probably know by now I got my signals crossed and was not able to contact you on my trip to New York City the first part of this week.

I have the general plans for the Bolivar Foundation fairly well drawn up. There are several matters which I need to discuss with you concerning it at this stage.

I am leaving here Sunday to make a speech at the Illinois Horticultural meeting in Springfield, Illinois, on the Food Supply Division's work in Latin America. I will be back in Washington on the 15th or 16th and as things now stand I would like very much to see you on the afternoon of the 18th. My train will arrive there about 1:30 p.m. and I could see you anytime thereafter at your convenience. If this cannot be arranged, the morning of the 19th would suit me just as well, but if at all possible I should like to leave New York shortly after noon for Washington.

In replying please do so at this address and send a carbon copy to my home address at Newark, Delaware, since I may not be able to get in the office here when I arrive on Sunday.

Looking forward to seeing you in the very near future.

Sincerely yours,

K J Kadow

Kenneth J. Kadow
Food Supply Division

No. 4 Tanglewood Lane
Newark, Delaware

Figure 3. Memorandum signed by Kenneth Kadow, detailing his plans for the writing of the Bolivar Foundation project. Note in the official letterhead that the Office of the Coordinator has improvisedly become the Office of Inter-American Affairs. From Kenneth J. Kadow to Nelson A. Rockefeller. 7 December 1945. Collection: Family, Record Group: III 4B, Box: 01, Folder: AIA – Bolivar Foundation.

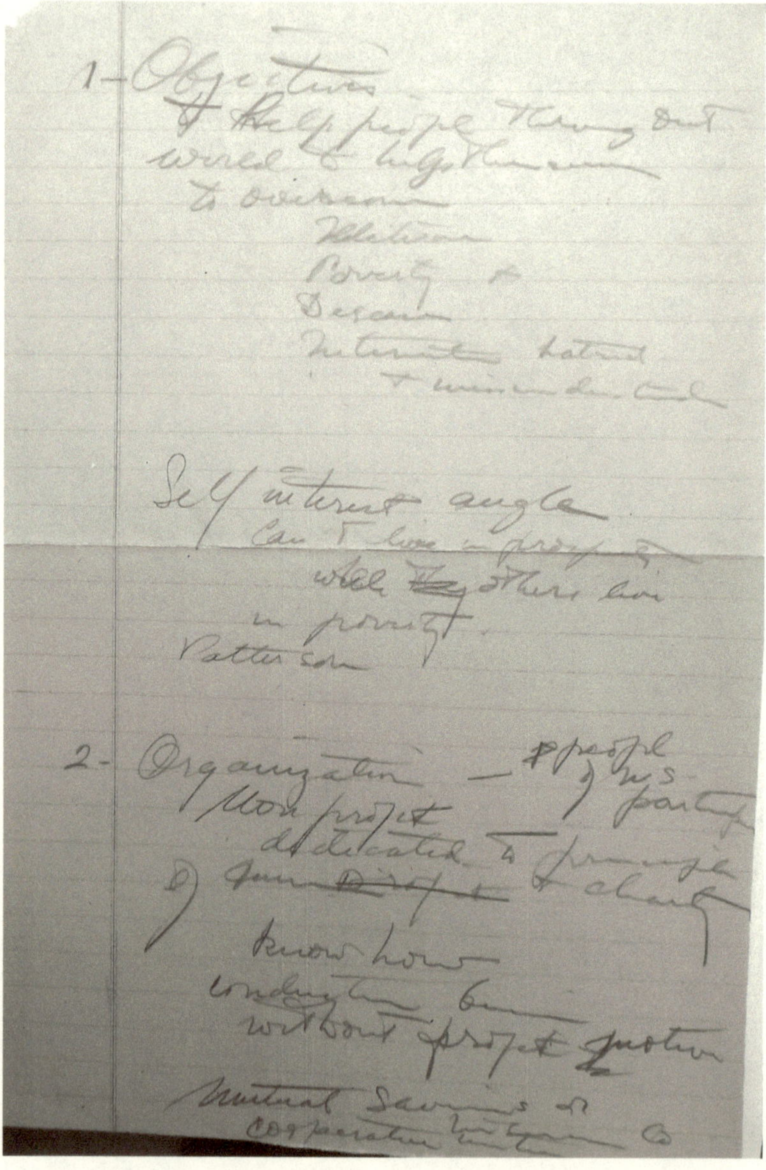

Figure 4. Drafting a brand new world. First page of AIA draft almost illegibly written by Nelson Rockefeller. Rockefeller Archive Center. Collection: Family. Record Group: III 4. B. Box 01, Folder AIA – Simon Bolivar Foundation.

during the war were, in many cases, no longer justified.[28] Post-war modernisers sought mechanisms for the adoption of new technical knowledge, so that local leaders themselves could ensure the continuity of the process.

Theoretically, this would kick-start dynamics by which nations could attain advanced stages of development without recourse to paternalistic help: 'Help people to help themselves', wrote Rockefeller on his sketchpad, inspired by the pragmatism philosophy. These localised experiences were expedcted then to result in publications about the programme, reporting failures or successes.[29] Thus, as Rockefeller's initial sketch included aspects of training and technical cooperation between the United States and other countries, his plan focused more on the realisation of a somewhat flexible experience, based on a trial-and-error system, than on simply applying a specific, rigidly defined model.

By early 1945, the Bolivar Foundation was set to operate only in Venezuela. Then, in September of that year, Nelson Rockefeller wrote to the then US ambassador to Venezuela, Frank Corrigan, stating that, with the involvement of 'enthusiastic' Gene Holman, President of Standard Oil of New Jersey, the work of the new foundation could extend throughout the hemisphere.[30] Moreover, from 1945 the group discussed the Bolivar Foundation's future management, with Kadow suggesting Dee W. Jackson to head the Economic Development Division – Jackson was then working at the American Embassy in Brazil, after a role at the General Motors Company in the previous decade.

As noted above, the initial design of the agency was closely linked to Nelson Rockefeller's ideas and relationships. Not coincidentally, the other four members of the new project had all served in the OIAA during the war. Lockwood was an OIAA attorney and became a legal adviser to Nelson Rockefeller; former reporter Francis Jamieson was director of the Press Division at the OCIAA; Berent Friele was a former director of the OIAA in Brazil; and Harrison was OIAA's assistant coordinator. As mentioned earlier, Kenneth Kadow had worked in the Food Supply Division (FSD), also at the OIAA.[31] John Lockwood acted as a legal consultant for the agency's founders during this time. In addition to Nelson himself, the Board of Trustees aimed to include an influential circle of politicians such as Franklin D. Roosevelt, Henry Wallace and Harold Stassen

28. James Maddox and Howard Tolley, *Case Studies of Training Through Technical Cooperation*, [s.l.]: NPA, [1956], p. 11.

29. Nelson Rockefeller papers. Bolivar Foundation papers. AIA-IBEC Box 1 RAC.

30. From Nelson A. Rockefeller to Frank P. Corrigan. 26 Sept. 1945. Collection: Family, Record Group: III 4B, Box: 01, Folder: AIA – Bolivar Foundation.

31. Cobbs, *Good Work at a Profit*, p. 117.

– then Governor of Minnesota and critic of American isolationism – as well as local politicians in places where the foundation was to maintain relations, and the foundation's director.[32] Kadow believed this would raise interest among Latin American executives and in the foundation, given that few American politicians had shown concern about Latin American problems before.

Nelson Rockefeller was not an expert in agriculture. That was the work of Kadow in the Food Supply Division. Thus Rockefeller chose Kadow to shape the ideas scribbled the previous year: after years working in the Office, Rockefeller considered Kadow an expert 'with a background of university work as well as broad experience in actual farming operations'.[33] Accepting the new mission, on 6 December 1945, Kadow apologised for the delay in response.[34] This was not unnecessary, since, after years in public life, Rockefeller was looking for new plans and needed quick answers: the OCIAA was practically a memory already. The Bolivar Foundation's ideological groundwork remained close to Nelson Rockefeller's vision, though, not least in the definition of the problems addressed. The Bolivar Foundation 'recognizes that misery, hunger, disease and ignorance in any part of this hemisphere forms a constant threat to welfare and security of all', stated the document delivered by Kadow in December 1945. It also sent a direct message to US executives in Latin America: 'It recognizes that social prosperity goes hand in hand with economic prosperity.'[35] For Kadow, whose thinking reflected that of Rockefeller, this constituted a democratic guarantee in the face of recently defeated Nazism and Communist expansion.[36] The agency's proponents sought to persuade US entrepreneurs – from Creole to Coca-Cola and beyond – to invest in their new enterprise.

---

32. From Kenneth Kadow to Nelson A. Rockefeller. Re: Board of Trustees. Newark, Delaware, 24 Dec. 1945. Collection: Family. Record Group: III 4 B. Box 01, Folder AIA – Simon Bolivar Foundation.

33. From Nelson Rockefeller to Robert J. Kleberg Jr. 21 Feb. 1946. Collection: Family, Record Group: III 4B, Box: 01, Folder: AIA – Bolivar Foundation.

34. The Bolivar Foundation. Attached to From Kenneth J. Kadow to Nelson A. Rockefeller. 7 Dec. 1945. Collection: Family, Record Group: III 4B, Box: 01, Folder: AIA – Bolivar Foundation.

35. Ibid.

36. H.F. Prioleau. Memorandum. Proposed Latin American Foundation. 28 Sept. 1945. Collection: Family, Record Group: III 4B, Box: 01, Folder: AIA – Bolivar Foundation.

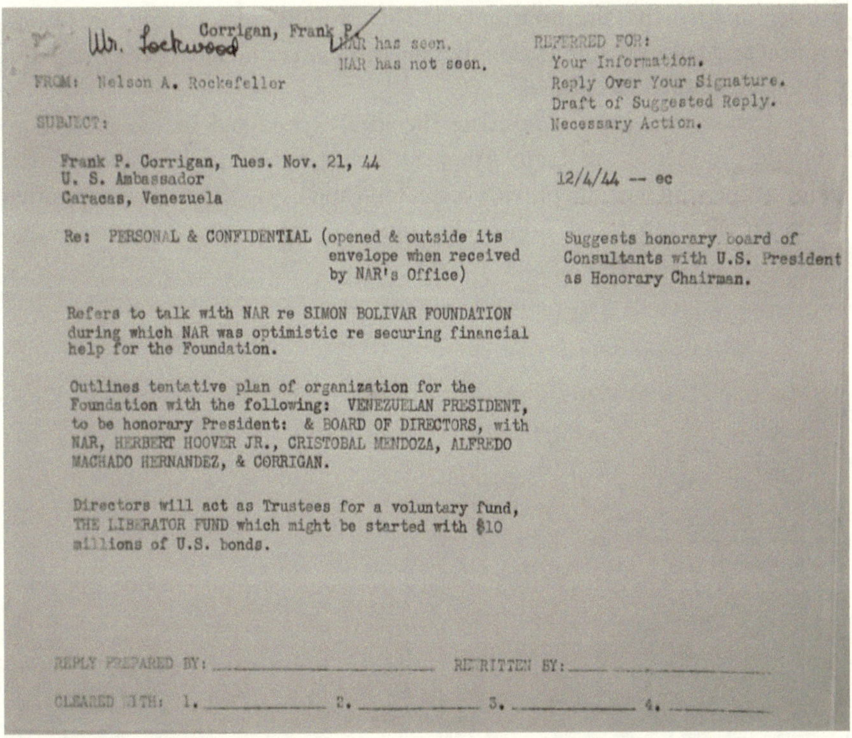

Mr. Lockwood Corrigan, Frank P. NAR has seen.
NAR has not seen.

REFERRED FOR:
Your Information.
Reply Over Your Signature.
Draft of Suggested Reply.
Necessary Action.

FROM: Nelson A. Rockefeller

SUBJECT:

Frank P. Corrigan, Tues. Nov. 21, 44
U. S. Ambassador
Caracas, Venezuela

12/4/44 -- ec

Re: PERSONAL & CONFIDENTIAL (opened & outside its envelope when received by NAR's Office)

Suggests honorary board of Consultants with U.S. President as Honorary Chairman.

Refers to talk with NAR re SIMON BOLIVAR FOUNDATION during which NAR was optimistic re securing financial help for the Foundation.

Outlines tentative plan of organization for the Foundation with the following: VENEZUELAN PRESIDENT, to be honorary President: & BOARD OF DIRECTORS, with NAR, HERBERT HOOVER JR., CRISTOBAL MENDOZA, ALFREDO MACHADO HERNANDEZ, & CORRIGAN.

Directors will act as Trustees for a voluntary fund, THE LIBERATOR FUND which might be started with $10 millions of U.S. bonds.

REPLY PREPARED BY: ______ REWRITTEN BY: ______

CLEARED WITH: 1. ______ 2. ______ 3. ______ 4. ______

Figure 5. Nelson Rockefeller intended to attract influential politicians like then US President Franklin Roosevelt, as well as to save a permanent seat for the president of Venezuela. In the above memo, we see Rockefeller's optimism regarding the attempt to organise the Bolivar Foundation and the establishment of a budget fund. From Nelson A. Rockefeller. Subject: Frank P. Corrigan, Tuesday, 21 Nov. 1944 (Personal and confidential). Caracas, Venezuela, 21 November 1944. Collection: Family. Record Group: III 4. B. Box 01, Folder AIA – Simon Bolivar Foundation.

The delay in Kadow's response to Rockefeller stemmed from Kadow's attendance the same week at the Illinois Horticultural Meeting in Springfield, Illinois, where he presented the experiences of the Food Supply Division in Latin America. The following day, he outlined his vision of the project to establish an agency: originally entitled 'Foundation Purposes and Plans by Kenneth J. Kadow'; the revision of 31 December would pencil in the name chosen for the initial venture. Thus, the document was renamed 'Bolivar Foundation Purposes and Plans'. The reference to Simon Bolivar served a possible initial strategy of the foundation – to show respect for the myths of Latin America and demonstrate that the insertion of US institutions did not mean foreignism, political and cultural domination, but an amalgamation, an approximation of Anglophile and Latin cultures.

Kadow was able to translate the ideals contained in the project: to promote the increase of Latin American living standards through technical cooperation, which would provide better food and living conditions, supported by the growing process of industrialisation.

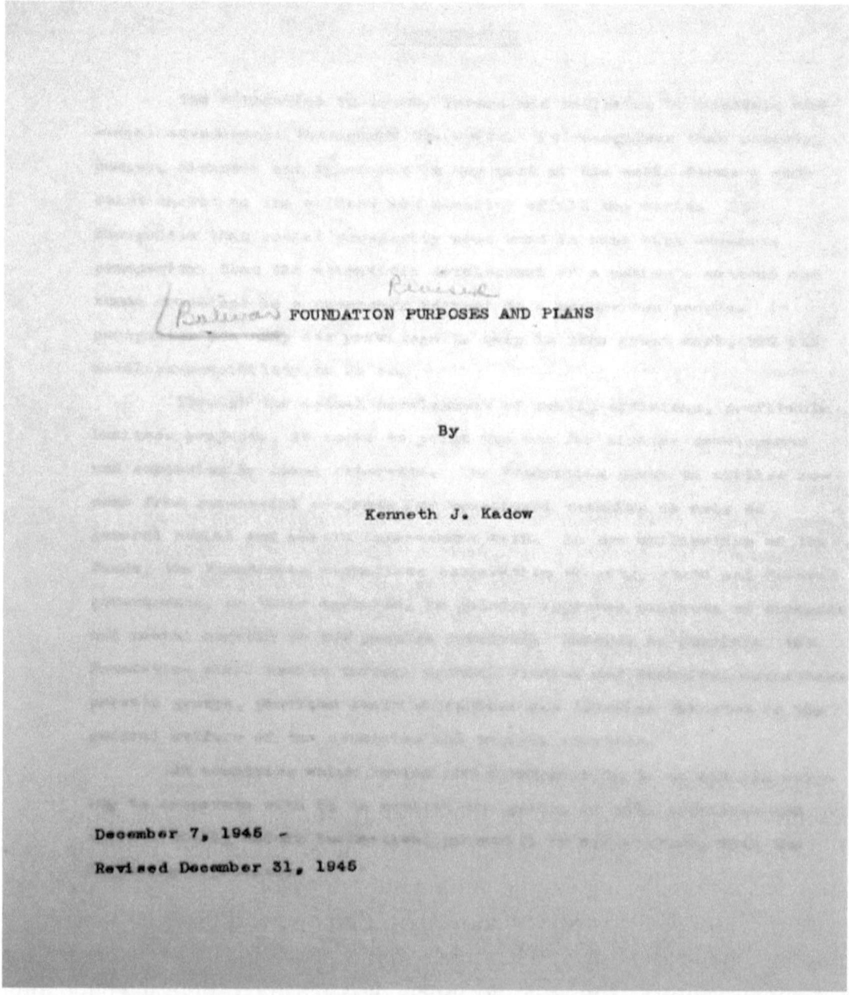

FOUNDATION PURPOSES AND PLANS

By

Kenneth J. Kadow

December 7, 1945 -

Revised December 31, 1945

Figure 6. Memorandum containing the revised version of a foundation proposal. The Bolivar Foundation. Attached to From Kenneth J. Kadow to Nelson A. Rockefeller. 7 December 1945. Collection: Family, Record Group: III 4B, Box: 01, Folder: AIA – Bolivar Foundation.

The aforementioned memo of 7 December demonstrates the fundamental role of Kadow in the conception of the programmes.[37] Kadow expressed his willingness to break with the traditionally accepted models of technical cooperation, seeking to submit the processes of education to the initiatives of entrepreneurship. Attracting the attention of executives before educators was part of the project of the Bolivar Foundation, since the agency would depend on the investment of companies such as Creole Petroleum to develop its activities. In seeking counsel on his entire proposal, Kadow remarked that the Bolivar Foundation idea was

> a radical departure from ordinary accepted concepts of foundation or educational project. It is highly probable that the average educator would not approve of it but I am quite certain hardheaded businessmen would see its advantage at once.[38]

With the project in hand, Nelson Rockefeller wrote in early 1946 to Robert J. Kleberg Jr., President of the King Ranch of Texas and oil business entrepreneur, to announce his intentions to maintain his programme in the region:

> Confidentially, I have been working on some plans to develop a Foundation, which can carry on some of the ideas, and work we started in Latin America during the war, putting it on a self-supporting basis. As the activities will be largely in the field of agriculture and economic development, I am anxious to get your reactions and very frank comments.[39]

It was the first presentation of the Bolivar Foundation project. Kadow later went to Texas for several days to analyse the operation and management of agricultural activities at King Ranch in Kingsville, probably in May 1946.[40] Previously, in February, Kadow had also met with Dr Haskill of the United States Department of Agriculture (USDA), who would be making available the bulletins published by the institution.[41] In April, he went to the West Coast of the United States where he exchanged experiences with Rafael Oreamuno.

---

37. From Kenneth J. Kadow to Nelson A. Rockefeller. 7 Dec. 1945. Collection: Family, Record Group: III 4B, Box: 01, Folder: AIA – Bolivar Foundation.

38. Ibid.

39. From Nelson Rockefeller to Robert J. Kleberg Jr. 21 Feb. 1946. Collection: Family, Record Group: III 4B, Box: 01, Folder: AIA – Bolivar Foundation.

40. Kleberg wrote to Rockefeller: 'I did the best I could in helping him and thinking out loud in connection with the problem he was working on.' From Robert Kleberg Jr to Nelson A. Rockefeller. Kingsville, Texas, 3 May 1946. Collection: Family. Record Group: III 4 B. Box 01, Folder AIA – Simon Bolivar Foundation.

41. From Kadow to Nelson A. Rockefeller. 26 Feb. 1946. Collection: Family. Record Group: III 4 B. Box 01, Folder AIA – Simon Bolivar Foundation.

Nelson Rockefeller himself wrote to Rafael in April 1946: 'Some time ago you and I discussed the possibility of our helping in connection with the operation of the Turrialba School if we went ahead with the Foundation idea', referring to one of IAIAS's units. Next, Nelson described what would become the hallmark of his projects in Latin America – the realisation of a small experiment that, if successful, could become a model: 'Very confidentially, we are now planning to proceed on a small scale with the organization of our program which will probably be known as the American International Association.'[42]

The contents of the letter sent to Oreamuno about the Bolivar Foundation approximated the ideas outlined by Kadow and Nelson Rockefeller in December 1945; but correspondence with the Costa Rican colleague already indicated the name change to American International Association, which possibly embraced a more comprehensive conception – and which materialised in 1946. By this time, however, according to historian Elisabeth Cobbs, OIAA staff were unwilling to let go of programmes created during the war.[43] In addition, Latin America was Nelson Rockefeller's area of operation and the continent still represented great possibility for his political ascension and influence in the region: Nelson had always believed that abandoning the Good Neighbor Policy would lead to a disaster for American business interests in Latin America, including Standard Oil.[44]

As the war ended and OIAA funding dwindled, two important actors lost their influence: Adolf Berle, assistant secretary for Latin American Affairs, and Undersecretary Sumner Welles. Nelson had to try to succeed Berle, a position he finally attained in August 1945.[45] Though Nelson Rockefeller's political and economic intentions motivated him to maintain close relations with Latin America, the end of World War II left him fearing that a repeat of the 1929 Wall Street crash was possibly around the corner in the United States. Since abundant food production to supply allied troops was no longer necessary, international cooperation represented a way to avoid overproduction. There seemed to be plenty of reason to believe that agriculture was of utmost importance in avoiding a new Great Depression: at least this was the view spread by Boyce Morgan, Kiplinger Washington Agency's correspondent, whose writings reached Nelson Rockefeller. The document warned: 'Remember the

42. From Nelson A. Rockefeller to Rafael Oreamuno. 4 Apr. 1946. Collection: Family. Record Group: III 4 B. Box 01, Folder AIA – Simon Bolivar Foundation.

43. Cobbs, *Good Work at a Profit*, p. 116.

44. Ibid., p. 185.

45. Ibid., p. 187.

"farm problem"... that plague of assorted troubles in agriculture and its allied industries which grew out of the last war, made headlines in the '20s and '30s? Well, once more we're in a period of post-war readjustment'. Finally, it asks: 'Is it "Look out, boys – here we go again?"'[46] This fear was far from unusual; at the March 1945 Inter-American Conference on the Problems of War and Peace in Mexico, American representatives who signed the Minutes of Chapultepec aimed to avoid a possible return of the Great Depression. Assistant Secretary-General Nelson Rockefeller himself declared: 'the United States was full of ideas, workers and products needed markets' or, according to Rockefeller's rhetoric, evoking one of the great North American myths, 'frontiers'.[47]

Roosevelt reinforced Rockefeller's worldview. In July 1944, Roosevelt declared at the Bretton Woods Conference that the United States should be the economic guardians of those hard times while 'memories of the Depression dominated the minds of the delegates', and Bretton Woods planners were determined that past circumstances should not recur. Their objective, according to historian Michael Heale, was to 'distribute happiness throughout the earth' and the key to this goal would be a global marketplace in which free trade might flourish together with international control over national monetary systems.[48] Two international governmental agencies were established to facilitate this healthier global economy. The World Bank was to extend credit to countries to rebuild their economies and promote the economic development of emerging nations. The International Monetary Fund aimed to promote international currency stability, primarily by providing financial assistance to countries with serious balance of payments problems. The Bretton Woods Conference representatives agreed that

> [the] monetary system would rest on the US dollar and gold. The United States, in effect, would be the world's banker. Unsurprisingly, both the World Bank and the IMF soon became largely subject to the will of the American government.[49]

The immediate post-war uncertainties forced these members of the Western financial and political elite to adopt what they believed was the right mindset, since a new crisis of overproduction could generate new economic and financial crises. Renewed interest in Malthusian ideas within post-war debates was

46. Boyce Morgan, *Are We Facing Another Postwar 'Farm Problem?'*, 25 Feb.1946. Collection: Family, Record Group: III 4B, Box: 01, Folder: AIA – Bolivar Foundation.

47. Cobbs, *Good Work at a Profit*, p. 197.

48. M.J. Heale, *Twentieth-Century America. Politics and Power in the United States, 1900–2000* (London: Arnold, 2004), pp. 139–40.

49. Ibid.

therefore certainly not a coincidence. Several international agencies, such as the United Nations' Food and Agriculture Organization (FAO), argued that population growth was above food production levels; in the early Cold War, increasing food production was high on the strategic agenda. Though distant in time, Malthus' worldview formed part of the repertoire of discussion. What is more, the setting-up of the Rockefeller Brothers Fund (RBF) in the 1940s brought together brothers John, Nelson, Winthrop and David, carving out more and more space for philanthropic activities. While Nelson focused on agriculture in Latin America, John Rockefeller III addressed the world's population growth; the RBF provided essential support to John's Population Council during the early years of his work and later supported the IRI Research Institute, especially its basic crop programme in Brazil and Venezuela.[50]

The political and economic interests of the Rockefeller family motivated the continued activities of its organisations in Latin America; economic pressures and uncertainties generated by the end of World War II created a context in which international cooperation and production strategies could help in avoiding a new global financial crash. It was precisely in this context that the Bolivar Foundation became the American International Association, as we will see in the following section.

Philanthropy and the Creation of the American International Association for Economic and Social Development

The Bolivar Foundation became the AIA, created and based in an office at 30 Rockefeller Plaza, New York City. Originally, the group framed the AIA as a philanthropic organisation aiming to provide agricultural technical assistance for countries considered less developed. Later in 1946, Kenneth Kadow built upon Rockefeller's initial idea to define what would become the principles of the AIA:

> Based upon a faith in the inherent dignity and worth of the individual and in the capacity and desire for self-improvement of human beings of whatever nationality, race, creed or color, and upon a conviction that the welfare of each nation and person in the modern world is closely related to the welfare and opportunities for advancement of all the people of the world, this Association

50. David Rockefeller, *Memoirs* (New York: Random House Trade, 2003), p. 154. From 1956 to 1959, the RBF made a donation equivalent to $ 525,000 for AIA to develop projects in Brazil. From Walter L. Crawford to The Board of Directors of AIA. Subject: Grant to AIA from Rockefeller Brothers Fund for Brazil Program. 6 Jan. 1956. Collection: Family; Record Group: III 4B; Box: 01; Folder: 7B, AIA Brazil.

> is organized for the purpose of promoting self-development and better standards of living, together with understanding and cooperation, among peoples throughout the world.[51]

The two men thought that the American experience of social and economic development could guarantee better possibilities for people of 'any nationality'. Rockefeller commented on the objectives of the AIA in a confidential message to his father in 1946. He explained to John Jr. that the type of cooperation proposed by the agency sought to eradicate poverty, disease and illiteracy and would continue the philanthropic tradition of the Rockefeller Family.[52] Scholars have thus described the AIA's early activities in Latin America as philanthropic in the classical sense of the term: the concept of philanthropy is not only the allocation of private resources to activities of public interest, but also work in the interest of humanity in general.[53] In Latin America, the philanthropic associations of the nineteenth and early twentieth centuries had a predominantly religious character, created by privileged social sectors with the purpose of providing relief to others in need, motivated by charitable impulses.[54] Moreover, these associations played a fundamental role in the construction and maintenance of local power, by pacifying possible conflicts and precariously stepping in to replace fragile and incipient states.[55]

Nelson Rockefeller felt that charity and business did not have totally delimited boundaries, but they did interact: 'Nelson had a hard time adjusting himself to the fact that business and charity are two different things', wrote Lockwood.[56] Originally, the idea of the AIA was, on the one hand, to raise resources and, on the other, to invest these resources in philanthropic activities. However, New York legislation did not allow an activity in these terms: it would be necessary to create two institutions with distinct objectives; thus,

51. Dalrymple, *The AIA Story*.

52. From Nelson A. Rockefeller to Mr John D. Rockefeller, Jr. Subject: Proposed American International Association. 27 Apr. 1946. Collection: Family; Record Group: III 4B; Box: 11, Folder: 104. Nelson convidou seu pai para presidir a AIA, mas John Jr não aceitou a tarefa.

53. Maria Gabriela Marinho, *Norte-americanos no Brasil. Uma história da Fundação Rockefeller na Universidade de São Paulo (1934–1952)* (Campinas: Autores Associados, São Paulo: Universidade São Francisco, 2001), p. 14.

54. Claudia Maria Ribeiro Viscardi, 'Mutualismo e filantropia', *Locus. Revista de História* 10 (1) (2004): 100.

55. Ibid.

56. Cary Reich, *The Life of Nelson A. Rockefeller: Worlds to Conquer (1908–1958)* (New York: Doubleday, 1996), p. 407.

the Bolivar Foundation became the AIA in July 1946 and later, in January 1947, it adopted for itself the actions of philanthropy. The International Basic Economy Co., meanwhile, began activities in the agricultural industry. With this, the AIA was the Sunday agency –where the millionaire could carry out his activities of charity – while IBEC would be the 'weekday' company directed to the realisation of business.[57] In this manner, some of the projects that could generate profits became of interest to IBEC, for example, the prospect of creating a fertiliser industry. Nevertheless, Rockefeller still insisted that even this weekday enterprise had to have an overarching social purpose. Just like the AIA, IBEC's certificate of incorporation attached a preamble stating its social concerns. The company declared that, by promoting 'economic development in various parts of world', it would 'increase the production and availability of goods, things and services useful to the lives or livelihood of their people', and would 'better their standards of living'.[58]

Starting from a theoretical myriad that included capitalism, philanthropy and rural development, Rockefeller based his thesis on the idea that American capital should participate in the economic development of the country in which it is invested. Similarly, speaking of IBEC, he argued that, in the post-1945 context, American capitalism would drive in a new direction: 'People before profits'. In early 1949, Rockefeller had the opportunity to more clearly express his view on the role of capitalism: 'We believed that American capitalism was ready to play a new part in world affairs', not 'seeking just the areas, which promised the greatest profit, but going to the areas of greatest needs'. With missionary rhetoric, he continued: 'We believed that it was ready to go where it could produce the most goods and render the greatest services' and, finally, 'that it would have the ingenuity and resourcefulness to accomplish these things on a sound and profitable basis, which would contribute to the well-being and real wealth of the people it served'.[59]

The philanthropic practices and religious ideals that grounded the AIA were also be associated with political or economic interests. Just as IBEC could profit from fostering research in Latin America, David Rockefeller also indicated that Chase National Bank's business kept on growing south of Rio Grande. In late 1947, David declared that he was frustrated with the difficulties of trying to convince clients to negotiate with Chase agencies in Paris and London and asked to be transferred to the Latin American section of the Foreign Affairs

57. Ibid., p. 408.

58. Ibid., p. 407.

59. 'People before profits', *The Science News-Letter* 55 (15) (9 Apr. 1949): 227.

Department. According to David, Latin America had become a more important region for Chase, and his own interest in the region's business, culture and art had grown.[60]

Nelson's younger brother also embraced this point of view when he became involved in the AIA's work in 1948. Following a visit to the Chase National Bank agencies in Puerto Rico, Cuba and Panama, David recalled a memo he addressed to his uncle Winthrop Aldrich in March 1948, where he noted the need for Chase to build different relations with local governments because nationalism was on the rise in Latin America.[61] David shared with Nelson the view that the rise of nationalism was a reaction to imperial policy practised for centuries, and that a change of methods was necessary. David understood that new times demanded a new attitude from Chase, rethinking policies towards Latin America; in his memo, David also wrote that their Southern neighbours would hardly tolerate American institutions on their soil without the latter participating in the local economy. In short, maintaining the Rockefeller family's oil or banking business would require negotiation with this wave of nationalism.[62] Later in the 1950s, David Rockefeller became an important decision-maker of the IRI Research Institute, providing funds from Chase, oil companies and the Rockefeller Brothers Fund for agricultural experiments.

To reduce nationalist resistance, the strategy used was to initiate a philanthropic project, in the belief that different populations, regardless of their previous history, religious culture or ethno-racial constitution, could emulate the considerable progress associated with the historical experience of the United States. In theory, values such as experimentation, self-organisation and democracy would help Latin American societies eliminate traditions that were holding them back, and thus achieve an economic and social model compatible with the new post-war times. In this perspective, the AIA's original project 'regards an opportunity to participate in man's more rapid development not only as its privilege but also as its moral responsibility'. Science would be a benchmark to operate the AIA's project: 'demonstrations of science's usefulness on a sound commercial basis will result in its adaptation by local peoples as a useful force for general development'.[63]

60. Rockefeller, *Memoirs*, p. 141

61. Rockefeller, *Memoirs*.

62. Ibid.

63. The American International Association for Economic and Social Development. An explanation of its objectives and method of operation by Kenneth J. Kadow for Nelson A.

In the period between the conception of the AIA project and its implementation, however, many things changed. As early as the late 1940s, with the beginning of programmes in Latin America, the actions of the AIA transcended the initial borders of the informal US Empire. A first example can be seen in the Venezuelan case, discussed in the next chapter.

Rockefeller. 19 Feb. 1946. Collection: Family. Record Group: III 4 B. Box 01, Folder AIA – Simon Bolivar Foundation. p. 2.

CHAPTER 3.

VENEZUELA: THE LAUNCH OF THE AIA'S PROGRAMMES IN LATIN AMERICA

A good idea seems to be harder to sell than a gold brick
(Frank Corrigan, US Ambassador in Venezuela)

Before US Republicans spread fearmongering about communism, in Democrat Harry Truman's second term and throughout the 1950s, Republican Nelson Rockefeller also asserted that protecting American security was a goal behind actions to keep nations 'free'. This pro-freedom rhetoric was already in use in the immediate post-war period and became commonplace during the Cold War, mainly after the Chapultepec conference in 1945. The purpose of this meeting was to create a defence agreement for the Americas, taking the view that a possible attack on any country in the region would be considered an assault on all American allies. With World War II ending, Nelson Rockefeller no longer saw the Nazis as the main danger, durably shifting his critical focus to communism.[1]

Historians often argue that there were two different phases in Latin America: the first, beginning in 1944, 1945 or 1946, depending on the country, has three distinct but interrelated aspects: democratisation, a consolidation of the political Left and labour militancy. The second – starting as early as 1945 in some cases, expanding over the following two years and reaching major proportions in 1948 – is characterised by greater control over the organised labour movement, with stronger state power; the communist parties suffered repression; the reformist parties took a turn to the right and democratic advances were contained.[2] Therefore, in the mid-1940s, elections all over Latin America achieved relatively high popular participation, while, for the first time a number of so-called progressive political parties and movements came to

1. Colby and Dennet, *Thy Will be Done.*

2. Leslie Bethel, 'Introduction. The postwar conjuncture in Latin America: democracy, labor, and the left', in Bethel and Ian Roxborough (eds), *Latin American Between the Second World War and Cold War, 1944–1948* (New York: Cambridge University Press, 1992), p. 2.

power.[3] Democracy set the tone of public debate and shaped popular expectations of Latin American politicians. Nelson Rockefeller did not attempt to distance himself from this tendency – for example, when he addressed Romulo Betancourt, from the Revolutionary Government Junta of Venezuela, pointing out the necessity for American capital to help develop the country, Rockefeller stated:

> the dynamic force of private enterprise, acting within the framework of a democracy, has the necessary creative energy to stimulate the production of such item as food and other products of prime necessity required by the Venezuelan economy.[4]

The Truman government's announcement of the Marshall Plan – financial aid for the reconstruction of Europe with the intent to consolidate the continent's market economy – increasingly reinforced the policy of containment of communism that Nelson Rockefeller had advocated years earlier. Even though US actions were directed toward Europe, the possibility of attaining leadership in the region encouraged the Brazilian government of Eurico Gaspar Dutra to break off from the communists, leading to a rupture in Brazil's diplomatic relations with both the Soviet Union and China.[5]

This chapter discusses actions directed at Latin American countries by the AIA at a time when the United States focused its foreign aid efforts on Europe. To do this, I examine the AIA's initial projects in Venezuela.

The AIA Experience in Venezuela

In 1944, Nelson Rockefeller asked the US ambassador to Venezuela, Frank P. Corrigan, for his opinion on the potential roles of an agency like the Bolivar Foundation in the country. Responding in November, Corrigan asserted that, even in the face of possible difficulties in attracting resources, 'I am of the opinion that we should begin. The Foundation has been the subject of talks for almost five years and if you and I do not take it, it may take five more.'[6] In addition to

3. Ibid.
4. From Nelson A. Rockefeller to Mr. Romulo Betancourt. English translation. 19 June 1947. Collection: Family; Record Group: III 4B; Box: 27; Folder: 269.
5. Peggy Beçak, *Evolução das relações comerciais Brasil – Estados Unidos de 1945 a 1995: no contexto da política externa e dos 'interesses nacionais'* (São Paulo: USP, 2007; Ph.D. Diss. in History of Economy), p. 117.
6. From Frank P. Corrigan to Nelson A. Rockefeller. Personal and confidential. Caracas, Venezuela, 21 Nov. 1944. Collection: Family. Record Group: III 4 B. Box 01, Folder

encouraging Rockefeller, Corrigan made it clear that, since the days of OIAA, the US government had been planning a similar project. With the end of World War II approaching, Rockefeller foresaw that the government of Isaiah Medina Angarita could quickly help shape a relatively new political and economic agenda for the post-war period. Corrigan suggested that the Board of Directors could manage a fund called the Liberators Fund, with an initial contribution of $10 million. The Board would be made up of Nelson Rockefeller, Herbert Hoover Jr. – son of former President Herbert Hoover and at the time overseeing new oil contracts for US Oil Companies in Venezuela – former Venezuelan Finance Ministers Cristóbal Mendoza and Alfredo Machado Hernandez, and the US Ambassador himself. Finally, he suggested that the President of Venezuela should also be invited to become the institution's honorary chair to foster diplomatic rapprochement. In general, the fund would sponsor various projects such as 'language and culture, art, literature, agriculture, fisheries, education, banking and finance', among other general matters.[7]

In January 1945, Rockefeller replied to Corrigan that, due to preparations for the Mexico City conference, he could only review the matter in early March.[8] Corrigan responded in April that he would continue to be available,[9] in July remarking that Rockefeller's personal input would be helpful to persuade Eugene 'Gene' Holman, geologist and then head of Standard Oil of New Jersey of the merits of the scheme, since 'A good idea seems to be harder to sell than a gold brick.'[10] Following this suggestion, in September, Rockefeller optimistically reported to Corrigan that, in conversation with Holman, the idea arose that a Foundation like Bolivar should not only act in Venezuela, but 'spread over the Hemisphere as a whole'.[11] Nevertheless, the oil companies were reluctant to finance the entire operation: Standard Oil responded on 1 October 1945 that it agreed with the project but that Latin American governments should invest the $10 million suggested into the fund.[12]

AIA – Simon Bolivar Foundation.

7. From Frank Corrigan to Nelson Rockefeller, Personal and Confidential. Caracas, 21 Nov. 1944.

8. From Nelson Rockefeller to Frank Corrigan. 16 Jan. 1945.

9. From Frank Corrigan to Nelson Rockefeller, 27 Apr. 1945.

10. From Frank P. Corrigan to Nelson A. Rockefeller. Personal. 21 July 1945. Collection: Family. Record Group: III 4 B. Box 01, Folder AIA – Simon Bolivar Foundation.

11. From Nelson A. Rockefeller to Frank P. Corrigan. 26 Sept. 1945. Collection: Family, Record Group: III 4B, Box: 01, Folder: AIA – Bolivar Foundation.

12. From John Brice to Eugene Holman, New York, 1 Oct. 1945.

However, political tension in Venezuela grew during that period – due to the government's refusal to legalise popular elections for president – culminating in the overthrow of Angarita on 18 October 1945. In his place, a former political exile took the presidency, Rómulo Betancourt, leader of the *Acción Democratica*, a party created in 1941 and linked to the Socialist International. As historian Shane Hamilton points out, 'leftist demands for the removal of U.S. capitalist influence in the country increased during the war, particularly after the 1941 formation of the social democratic political party *Acción Democrática*'.[13] During the new government's formation, Rómulo Betancourt established the provisional ruling junta in October of 1945. Rockefeller then wrote to Corrigan expressing concern about events in Venezuela, and especially for his ally and former president (1935–1941) General López Contrera.[14] At stake were not just Contreras or the Bolivar Foundation, but also the interests of the Rockefeller family's oil companies. Betancourt had regarded Nelson Rockefeller as a political adversary since at least 1939, when he published an article about the multi-millionaire's visit to Venezuela, calling him 'Johnny Ten Cents' and describing him as 'a hypocrite pretending at playing a humanitarian role while oblivious to the real need of the Venezuelan people'.[15] Betancourt and other actors of the 'Generation of '28', exiled by Dictator Juan Vicente Gómez for their anti-imperialist critiques, were interested in reviewing contracts with US and British oil companies.[16] Moreover, agricultural modernisation had raised tensions since the Juan Vicente Gómez dictatorship, affecting both oil income and the latifundia, of which the dictator was the chief representative.

The American ambassador, on behalf of his country's business classes, took the opportunity to mediate between Rockefeller and Betancourt, who in turn moderated his anti-imperialist rhetoric in pursuit of a policy of 'social peace'. In his meeting with the Venezuelan leader, Corrigan stated that Betancourt responded well the idea of creating a foundation:

> In my first long interview with Betancourt … I took occasion to broach the idea of 'a foundation' to which both government and industry could look for expert advice and help with regard to the momentous social responsibility in which they are partners. The idea was well received and I think this period of interim government, which will last for a year at least before a new constitution

13. Shane Hamilton, 'Distributing legitimacy: the politics of milk in post-World War II Venezuela', *History of Retailing and Consumption* 5 (1) (2019): 31.
14. From Nelson Rockefeller to Frank Corrigan. 17 Nov. 1945.
15. Rivas, *Missionary Capitalist*, p. 69.
16. Ibid., pp. 69–70.

can be drafted and a constitutional government elected, presents a God-given opportunity to obtain an advantage to draw lasting benefits out of an unusual situation'.[17]

The receptiveness of the Venezuelan centre-left generated surprise and, perhaps, a certain relief for both oil tycoons and those interested in investing in the country. This was because food supply problems in Latin America in general and Venezuela in particular meant that programmes to modernise agriculture were also on the agenda for nationalist leaders. 'Betancourt's vision for the future of Venezuela was of an urbanizing, industrializing nation where workers' rights were respected', according to historian Shane Hamilton, 'and middle-class consumers benefited from the nation's resource wealth, yet without alienating landowning elites and foreign capitalists from the country's economy or political processes'.[18] As Latin American leaders sought to develop comprehensive policies for industrialisation and food production, on the other hand, abundant food production in the United States initiated what Bryan McDonald called 'food power.' This arose because 'food, beyond providing sustenance, can also have a role in politics' in demonstrating 'the superiority of America's way in providing a modern standard of living'.[19]

With the imposition of quotas limiting the export of US-produced food – due to the decline in food production during the war – Venezuela needed to increase the availability of lard, corn, flour and meat, leading Betancourt to create the *Corporación Venezolana de Fomento* (Venezuelan Development Corporation, CVF) in 1946. However, the operational dynamics of the CVF did not achieve the desired results and, while Rockefeller created the AIA in July 1946 and turned to small-scale projects in Brazil, food production in Venezuela continued to decline. At the end of 1946, the food supply crisis was near a solution because the oil companies raised funds and, finally, interest in connecting to the decision-making spheres of government led the newly created IBEC to found a subsidiary called *Venezuelan Basic Economy Corporation* (VBEC). 'The firm's mission was relatively straightforward: it would invest in new enterprises devoted to lowering the price of food, primarily by "improving methods of food distribution" and boosting agricultural production.'[20] With

17. Frank Corrigan to Nelson Rockefeller, Caracas, Venezuela, 6 Nov. 1945. Collection: Family. Record Group: III 4 B. Box 01, Folder AIA – Simon Bolivar Foundation.

18. Hamilton, 'Distributing legitimacy': 31.

19. Bryan McDonald, *Food Power. The Rise and Fall of the Postwar American Food System* (New York: Oxford University Press, 2017), p. 2.

20. Hamilton, 'Distributing legitimacy', 31.

this, IBEC and the AIA, US commercial companies and the Venezuelan state would promote policies of agricultural and industrial development.[21]

In early 1947, a more concrete idea about IBEC's role in industrialisation[22] enabled the AIA to operate in the country through a programme aiming to 'raise standard of living', 'preserve freedom, human dignity and opportunity to improve life of individual by increasing production of goods and services in demand on efficient economical basis'.[23] Comparing to the agricultural modernisation initiated during the war in Mexico – later known as the green revolution – Dalrymple believed that 'Venezuela will go ahead faster than Mexico did – or Perón can',[24] through non-profit programmes in agriculture, health and education and demonstration and training projects carried out by the AIA. Likewise, the AIA would provide technical services to government and private groups, while the VBEC was to form companies on a sound business basis. By year's end, the AIA provided $25,000 for studies in nutritive foods, improving agriculture and food production practices, resulting in the creation of two of the most important projects: the *Consejo Interamericano de Educación Alimenticia* (Inter-American Council of Nutrition Education, CIDEA) and the *Consejo de Bienestar Rural* (Rural Welfare Council, CBR)[25] – to be discussed later in this chapter. The OIAA 'servicio' model inspired both projects, 'keeping with the pattern established by the Rockefeller Foundation and later the IIAA, the AIA's services were jointly funded by the AIA and the Venezuelan government, with the understanding that Venezuela would eventually absorb useful and effective programs'.[26] As in Brazil, 'financial contributions by the participating organisations were put on a sliding scale, with the AIA paying more in the early years and the Venezuelan government more over time'.[27]

21. Rivas, *Missionary Capitalist*, p. 75.
22. Hamilton, 'Distributing legitimacy', 131.
23. Dalrymple, *The AIA Story*, p. 63.
24. Ibid., p. 64.
25. Ibid., p. 65.
26. Rivas, *Missionary Capitalist*, p. 145.
27. Ibid. 'The idea underlying the *servicio* was that Latin American nations gained needed technical assistance in establishing programs of modern health and agriculture that they could carry on themselves. U.S. agronomists and public health experts offered their expertise in such projects as malarial control, hookworm eradication, and water filtration. Latin American countries gained valuable experience in the practical application of recent knowledge in public health and agriculture. To ensure that Latin American nations could eventually absorb the programs into their public administration, the program emphasized education and training of local personnel. The funding arrangement,

A humble start to increasing basic crop production followed the fall of the Gomez dictatorship, when the state adopted its 'sanitize, educate and populate' ideology and intensified the anti-malaria campaign. This allowed the incorporation of land to agriculture and the rescuing of export agriculture. According to Rojas López, although haciendas and commercial houses had reduced their agricultural activities, there was an increase in family farming of vegetables, fruits, legumes and cereals.[28] In part, this experience became a model that fertilised the soil for post-war experiences. One of OIAA's employees during the war, John Camp, became head of the AIA in Venezuela and played a key role in the creation of the CIDEA. This project arose in 1948 through a contract between Camp and José Ortega Durán, of the *Instituto Pro-Alimentación Popular* (Institute for Popular Food). The government started to combat nutrition problems through mobile units, or using strategies such as press, magazines, radio, movies, television, comic books, flannel and flip boards, scholarly journals and books with the purpose of disseminating nutrition techniques.

John Camp was involved from the beginning of 1947 in the survey of infrastructure problems, such as a discussion with the multinational Cargill about the need for corn storage.[29] And besides increasing the provision of silos, the CIDEA expanded the exposure of peasants and the working class to information material, whether nutritional, agricultural or related to hygiene and health. With this, a great battlefield opened in the Cold War of development in Latin America, where leaflets and educational films – emulating the strategy of the earlier OIAA – would free Latin Americans from ignorance, as expounded by the founding text of the AIA.

During the late 1940s, CIDEA disseminated its mobile units – station wagons with 16 mm equipment, sound projector, microphone, turntable, generator, and films and records – which projected educational films in the evenings in the squares of small towns or cities. At the same time, CIDEA's

---

a sliding scale of contributions, also promoted eventual local control. Usually, the IIAA provided a larger percentage contribution than the host country in order to establish the program. Over time, the host government paid higher proportions of the cost until finally reaching complete financing of the program, at which time the IIAA's involvement would end'.

28. J.J. Rojas López, *Del agrarismo histórico a los desafíos del desarrollo territorial em Venezuela* (Caracas: 2016).

29. From Stacy May to Nelson Rockefeller. Background on Venezuelan corn storage for Cargill Discussion. New York, 10 Apr. 1947.

advertising penetrated radio and newspapers: as the most widespread means of communication, radio programmes incorporated news and guidelines on nutrition and health, such as the children's programme *Aventura de la Vitamina Valiente*, or the 'Adventure of the Valiant Vitamin'.[30]

The *Consejo de Bienestar Rural*, or Council for Rural Welfare, and CIDEA arose at the same time, as part of an agreement between the Technical Institute for Immigration and Colonization, later National Agrarian Institute, and the AIA. The initial objective was to stimulate extension programmes served by rural youth groups and local health services in the states of Carabobo, Táchira, Nueva Esparta, Lara and Bolívar. The 'servicio' model provided for a gradual reduction in disbursement of resources by the AIA and its funders until, at the end of the programme, the local government would completely absorb the institution. The contracts would last three years and become renewable thanks to an increased Venezuelan financial contribution. Thus, over six years (1948–1954), the programme fostered activities in supervised credit, tractor training, community centres and training 'at all levels, from the illiterate peasant to high government officials', at least this was the AIA's ideal.[31] Contemporary with the pilot ACAR (*Associação de Crédito e Assistência Rural de Minas Gerais* (Rural Credit and Assistance Association of Minas Gerais, ACAR/MG), programme in Minas Gerais, initiated in 1948, the supervised credit programme aimed to organise the rural life of small and medium sized Venezuelan farmers. Like the Food Supply Division, the programme achieved a high rate of return on investment, of around 91 per cent. Robert Hudgens learned with the FSA about the importance of supervised credit for rural development, believing that the Venezuelan government could achieve the same.

The CBR was a Venezuelan civil society organisation whose general objectives entailed contributing to the promotion of agricultural production and the improvement of living standards in rural areas. Until the closing of the AIA in 1968, the CBR investigated, at the request of government-related entities, projects such as land reform, roads and ecological studies. According to Yolanda Arnal, the CBR hired 135 Venezuelan and 103 foreign specialists, including technical assistants, carrying out a total of 339 studies and projects up to 1966.[32] Like the AIA, the CBR promoted the development of pilot projects

30. Dalrymple, *The AIA Story*, pp. 73–75.

31. Ibid., pp. 80–81.

32. Yollanda Texera Arnal, 'Extranjeros en el Ministerio de Agricultura y Cría de Venezuela. 1936–1958', *Bitácora-e Revista Electrónica Latinoamericana de Estudios Sociales, Históricos y Culturales de la Ciencia y la Tecnología* (2014, n 2): 51.

Figure 7. Map of Venezuela.

widely distributed among Venezuela's villages; in 1949, the Council initiated a programme of community centres, organising 21 of these in the following five years. Later, the CBR reported on its experiences to the Seminar on Agrarian Reform, presenting themes reminiscent of Bolivar Foundation draft: 'The problem today is not to solve the people's problems, but to help them solve their problems. Helping them to solve their problems.'[33]

In the second half of the 1940s and throughout the 1950s, CBR stimulated the creation of community centres, which provided spaces for the dissemination of nutrition, health and hygiene practices. Agricultural techniques were also a priority; the Venezuelan government and the AIA established a partnership for managing agricultural machinery in peasant settlements – as in the region of Lake Valencia, state of Carabobo – training 2,000 drivers by 1956. In addition, other regions of the country offered Extension training programmes, mainly in the centres of Palo Negro and San Francisco de Asís, through 5-V clubs.[34] In addition, the Rockefeller Brothers Fund contributed

33. Dalrymple, *The AIA Story.*

34. Dalrymple, *The AIA Story*, pp. 91–96.

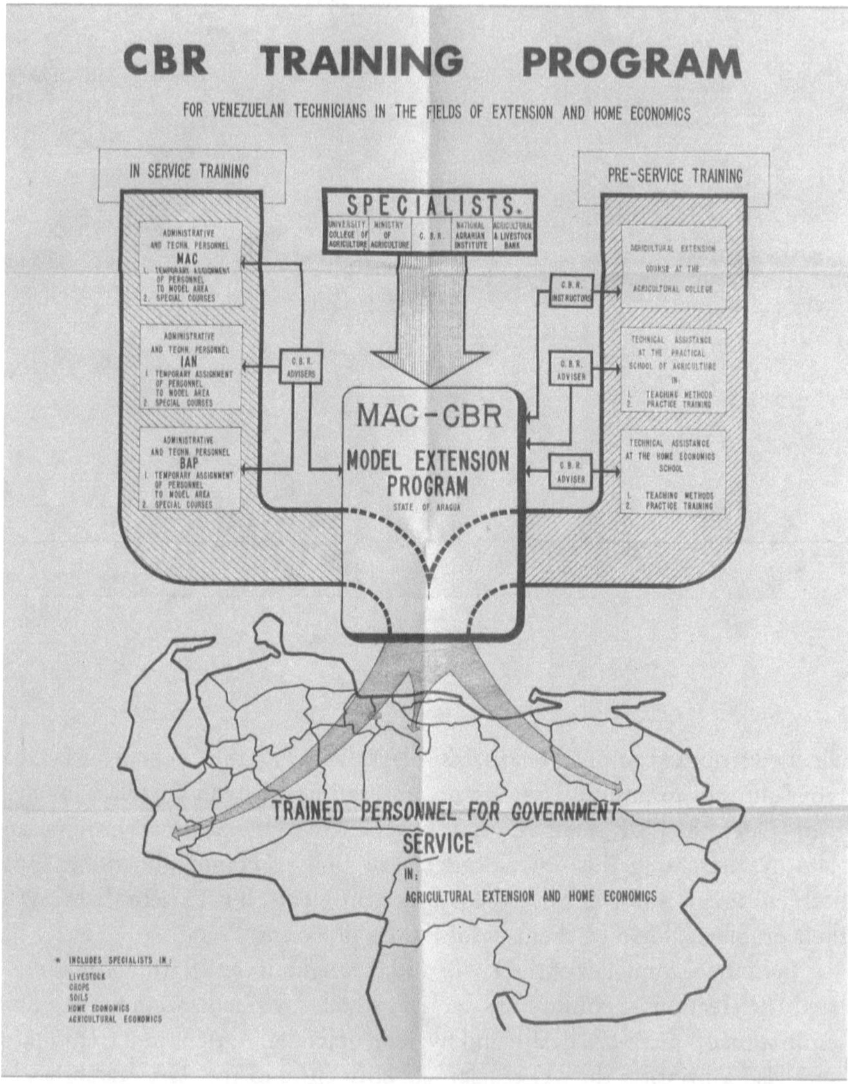

Figure 8. CBR Training Program. American International Association for Economic and Social Development (AIA) records (FA079). General, 1947-1968. Box/Reel: Box 4. Folder/ Frame: Folder 37. Folder Title: American International Association for Economic and Social Development (AIA) – New York Office – Projects – Council of Rural Development (CBR) – General. Date: 1960.

$50,000 to the AIA for the CBR's rural rehabilitation programme in Venezuela. This programme, born of the AIA's cooperation with the Venezuelan government, aimed at improving agricultural and rural living standards by training technicians, conducting special studies of agricultural and resource problems, and organising rural youth clubs.[35]

These clubs are a 'key piece of agrarian Americana', originally known as 4-H – head, heart, health and hands – 'the homespun youth clubs that, over roughly a century of existence, taught millions of rural children how to be farmers and homemakers'. Founded in 1902 in Ohio as 'tomato club' and 'corn club', a clover pin with an H in each leaf was developed around 1910 and they became officially known as 4-H Clubs in 1912. According to Gabriel Rosenberg,

> Federal interest in agricultural youth clubs initially emerged out of efforts to materially improve conditions in America's rapidly expanding farmlands in the late nineteenth century, but it was tied as well to efforts to reconcile the nation's seemingly urban destiny with its agrarian past. The increase of cultivated acreage and production across the United States during this period brought attendant concerns about pervasive rural poverty, moral and physical degeneracy, and inefficient farming techniques that complicated equally pervasive celebrations of the homesteading farmer as the source of national character. Middle-class reformers, both urban and rural, promoted 'progressive' and 'scientific' practices in the countryside, intending to improve rural living conditions, increase the nation's agricultural bounty, and safeguard the countryside's reproductive future.[36]

The 4-H clubs became one of the instruments of the Cooperative Extension System created in 1914 through the Smith-Lever Act, and were diffused around the country in the 1920s. At the international level, some experiments were carried out in Wales, England and Australia in the 1920s. In turn, the 5-V in Venezuela and the 4-C in Haiti started their activities in 1939, with versions in Korea in 1947 and Japan in 1948. Kenya's version in 1949 and the 4-T in Ethiopia in 1956 became precursors in Africa. After WWII, rural youth clubs spread to almost all of Latin America by means of the creation of the Inter-American Rural Youth Program, through the Inter-American Institute of Agricultural Sciences of the Organization of American States and the AIA. According to Rosenberg, the spreading of 4-H clubs in the United States demonstrates the power of government over supposedly-free rural communities; at the international level, these programmes adjusted to the historical context

35. Rockefeller Brothers Fund, *Report* (New York, 1958). p. 7)

36. Gabriel N. Rosenberg, *The 4-H Harvest: Sexuality and the State in Rural America* (Philadelphia: University of Pennsylvania Press, 2016).

Figure 9. A Venezuelan campesino tackling an informative graphic pamphlet during his labour. This picture represents the AIA's dream of diffusing technical knowledge in the so-called most remote parts of the world. Rockefeller Archive Center, Collection 1027 AIA, Series 2, Box 2, Brazil.

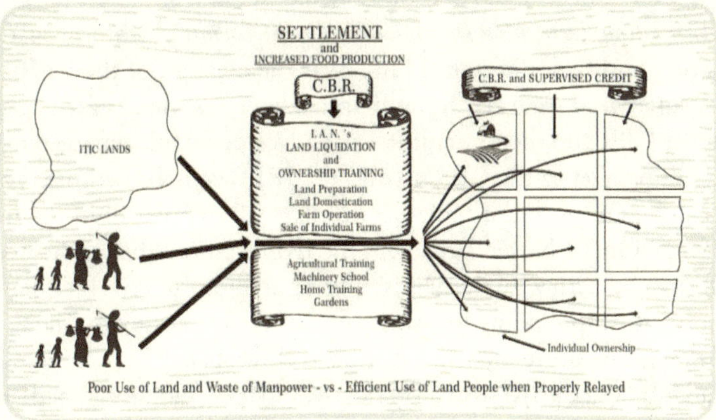

Figure 10. CBR advertisement, stimulating 'efficient use of land people when properly relayed'. American International Association. American International Association for Economic and Social Development (AIA) records (FA079). General, 1947-1968. Box/Reel: Box 4. Folder/Frame: Folder 37. Folder Title: American International Association for Economic and Social Development (AIA) – New York Office – Projects – Council of Rural Development (CBR) – General. Date: 1960.

as well as to local political and agrarian interests. For example, in the 1970s, the Brazilian dictatorship aimed to develop more than just a rational farmer; the government wanted to rouse disciplined and patriotic feelings among rural youth.[37]

Back to the Venezuelan example. Considering the AIA's view that US capital should be involved in the development of the countries where it was doing business, Nelson and his allies sought to demonstrate that AIA, IBEC and its subsidiary VBEC were not just 'another yanqui plot to bleed the country'.[38] With the support of oil companies investing in both the AIA and VBEC, the creation of economic partnerships between the public and private sectors served to change the image of American companies and projects in Venezuela.[39] Thus,

37. Claiton Marcio da Silva, 'Uma contribuição para o desenvolvimento de sua comunidade e da Pátria: juventude rural e Clubes 4-S durante a ditadura militar na região oeste de Santa Catarina (1970–1985)'. *Cadernos do Ceom* **23** (33) (2013).

38. Reich, *The Life of Nelson A. Rockefeller*, p. 410.

39. Ibid.

one of the first projects that AIA consolidated in Latin America, in agreement with the *Instituto Técnico de Imigración y Colonización* (Technical Institute of Immigration and Colonization, ITIC), was the creation of the CBR in Venezuela. A supervised rural credit programme, later enshrined in the agreement between the CBR and the Agricultural and Livestock Bank, emerged from this project.[40] In parallel to the CBR's work, the IRI Research Institute promoted field research and produced bulletins translated into Spanish in the first half of the 1950s. On 19 November 1953, the IRI discussed the results of experiments in rice and corn with the Minister of Agriculture and the President of the Agrarian Institute, providing them with copies of the rice report. The President of the Agrarian institute reported that his technical staff from the Colonia at Turen had followed the IRI work very closely, and the Colonia planned intensive investigation, as well as some field-scale trials, for 1954.

In fact, the IRI collaborated with CIDEA and CBR during early 1950s, especially after the arrival of Jerome Harrington, a young US technician trained in horticulture, plant pathology and business administration at the University of California in 1944. Harrington worked as an agricultural research assistant to the Hawaiian Pineapple Company immediately following his graduation, especially focusing on irrigation, soil fumigation and insect control problems. Later, he resigned to attend Harvard Business School; he graduated in June 1950 and became administrative assistant to the Vice President of IRI, Hertley Rowe, from the United Fruit Company. Along with Frederick Johnson, a graduate of Cornell University College of Agriculture who first worked in Latin America on rice problems in Ecuador with IBEC, the experts 'made significant contributions to improvement of soil tillage and weed control practices in Venezuela'. Despite their efforts, five years after the IBEC and VBEC planning stages in 1947, not much progress had been made regarding Venezuelan and Brazilian needs to increase food production and distribution: 'the situation has not changed appreciably over the past five years', stated an IRI report. 'It was because of this importance of agriculture, and the crying need for research in it', necessitating the organisation's creation, that 'IRI was set up to work in the field'. In consequence, in the half decade following extensive debates, IBEC and VBEC invested \$ 125,000 in corn and rice programmes in both countries; \$ 60,000 in chemicals and \$ 65,000 in coffee processing in Brazil: the whole Rockefeller group realised that both countries needed more than pamphlets to achieve something similar to the US development model. FAO statistics showed

40. José Paulo Ribeiro and Geraldo Machado, *A situação atual da extensão no Brasil* (Rio de Janeiro: Fundação Antunes, 1964), p. 35.

6,189 tractors in use Brazil in 1949 and an average of one tractor for every 6,000 acres of land cultivated. This compares with an average of one tractor for every 1,800 acres of cultivated land in Latin America as a whole. In Venezuela, the ratio was one tractor for 330 acres of land while in the United States there was an average of one tractor per 95 acres of cultivated land.[41]

For the experts, this dramatic situation justified an increase in IRI's operations in Brazil and Venezuela. In the meantime, IRI would provide an interconnection between commercial and philanthropic agencies such as IBEC, VBEC and AIA through experimental research and the production of technical bulletins. In 1952, for instance, the AIA, funded by the oil companies, presented annual expenditure of about $250,000 to cover the cost of Venezuelan operations. Early experiences in corn production demanded complete mechanisation and bulk handling from seedbed preparation through drying and into fumigated storage. In Venezuela, the agrarian experts considered it essential to produce crops at reasonable costs in the face of low labour productivity and inadequate labour availability. It was thus necessary to develop high-mounted spray equipment to permit control of post-maturity weeds, which, if uncontrolled, made mechanical harvesting impossible.[42] Moreover, the 'troubled' poor seed germination of the Brazilian Rice Program, showed 'results quite similar to those observed in Venezuela', according to IRI president Robert Russell, 'a renowned chemical engineer who served as President of Standard Oil Development Company'. Since joining the IBEC group of companies in 1947, he had worked on basic food crops, particularly corn and rice, and he served as Vice President of IBEC until made President of the IBEC Research Institute in November 1950. Despite the poor results, Nelson Rockefeller continued with farming entrepreneurship in the country, owning four properties – two in the Llanos for cattle breeding and cattle fattening, another developing a rice programme and a last one near Valencia, an industrial centre with cattle, corn, pepper and maize operations.

By the first half of the 1950s, Nelson Rockefeller had a fairly integrated system gravitating around him: the IBEC, VBEC, AIA and IRI working more or less in contact, providing everything from field experiments to storage. He was thus able to proudly state during his nomination as US Vice-President in the 1970s: 'I introduced the growing of rice into Venezuela, as I have many other agricultural innovations.' However, the white leaf fungus (*hoja blanca*),

41. Memorandum. Re: Increase in scope of Ibec Research Institute Activities. Collection: IRI RESEACH INSTITUTE, Record Group: 3.1, Box 475. Folder: 2891.

42. Ibid.

dramatically destroyed entire rice plantations. 'I experimented with 3,000 different varieties of rice until I found one drought resistant, and that is now used in Venezuela',[43] he told Congress. Meanwhile, CBR, IBEC supermarkets and other projects continued with or without connections to the Rockefellers.

The AIA's experience in Venezuela is likely to caused it some initial embarrassment, since Nelson Rockefeller would thereafter need to negotiate with nationalist forces who opposed US influence in the Venezuelan economy. Even though this case speaks of another country's specific context, it provides a background against which to interpret Rockefeller's willingness to establish AIA programmes in Brazil, which he saw as a welcoming and fertile environment. The next chapter seeks to demonstrate how the initial period of the AIA's work in Brazil involved intricate negotiation, sometimes imperceptible in the existing bibliography on this topic.

43. Hearings before the Committee on the Judiciary House of the Representatives. Second Session on Nomination of Nelson Rockefeller to be Vice President of the United States. (Washington: US Government Print Office, 1974).

CHAPTER 4.

BRAZIL: FROM BASIC AGRICULTURAL PROGRAMMES TO THE NATIONAL SOCIAL WELFARE FOOD SERVICE

This chapter demonstrates how technical cooperation programmes between the AIA and Brazilian institutions began between 1946 and 1950. More specifically, it chronicles the agreement between the AIA and the Brazilian government that generated the *Serviço de Alimentação da Previdência Social*, or Social Welfare Food Service (SAPS). While Venezuela experienced a surge in centre-left movements during the same period, mainly through the government of *Acción Democrática*, in Brazil the initial Communist Party opposition diminished after President Dutra made the party illegal in 1947. At the same time, Getúlio Vargas, a proponent of nationalist oil policy – just the opposite of Standard Oil's interests – was out of the political game between 1945 and 1950, when the AIA asserted itself in Brazil. I argue that political resistance to Rockefeller's projects did not happen in the sphere of social struggles, that of political parties, or that of lack of support from oil companies – as in Venezuela – but in the struggle about which agricultural modernisation project would be best suited to the country. To establish its programmes in Brazil, the AIA found 'friends', in its own agents' words, but also 'reactionaries'.

The AIA's projects in Brazil differed from the Venezuelan ones on a crucial point: while in Venezuela the programmes had a national reach, the Brazilian experiences were restricted to municipal and regional levels until 1956 – a function of the great territorial extent of the country. However, I characterise the period between 1946 and 1950 as a time when the AIA was just an idea in search of a programme: Nelson Rockefeller and his agrarian ideals were looking for ways to cooperate with Brazilian institutions, while the response of Latin American political elites was not enthusiastic. In addition, just as Betancourt's reactions generated a reorganisation of programmes in Venezuela, the AIA encountered resistance in Brazil, but of a different nature. Brazilian bureaucrats, far from rolling out the red carpet for the AIA's unshakeable belief in ideals of development and modernisation, initially saw the North American experts as inopportune guests. As we will see below, the situation would change but, between 1946 and 1950, few members of the Brazilian elite showed a genuine interest in the work of the AIA, even those who welcomed the agency. This is fundamental to understanding how negotiation strategies changed, as we will see in later chapters. For now, I focus on the initial programmes and on whom the Americans would trust with their work agenda.

Ideas on Paper: A 'Big Programme' for Brazil

The AIA's activities in Brazil began in 1946 when an outbreak of swine cholera spread through the states of São Paulo, Rio Grande do Sul, Paraná and Minas Gerais. In response, the AIA assisted the Brazilian government by making available a US veterinarian who introduced vaccines, among other techniques.[1] After this first project, the AIA planned to develop activities related to agricultural production, nutrition and health projects: thus, on 21 May 1946, John Lockwood sent Nelson Rockefeller details of the first concrete proposal for the future actions of the AIA (officially founded only in July of that year) in Brazil. According to the document, Lockwood saw the wellbeing of the population as something to be achieved through agricultural transformation, seeking to make modern techniques and methods increasingly available.[2] He envisioned that this process should start with specific activities, such as soil improvement via fertilisers, the use of selected seeds and the breeding of domestic animals. He also argued for an increase in storage facilities, adequate transport development, better marketing methods, better use of natural resources, and higher educational levels and better standards of health in rural areas.[3]

In other words, the AIA proposed to start establishing an industrial network in Brazilian agriculture, adapting what had begun in the 1920s in the United States. As historian Deborah Fitzgerald points out, in the period between the end of World War I and the Great Depression, a complex network of relations emerged in the United States. It brought together various actors and agencies involved in agriculture, made up of 'economists, farm managers, employees of agricultural colleges, farm and home demonstration agents, rural banks and insurance companies'. It also included 'agricultural businesses such as those centered on farm machinery and seeds', whose main purpose was to industrialise the whole agricultural enterprise; this network created

1. Dalrymple, *The AIA Story*, pp. 16–17.

2. From John E. Lockwood to Nelson A. Rockefeller. American International Association. Program for Brazil. 21 May 1946. Collection: Family. Record Group: III 4 B. Box 01, Folder AIA – Simon Bolivar Foundation.

3. Ibid.

and maintained a philosophy based on science, technology and the spirit of rationalism that characterises this agriculture model.[4] According to Fitzgerald, 'this process should also be considered industrial because the most prominent and often unnerving elements of this transition were technological and scientific innovations'.[5] Historically, 'the dramatic changes in twentieth-century farming were usually described as stemming from the twin forces of science and technology, in the form of tractors, hybrid seeds, pesticides, electrification and so forth'. However, the author highlights a set of relationships that drove industrial agriculture when 'a recipe for modernization seemed written in the very process' – that a farmer adopted tacitly when, for example, he adopted a tractor. In this complex, Fitzgerald also included the importance of financial relationships with banks, like fuel and mechanical repairs being elements of a system without which the tractor would not exist or would not succeed.[6]

The AIA's proposal for Brazil was reminiscent of the process described by Fitzgerald in the United States, aiming to render the agricultural production process increasingly interdependent. Following Lockwood's suggestions, the initiatives proposed two methods – the association's promotion of intensive and extensive farming[7] that would rebuild the organisation of agricultural production in Brazil from the ground up. The intensive method aimed at improving the soil using fertilisers and encouraging the creation of an economic sector to produce, import and market these fertilisers. According to Lockwood's proposal, both the AIA and the Brazilian government would fund the initiative. This approach characterised the AIA in both Brazil and Venezuela, the agency's resources combining with capital from the host country. Secondly, the extensive method aimed at incorporating fertilisers into soil treatment through a demonstration work programme, similar to the United States Extension Service in the early twentieth century. Broadly speaking, the programme brought in a training agent to demonstrate to farmers how a particular innovation should be undertaken. The ideal of demonstration work is attributed to college instructor Seaman A. Knapp (1833–1911), during the boll weevil control campaign of 1903–1904: 'What a man hears, he may doubt; what he sees, he may possibly doubt; but

4. Ibid., p. 6

5. Deborah Fitzgerald, *Every Farm a Factory. The Industrial Ideal in American Agriculture* (New Haven: Yale University Press, 2003).

6. Ibid.

7. From John E. Lockwood to Nelson A. Rockefeller. American International Association. Program for Brazil. 21 May 1946. Collection: Family. Record Group: III 4 B. Box 01, Folder AIA – Simon Bolivar Foundation.

what he does, he cannot doubt',[8] stated Knapp. According to this ideal, the only thing that could persuade a farmer to adopt a new practice was the concrete demonstration of its economic advantages – and Lockwood based his beliefs about reforming Latin American agriculture on this ideal, at least initially.

Following this rationale, according to the AIA's members, it was necessary to develop this type of demonstration to teach Brazilians the importance of using fertilisers and modern farming methods. The prescription at first seemed simple: to follow Knapp's management of boll weevil in the United States, whereby he showed rural workers how to solve problems in innovative ways and to change their practices, through lectures and conversations combined with sales of agricultural inputs. Concerted action between the AIA, the federal and state governments, and agricultural organisations held this kind of process to be an important element in the programme's maintenance. Circulation of ideas in the written press, radio and films[9] – to introduce the use and facilitate the sale of fertilisers – was an important part of this strategy for social and technological change.

For this reason, the AIA's first programme started by evolving nine projects in Brazil. The first, the 'Brazil Project n. 1, Hybrid Seed Corn, São Paulo, Brazil', intended to develop hybrid corn seeds in the country with IBEC's financial support. In the opinion of the AIA's administrators, both quantity and quality of seeds were Brazil's main agricultural development challenges. Because it entailed high production costs, the project would start with two experimentation units for hybrid corn seeds. According to the AIA's strategy of mixing itself with the capital and initiatives of the countries that developed projects, success in experiments with hybrid corn would lead to expansion of the projects. Within this first experiment, as narrated by Lockwood, a group of young Brazilians, employed by the AIA's office and trained in the United States, started producing hybrid corn seeds in Minas Gerais under the name Agroceres.[10]

The results of working with fertilisers in project n. 5, 'Commercial development of Brazil's fertilizer deposits', also show a more effective relationship with the national authorities. The experiments developed by Rockefeller

8. Murray Benedict, *Farm Policies of the United States, 1790–1950: A Study of their Origins and Development* (New York: Twentieth Century Fund, 1953). p. 152.

9. From John E. Lockwood to Nelson A. Rockefeller. American International Association. Program for Brazil. 21 May 1946. Collection: Family. Record Group: III 4 B. Box 01, Folder AIA – Simon Bolivar Foundation.

10. Ibid.

helped to elaborate agricultural policies in Dutra's government, by encouraging participation of private initiative in development projects. Valentim Bouças, Getúlio Vargas' former personal financial advisor, one of the Brazilian participants at the Bretton Woods conference (1944) and a consultant to Abink Mission, requested information on the work of the AIA in Brazil. Bouças stated that this information would enable him '[to obtain] the most valuable sources of information to outline the project submitted to the Government'.[11] In 1946, Lockwood testified that the use of fertilisers in Brazil should follow the US model; in his interpretation, fertilisers had provoked intense changes in American agriculture.[12] In the Brazilian case, the President of Republic questioned Mr. Bouças about what 'we do in that field'. The Brazilian government considered the use of fertilisers a 'very serious' issue for the country's development. The AIA had no interest in manufacturing fertilisers, as Kadow made clear to the Brazilian representative, and many Brazilian groups were interested in manufacturing phosphate and nitrate fertilisers. 'They did not need the AIA's assistance in this regard'.[13]

On the other hand, the AIA's expertise in developing fertiliser experiments in Brazil interested the Brazilian government. The AIA continued to coordinate this project, recommending that Hungarian chemist and agronomist John S. Csiky continued using lime and raw rock phosphate to conduct the corn, soybean and wheat programmes.[14] Dr Csiky conducted experiments in outdoor greenhouses; the New York staff member Lawrence H. Levy suggested that the experiment could be carried out on the property of Semente Agroceres.[15] Instead, the AIA selected five areas and made them available at no cost in the state of São Paulo – owned by SA *Fomento Agro-Pecuária*, and on the farms of Teodoro Quartim Barboza and Olívio Gómez. Other properties situated in the Northern region of Paraná, on a farm owned by the company *SASA,* represented different types of soil. Finally, Dr Csiky conducted experiments

11. From Valentim F. Bouças to Nelson A. Rockefeller. Rio de Janeiro, 9 May 1947. Family. Record Group: III 4 B. Box 13, Folder 134.

12. From John E. Lockwood to Nelson A. Rockefeller. American International Association. Program for Brazil. 21 May 1946. Collection: Family. Record Group: III 4 B. Box 01, Folder AIA – Simon Bolivar Foundation.

13. From Kenneth Kadow to Morrison G. Tucker. Memorandum. Subject: Fertilizers. Rio de Janeiro, 21 May 1947. Family. Record Group: III 4 B. Box 13, Folder 134.

14. From Lawrence H. Levy to Executive Committee of the AIA. Memorandum. Fertilizer Experiments in Brazil. 15 Oct. 1947. Family. Record Group: III 4 B. Box 13, Folder 134.

15. Ibid.

to determine the exact amount of lime needed for agricultural production in the cultivation of maize, beans, wheat and alfalfa.[16]

In this initial period, the AIA proposed other projects as small demonstration experiments: project n. 2 entitled 'Model Demonstration Farm & Training School', developed for the state of São Paulo, aimed to introduce modern agricultural methods and varieties in poultry and swine production. The project sought to demonstrate the practice of mechanisation, and promote vocational training in cooperation with colleges and schools of agriculture. The third project, 'Vegetable and fruit canning factory', planned for the northeastern states of Paraíba or Pernambuco, aimed at introducing tomato and pineapple cultivation in dry areas under irrigation. Project n. 4, 'Cattle, horse and mule breeding ranch', aimed at producing meat and domestic animals for on-farm labour. Project n. 7, named 'Livestock and parasite control investigations and demonstrations' had the objective of curbing certain types of worm infestations, targeting several states, including São Paulo and Minas Gerais. The maintenance of these activities connected to another project, n. 8, titled 'Brazil, community services program'. In turn, project n. 9, 'Organizing a 4-H club program for Brazil', proposed that the federal and state governments reorganise their various attempts to educate rural youth, which the AIA considered 'poorly developed and executed' in Brazil. The modernisers argued that, once a plan was conceived and implemented with the methodology used by the 4-H Clubs in the United States, the project would very quickly result in the implementation of primary- and secondary-level courses in target areas. This would then stimulate creation of competitive programmes at the federal and state level, with the distribution of awards as a means of recruiting young people, 'inevitably resulting in better agricultural practices and rural living conditions'. The project's strategy was that Nelson Rockefeller would negotiate creation of these programmes at the national level, giving the team the advantage in starting work to reorganise them at both federal and state levels.[17]

Not all projects had the desired results, though. For instance, projects n. 1 and n. 5, which dealt with the production of hybrid corn and fertilisers, respectively, were closer to IBEC, while the AIA continued with the experiments initiated in projects n. 7 and n. 8, which resulted in the programmes of Santa

16. American International Association for Economic and Social Development. Fertilizer experiments in Brazil. Project n. AIA – 5 – Brazil. Proposed by Dee Jackson. 1 Dec. 1947. Family. Record Group: III 4 B. Box 13, Folder 134.

17. International Basic Economy Corporation. Legal report on status of corporation. 10 Jan. 1947. Family. Record Group: III 4 B. Box 01, Folder AIA – Simon Bolivar Foundation.

Rita, São José and, later, ACAR in Minas Gerais. In the same period, Berent Friele, Kenneth Kadow and Dee Jackson proposed a technical cooperation project between the AIA and the National Social Welfare Food Service under the Home Demonstration even before the consolidation of such programmes.[18]

Negotiating with 'Friends' and 'Reactionaries'

Getúlio Vargas created the SAPS in August 1940 – and the programme ran for 27 uninterrupted years, closing only during the civil-military dictatorship in 1967. Considered by the AIA as the 'best and most practical' nutrition programme in Brazil, SAPS was an autonomous agency, even though the Ministry of Labor oversaw it. Its purpose was to guarantee decent and cheap meals to the emerging industrial workforce by implementing a network of popular restaurants in the great centres. The government implanted the pioneer unit in Rio de Janeiro and the first director of SAPS was a geographer from Pernambuco, Josué de Castro. After 1943, SAPS generally had reading and music rooms and helped with job placements and adult literacy.[19] Coincidentally or not, Josué de Castro launched his classic book *Geography of Hunger* [Geografia da Fome] in 1946 – the same year that the AIA signed a cooperation agreement with the agency – making Castro one of the leading Brazilian intellectuals committed to fighting endemic and epidemic hunger. Later, Castro translated his *magnum opus* into more than 25 languages and even caught the attention of filmmaker Roberto Rosselini, who intended to shoot a film based on the book. In summary, *Geography of Hunger* denounced how the prevailing discourse in Brazil, based on determinist precepts, naturalised the problem with a Neo-Malthusian approach, similar to that defended by the Rockefeller Brothers Fund. On the other hand, Josué de Castro's criticism and his involvement with national and international universities and institutions such as the FAO – where he became President of the Executive Council in 1952 – consolidated an anti-Malthusianism stance that earned him nominations for the Nobel Peace Prize in 1953, 1963 and 1965.

Meanwhile, Louise Stanley, director of nutritional services at the USDA since 1923, and Anita Magolin, from the AIA's New York office, visited Brazil to plan implementation of a nutrition programme. The purpose of the AIA's

---

18. American International Association for Economic and Social Development. Project n. Brazil 1 – Revised. Title: Home Demonstration Service. Collection: Family, Record Group III 4B, Box 13, Folder 135.

19. Ana Maria da Costa Evangelista and Dalva Carolina de Menezes Yazbeck, 'Serviço de alimentação da previdência social (SAPS)', *Revista Virtú*, Juiz de Fora: Universidade Federal de Juiz de Fora, 2008. 7th ed., p. 2.

proposal was to create the Food Visitation Sector (SVA) to work with Home Demonstration and, in this sense, to integrate the actions of several national and international agencies such as the AIA and SAPS, through the SVA and ministries of Labor and Agriculture in several states of Brazil.[20] The USDA official observed that the agents who would carry out their work should speak the 'language of the people' – they should know the public with whom they would work.[21]

However, communication issues became clear as early as 1946. On 19 August of that year, the AIA approved an agreement with the SAPS – revised in November. The main reason for the changes was the Minister of Labor's view that the SVA, one of SAPS' divisions, enjoyed excessive 'autonomy'. For the Brazilian official, the SVA seemed to have greater financial and administrative autonomy than SAPS, meaning it would become larger and more powerful than the Minister himself. According to Dee Jackson, as the AIA would be donating a certain amount of money, the SAPS was interested in obtaining some form of control over financial and administrative operations.[22] In other words, the overlapping objectives of the two agencies – a Brazilian government unit and a US philanthropic organisation – made the reorganisation of the agreements necessary and caused difficulties in negotiations, resulting in the AIA not carrying forward this agreement in the 1950s.

The AIA suggested the reorganisation of activities itself when it decided to eliminate sending donations to the programme and decreed that the SVA would from then on be considered an integral part of SAPS. It was also suggested that AIA should provide an expert for the development of the programme – more specifically, a nutritionist who would guide SVA's projects, among other actions. At this early stage, negotiations between the AIA and the Brazilian government led to a reformulation of the agreement's initial ideas. The AIA relinquished some control over the initial programme because of legal issues – presented by the Brazilians – in exchange for a greater, if not total, influence regarding technical activities.

Prior to this, in April 1946, Major Humberto Peregrino was assigned to lead SAPS. After seeing the project's experiences in Fortaleza, in the Northeast

20. American International Association for Economic and Social Development. Project n. Brazil 1 – Revised. Title: Home Demonstration Service. Collection: Family, Record Group III 4B, Box 13, Folder 135. p. 3. [1947]

21. Ibid.

22. From AIA – Rio de Janeiro to AIA – New York. Memorandum. Subject: AIA Program n. Brazil 01. Rio de Janeiro, 25 July 1947.

Figure 11. 'At the invitation of Dr. Josué de Castro, Chief of the Institute of Nutrition in Brazil, Dr. Louise Stanley, an American nutritionist, addressed the members of the Nutrition Institute Course during the recent meeting held at *Santa Casa de Misericórdia.* Dr. Stanley's lecture on how the problems of nutrition in the United States had been faced and solved, aroused great interest among the members of the National School of Medicine who perform similar activities in this country'. Rockefeller Archive Center, Series 1 General, 1027 AIA Photograph Collection, Box 2, Folder 31.

region of Brazil, he was enthusiastic about the project of Home Demonstration developed in partnership with the AIA. Peregrino discussed this project with President Eurico Gaspar Dutra, who appreciated the objectives of the programme and the technical assistance offered by the AIA. The President agreed with Major Peregrino that an expansion plan should include not only establishment of a larger school in the State of São Paulo, but also that of an additional school in the Distrito Federal, as well as a fourth school. For these reasons, Major Peregrino was willing to cancel the agreement of 26 November 1946 and propose another one.[23]

23. Ibid.

However, at that time, President Dutra's position was somewhat cautious, as he was still elaborating a development plan and so did not yet have a defined position on the importance of private enterprise in relation to agricultural development and related activities. The government established a commission chaired by the Minister of Agriculture to take charge of the study of Brazilian economic issues, 'whose quick solution depends on large investments'. This commission would have 'the purpose of discriminating the [investments] that should preferably be left to private initiative' and 'the limits and conditions under which foreign capital and technical cooperation may be solicited or accepted'. Thus, according to the commission's discussions, private initiative would not have total freedom, and the Brazilian government planned to keep control over foreign aid.[24]

Berent Friele, who had years of experience in Brazil as a representative of OIAA, followed the committee's work and remarked that it would include many of 'our friends', such as Ary Torres. He also suggested that the current Minister of Agriculture, Daniel de Carvalho, would be one of these friends.[25] If the possibility of introducing some of the AIA's conceptions at the national policy level excited Friele, other issues made it difficult for the AIA to act. Analysis of a February 1947 conversation that took place between the Minister of Labor, Morvan Dias de Figueiredo, and Dee Jackson, however, shows that the relationship between the SAPS and the AIA – and the nationalisation of the Food Visitation Sector – was not the objective of the Minister. A former vice-president of the Federation of Industry of São Paulo state, Figueiredo argued against the AIA's position, asserting that food prices should increase.[26] According to Jackson, the Brazilian Minister was not in favour of the SAPS programme. In fact, according to an AIA official, 'he has never been' because he 'always had a negative attitude' towards the programme, labelling it 'luxurious' and something that SAPS 'could not sustain'.[27] Finally, 'he does not recognize the effective work', according to the agent of the AIA, complaining that Minister Carvalho could be considered a 'reactionary'.[28]

---

24. From AIA – Rio de Janeiro to AIA – New York. Memorandum. Subject: AIA Program n. Brazil 01. Rio de Janeiro, 25 July 1947.
25. From Dee Jackson to Berent Friele. Rio de Janeiro, 3 Oct. 1947. Family. Record Group: III 4 B. Box 13, Folder 135.
26. Ibid.
27. Dee Jackson. Memorandum for Project n. 1 (SAPS). 13 Feb. 1947. Family. Record Group: III 4 B. Box 13, Folder 135.
28. Ibid.

On the other hand, the AIA's 'friends', including José Evangelista and one of his assistants at SAPS, were investigated for poor administration, preventing SVA from participating in any sort of event until the matter was resolved. Evangelista's departure allowed the Minister of Labor the opportunity to criticise the agreement between the AIA and the SAPS, calling into question the autonomy given to the sector by the agreement. In this regard, Jackson commented: 'I expressed to the Minister our surprise that two Ministers of Labor would approve a contract which was not in accordance with Brazilian laws'.[29] This left the AIA officials in limbo, as the Minister's proposed changes to the agreement created an impasse. In February 1947, Jackson reported: 'seemingly well-informed sources advised us that the President of the Republic will replace Morvan Dias de Figueiredo as Labor Minister within the next few days and appoint a new Minister. Of course, then a new SAPS director will be appointed'. In these circumstances, it was advisable for the AIA to wait for renewal in both the Ministry and SAPS before starting another agreement or suggesting amendments.[30]

However, Morvan Dias de Figueiredo remained in office until 1948, and the AIA had to find ways to negotiate. To assist in establishing the agreement, two Brazilians with experience in federal administration had been assigned a year earlier to assist in studying the issues before submitting them for consideration. As a result, Major Peregrino 'not only accepted the clarifications presented', but also supported a point of view similar to that of the AIA. One of the issues discussed in the agreement was what would happen if the SAPS director wished to close the collaborative programme without the consent of the AIA; or if the AIA wished to withdraw from the programme without the consent of the SAPS director. In addition, in a conciliatory tone, Kenneth Kadow declared: 'the objections raised to the original project by the Brazilian Minister of Agriculture are understandable'.[31] However, as the SAPS chose a political instead of a technical board, according to the AIA, the assistance of this agency might not be effective. Kadow would thus state in 1948: 'I would like to suggest that we approve cooperation with SAPS on an annual basis'.[32]

29. Dee Jackson. Memorandum for Project n. 1 (SAPS). 13 Feb. 1947. Family. Record Group: III 4 B. Box 13, Folder 135.

30. Ibid.

31. Cooperação entre o SAPS e a AIA referente à execução do programa do 'Setor de Visitação Alimentar' no Brasil. Family. Record Group: III 4 B. Box 13, Folder 135.

32. From Kenneth Kadow to AIA. Brazil Project n. 1, Home Demonstration Service. 20 Aug. 1948. Family. Record Group: III 4 B. Box 13, Folder 135.

Prior to this, banker and VBEC manager Morisson G. Tucker, in a conversation with Nelson Rockefeller, had stated that the AIA should participate in choosing the Director of the Sector.[33] In summary, the criticisms generated during the consolidation of the agreement led the AIA to adopt a more cautious approach, ending the agreement around 1950.

After New York AIA representative Willian H. Alton visited Brazil and Venezuela in 1947, he wrote to Nelson Rockefeller to report on the progress made by John Camp and other agents towards achieving the AIA's goals. While Alton relativised the problems in Venezuela, he requested the AIA to provide direction for the programme, since little willingness was observed. According to him, Dee Jackson's management of the Rio de Janeiro office lacked aggression regarding the initiatives.[34] He suggested that John Griffing replace Jackson immediately; and the AIA sealed Jackson's dismissal in the coming months. Griffing then assumed the task of taking the AIA office forward.

The departure of Dee Jackson and, shortly after, of Kenneth Kadow, changed the way the AIA operated, especially in Brazil. The initial years featured development of small projects and an incessant fight over the hegemony of SAPS and SVA decisions. In the meantime, between the departure of Jackson and Kadow and the rise of Griffing and Walter Lion Crawford, agreements between the AIA and state governments fostered the emergence of two of the agency's main projects in Brazil: agricultural development programmes in the interior of São Paulo state and in Minas Gerais. The next chapter will discuss how the first programme obtained relative recognition; on the other hand, when the AIA began its work in Minas Gerais state, similar experiments already existed, sponsored by the state government, leading to a situation where Brazilians had little interest in the AIA modernisation programmes. In Minas Gerais, in turn, political elites enthusiastically adopted similar initiatives, building the basis for the nationalisation of the Extension Service in Brazil.

33. From Morrison G. Tucker to Berent Friele and Dee Jackson. AIA project – number 01 – Brazil Nutrition and Home Demonstration Program. Family. Record Group: III 4 B. Box 13, Folder 135.

34. From Willian A. Alton to Nelson Rockefeller. Memorandum. Report on visit to Venezuela and Brazil. Personal and confidential. 11 Nov. 1947. Collection: Family. Record Group: III 4 B. Box 01, Folder: Alton, W. H. p. 03.

PART II – OVER THE HILLS AND FAR AWAY: DUSTING OFF THE BOOTS IN LATIN AMERICA

CHAPTER 5.

THE BEGINNING OF THE AIA'S REGIONAL EXPERIENCES IN BRAZIL: THE EXTENSION SERVICE TRIAL IN THE STATE OF SÃO PAULO

This chapter examines the negotiations between the AIA and sub-national governments in the state of São Paulo and analyses the programmes that the AIA initiated there. In São Paulo, the AIA launched programmes in two cities, Santa Rita do Passa Quatro and São José do Rio Pardo, involving both the state and local governments, as well as farmers and entrepreneurs. It signed agreements with individual municipalities that were later extended, requiring support from the state government. On the contrary, the Minas Gerais experiment started with constituting a programme at the state level and seeking to expand it locally with the support of municipal governments – as discussed in the next chapter. Another difference lies in the fact that, in the hinterlands of São Paulo state, the AIA office carried out the programmes, enjoying the resources of the philanthropic agency with the support of sub-national governments and business elites. In Minas Gerais, the entity responsible for operationalising the projects had a mixed Administrative Board – including not only Brazilian and US experts, but also Brazilian politicians. This pooled the efforts of both the AIA and public power towards the modernisation of agriculture. Finally, the São Paulo experience was limited to installation of two local offices and terminated in 1956 for lack of financial and political support. Minas Gerais, however, started with a small programme that expanded gradually, reaching most of the state's territory in the early 1960s. This chapter will analyse the São Paulo experience while the next will focus on the work done in Minas Gerais.

The experiment in São Paulo is important for two reasons: it did not progress because there were already initiatives in place to modernise agriculture but, on the other hand, it brought with it some techniques that contribute to understanding how broad the concepts of modernisation and development are.

Agricultural Issues and Extension Service in the Hinterlands of São Paulo

It is undeniable that the discourses of the AIA and those of local Brazilian representatives were similar during the first years of the programmes developed

Figure 12. Map of the state of São Paulo.

in Santa Rita do Passa Quatro and in São José do Rio Preto, mainly during the government of Adhemar de Barros (1947–1951) and part of Lucas Garcez's tenure as state governor (1951–1955). However, plans to expand and intensify these programmes created a rift between the actors, prompting the AIA to focus exclusively on the state of Minas Gerais. After completion of AIA programme n. 7, entitled 'Livestock and parasite control investigations', the continuity of its activities was ensured by another project, n. 8, entitled 'Brazil, community services program'. Although started in Santa Rita do Passa Quatro, this project also gave birth to the agreement with the state government of Minas Gerais. This, in turn, made possible the creation of ACAR, a pilot programme in credit and rural development, on 6 December 1948. Earlier, the AIA established a central office in the state of São Paulo. Robert Hudgens headed it and its main technical director was John Griffing, head of the *Escola Superior de Agricultura e Veterinária* (Viçosa College of Agriculture, ESAV) between 1936 and 1939.

On 1 August 1948, negotiations between AIA and Santa Rita's municipal authorities began, aiming to establish a collaborative project. The negotiations involved both the mayor and local farmers. The Association carried out strategic demonstration work of bovine tick control techniques, on 29 August 1948, and, a few days later, the AIA, Santa Rita's city government and local farmers signed an agreement for technical assistance.[1] According to AIA documents, the demonstrations were fruitful, not only showing the possibility of tick control but also prompting farmers' interest in solving other problems. Months later, because of the spread of the AIA's experiments in the region, the municipality of São José do Rio Pardo requested technical assistance from the agency; the AIA's employees Lineo Brassoloto and Marcos Pereira then became responsible for work in São José and Santa Rita, respectively. The participation of farmers in São José would include their donating part of their milk production to the programme.[2]

In the rural communities of Santa Rita – a small city located in the centre-north of the state of São Paulo, in the region of Terras Altas Paulista – the AIA started five different projects, focusing mainly on artificial insemination, health services and rural youth clubs, with the participation of forty farmers.[3] At that time, the region was undergoing a restructuring of its economic activities, with the decline of coffee plantations and their replacement by dairy cattle. This followed a Brazilian pattern of modernisation, defended by large estate owners, who considered the rationalisation of production and productivity and the training of a skilled labour force to be necessary.[4] Moreover, modernisers inserted Extension Service and soil conservation into the modernisation debate; on the subject of soil, 'Dad' Griffing was emphatic: the great agricultural problem in Brazil was, he averred, the calamitous deterioration of the soil, with steady decline in production.[5] Brazil's agricultural system had been characterised by 'cut, burn, destroy and move on' cycles, with a detrimental effect on Brazilian agricultural productivity. The AIA proposed a different model: in 1953, years after the experiment had begun in São Paulo, AIA presented a set of solutions

1. American International Association for Economic and Social Development. A statement of organization, activities and objectives. Jan. 1949. Collection AIA, Box 10, Folder 85.
2. AIA. The first three years. Collection: Family, Record Group: II 4B, Box: 01, Folder AIA General 1946–1958, n. 02(a). p. 29.
3. AIA. The first three years. Collection: Family, Record Group: II 4B, Box: 01, Folder AIA General 1946–1958, n. 02(a). p. 29.
4. Sonia Regina Mendonça, 'Agricultura, Poder e Estado no Brasil: um projeto contra-hegemônico na Primeira República', in Sonia Regina Mendonça and Márcia Motta (eds), *Nação e Poder: As Dimensões da História* (Niterói: EDUFF, 1998), vol. 1, p. 103.
5. John Benjamin Griffing, 'Air view of the forest'. [1953]. Collection AIA, Record Group IV 3B, Box 02, Folder 12. p. 7.

based on technical assumptions that demonstrated the country's agricultural potential and the promises of organic fertilisation.[6]

The AIA modernisers, however, were not the first to introduce Extension Service ideals. US agronomist Peter Henry Rolfs, one of the founders and organisers of ESAV had introduced the first experiment in integrated rural development in the 1920s.[7] Meanwhile, the Ministry of Agriculture, together with agricultural agencies at state level, organised 'ruralist weeks', aiming to introduce agronomists and veterinarians giving lectures on agricultural topics for farmners. These included cattle vaccination, tick and berne control, tillage and other simple practices.[8] In the same way, the Ministry of Agriculture created Agricultural Stations, small demonstration farms working as models and spreading the correct use of agricultural machinery, soil conservation, crops and rational animal production.[9] Nevertheless, these experiments included, according to Brazilian agronomist Glauco Olinger, only 'a privileged few, generally those who had the support of influential people of the government'.[10] Already prior to WWII, the US model of Extension Service had become an unattainable dream, its demise compounded by the exodus of Brazilian agronomists (such as Miguel Bechara in the 1930s) to the United States. During and after the War, the ESAV introduced a more consistent experience in Extension at a state/regional level.

Former ESAV director 'Dad' Griffing used fervently to express ideals related to the model: the Extension department with its army of workers would disperse throughout the state, encouraging farmers to adopt the discoveries made. In addition, it would develop a specialised section to teach methods of extension.[11] To this end, Griffing sought to integrate the state agencies responsible for different activities, exemplified by the work of the AIA in co-operation with the Health Department of the State of São Paulo. Beginning in the early 1950s, he launched an 'agro-medical-social' clinic in the municipalities of Santa Rita and São José. Enacted by nurses, dentists and physicians,

6. Ibid., p. 10.

7. Glauco Olinger, *Ascensão e decadência da Extensão Rural no Brasil* (Florianópolis: EPAGRI, 1996), pp. 42–43.

8. Ibid., p. 44.

9. Ibid.

10. Ibid., p. 45.

11. Maria Rachel Fróes da Fonseca et al., 'Escola Superior de Agricultura e Veterinária', in *Dicionário Histórico-Biográfico das Ciências da Saúde no Brasil (1832–1930)* (Rio de Janeiro: Casa de Oswaldo Cruz/Fiocruz – http://www.dichistoriasaude.coc.fiocruz.br).

the services were itinerant and connected with activities related to agriculture, such as to support the production of vegetables or even hygiene and sanitation practices. According to official data, 566 families (4,396 people) had access to these health services or technical assistance in general in 1950. Providing both dental treatment and treatment for intestinal parasites, among other services, the cooperation between the AIA and the Health Department provided 6,700 medical consultations that year.[12] The AIA also expected to cooperate with other local or national agencies. Griffing wanted by these means to make the benefits of rural improvement programmes available to the entire rural population, not just a select few. Ultimately, he expected the adoption of new techniques in a given rural area to bring economic benefits greater than the costs. He criticised the Brazilian model programmes, since their costs were not rationalised and they were, therefore, more expensive than the value of benefits provided to the rural population.[13]

For the same reasons, Griffing objected to the proposed expansion of the 'agro-medical-social' clinics to twenty other municipalities in São Paulo state. Shortly before leaving Brazil due to health problems in 1953, he wrote to physician Paulo Cesar de Azevedo Antunes, then Director of the School of Hygiene of São Paulo, whom he considered 'one of the few in his country who is willing and able to think rational solutions',[14] suggesting a possible rural health programme. Paulo Cesar de Azevedo Antunes had collaborated with the Rockefeller Foundation since 1934; four years later, the Malaria Prophylaxis Service appointed him as director in an institution linked to the rural service of the Health Department of São Paulo state. After returning to work with the Rockefeller Foundation in 1939, conducting research in the Northeast Region of Brazil, he moved to the United States to train as a Doctor of Public Health at Johns Hopkins University (1941–1942). Back in Brazil, the *Serviço Especial de Saúde Pública* (or Special Service on Públic Health, SESP) invited Azevedo to work on the programme developed in the Amazon, where he remained until he became head of the Faculty of Hygiene and Public Health of the University of São Paulo.

12. American International Association for Economic and Social Development. p. 06. Collection: Family, Record Group: III 4B, Box 03, Folder 23, AIA, Ford Foundation.

13. John Benjamin Griffing, 'Theory and practice in rural improvement'. Collection: AIA (closed section), Box 01, Folder: operations, 1953.

14. From John B. Griffing to Paulo César de Azevedo Antunes. 30 Mar. 1953. Collection: AIA (closed section), Box 01, Folder: operations. p. 1.

Figure 13. The 'agro-medical-social' vehicle visiting the rural area of Santa Rita do Passa Quatro and São José do Rio Pardo. Rockefeller Archive Center, Series 1 General, 1027 AIA Photograph Collection, Box 2, Folder 31.

Azevedo envisioned an agreement between the AIA and the state government, consistent with Griffing's thinking that Brazilian leaders were more willing to observe problems from an idealistic point of view, instead of taking a pragmatic approach. For instance, the State of São Paulo funded and maintained with 'fabulous expenses', and few benefits, the system of agricultural technical schools: 'magnificent white elephants', claimed Griffing. To him, even the Rockefeller Foundation was idealistic, not pragmatic, since the cost of its programmes would be very high. For instance, a project using the model of the itinerant agro-medical-social clinics would have a very high cost if extended to twenty municipalities.[15] Before returning to the United States, Griffing spared no criticism for the way different government agencies in Brazil operated, proposing a rational model of work that could expand health services for these twenty municipalities. To this end, Azevedo Antunes started by selecting a technocratic team, seeking to hire people not by party affinity, but based on their technical skills. The programme ought to be educational and directed to the prevention of diseases, since, according to Griffing, at present Brazilian 'physicians [were] only interested in treating diseases', not getting involved in preventative campaigns.[16] The rationalisation here would be in the hiring of a nurse who could make regular visits to all the communities in a specific municipality. With some medicines and technical knowledge, this nurse could drive a Jeep and work on prevention as well as helping in simpler cases. In the itinerant model, by contrast, not all professionals would be busy at all times, generating expenses considered unnecessary.[17]

Even though the idea of the 'traveling nurse' was not put into practice by the Health Department, other similar projects in agriculture, health and education bore the mark of Griffing's pragmatism. The typical policies of the AIA in Santa Rita and São José were based primarily on Griffing's assumptions about the value of demonstration work, and adapted the tenets of Seaman Knapp to the post-war era. The results of the agronomists' performance would be so striking that they would lead farmers to repeat the practice for themselves and, over time, spread it within communities. They complemented the technique with technology assistance: for instance, if a sprayer were necessary to combat bovine pests, the AIA would provide it until the farmers could buy their own.[18]

For AIA modernisers like Griffing, modernising did not simply mean applying techniques developed in the United States. The idea of agricultural modernisation also related to adopting the most appropriate techniques for a given environment. Whether these techniques were labelled as modern or not, the result achieved, the efficiency and the rationality applied were the most important aspects to highlight. If, on one hand, agriculture, soil conservation, public health, sanitation, literacy and industry, among other possible activi-

15. From John B. Griffing to Paulo César de Azevedo Antunes. 30 Mar. 1953. Collection: AIA (closed section), Box 01, Folder: operations. p. 1.

16. Ibid., p. 2.

17. Ibid., p. 3.

18. John Benjamin Griffing, 'Theory and practice in rural improvement'. Collection: AIA (closed section), Box 01, Folder: operations, 1953, p. 2.

Figure 14. AIA attempt to integrate rural development and medical care in the state of São Paulo. Rockefeller Archive Center, Series 1 General, 1027 AIA Photograph Collection, Box 2, Folder 31

ties, facilitated the provision of scientific 'discoveries',[19] on the other hand, John Griffing applied traditional techniques such as trench silos. These were a traditional silage practice, involving taking advantage of the topography and digging only what was necessary to shelter pasture for the winter. In the perception of Brazilian technicians, the trench silo was backward comparing to the industrial silo; Griffing, though, insisted on the usefulness of traditional practices for their effectiveness and low cost.

The work of the AIA in São Paulo expanded during the early 1950s, from then on including Agricultural Clubs for rural youth, following the 4-H model. In 1948, the association had organised nine agricultural clubs with 102 participants, developing projects mainly on hybrid corn seeds, but also on Irish

19. From Joan to Mr. Nelson [Rockefeller]. Memorandum. Subject: General objectives of the American International Association for Economic and Social Development. Collection: [Family], Record Group: III 4B, Folder: AIA General 1946–1958, n. 02. p. 1.

Figure 15. filling the trench silo with corn straw. Rockefeller Archive Center, Series 1 General, 1027 AIA Photograph Collection, Box 2, Folder 31.

potatoes or other plant species.[20] By 1952, the clubs had 419 participants.[21] The clubs of Santa Rita and São José encouraged work with hybrid corn through the donation of seeds by *Sementes Agroceres S.A.* (SASA). The objective of this extension work was to reach older farmers through their relationships with younger family members who were empowered by the project to cultivate a small area on their parents' property, so as to demonstrate that modern practices were more productive. 'I learned to grow corn with my son',[22] a farmer would tell Griffing, adding that the profits made by younger people yielded a better standard of living.[23]

The introduction of modern knowledge through integrated rural extension service, including preventative health aspects for young and adult farmers,

20. John Benjamin Griffing, 'Air view of the forest'. [1953]. Collection AIA, Record Group IV 3B, Box 02, Folder 12. p. 5.
21. John Benjamin Griffing, 'Theory and practice in rural improvement'. Collection: AIA (closed section), Box 01, Folder: operations, 1953, p. 4.
22. Ibid., p. 5
23. Ibid.

Figure 16. Agronomist Marcos Pereira and 'Dad' John Griffin observing the work of Corn Clubs, an initial adaptation of 4-H Clubs in Brazil. Rockefeller Archive Center, Series 1 General, 1027 AIA Photograph Collection, Box 2, Folder 31.

aimed to enable the 'man in the field' to live and work in rural settings rather than migrating to cities. Halting the process of rural exodus would be a great gain, Griffing said.[24] Linked to this argument, in 1956, Afonso Paulino, president of Caixa Econômica do Estado de Minas Gerais – a state bank created to help fund development projects – stated in his inauguration speech for ACAR's office in the municipality of São João Nepumoceno: 'There is a lot of talk about the industrialization of Brazil. Yes, we are not opposed to industrialization, but it can only really succeed when we have solved our agricultural problems.'[25] In this sense, the ruralists themselves, characterised as defenders of latifundia and thus associated with rural Brazil's backwardness, were also advocates of the industrialisation project, even though they disagreed with nationalist and labour groups about the extension of social and labour legislation in favour of the rural population.

24. Ibid., p. 6.

25. Eis o discurso do Dr. Afonso Paulino. São João Nepumoceno, MG, 19 Aug. 1956. [clipping from EMATER Collection]

For advocates of large farms, the rationalisation of agriculture would play an important role in ensuring a dynamic industrialisation process. Although Griffing did not dwell on the issue of rural migration, he considered the phenomenon 'inordinate' and hoped that the work of rural extension would put an end to it. A May 1946 AIA paper, probably written by Kadow and prompted by Lockwood's suggestions, discusses the introduction of agricultural projects in Brazil requiring a long time to implement so as to avoid superficial results. Extensive work to introduce modern machinery in agriculture would take about ten years, according to the document. Providing technical expertise to farmers would make it possible to fix part of the farming population in the rural environment and would encourage the migration only of the technically 'unqualified'.[26]

Although operating for almost a decade in the hinterlands of São Paulo, the Rural Extension work was either warily accepted or encountered obstacles in political negotiation. To complete the picture, John Griffing's departure during the 1950s seems to have been the reason behind the programme's closure a few years later, though in other states a prosperous relationship was about to begin. Analysing the São Paulo experience, AIA local director Henry Bagley stated: 'Santa Rita's program was good as a pilot program, but failed because it did not ensure its own continuation when AIA withdrew'. Rural producers demonstrated little initiative, according to Bagley and, as soon as the AIA ceased to contribute financially, the farmers did not want to invest in the continuance of these activities. In São José, on the other hand, farmers continued their activities even after the AIA's formal withdrawal in 1956. The two programmes had different origins: while 'Dad' Griffing and state secretary Humberto Pascale began the work in Santa Rita, in São José the regional farmers' organisation introduced the experiment, requesting technical assistance and continuing when the AIA decided to quit investing in the programme.[27]

According to Henry Bagley's analysis, the São José project arose from local farmers' needs, which made it more likely to move forward. In a letter dated August 1956, addressed to the representative of the Rural Association of São José do Rio Pardo, Dionysio Guedes Barreto, Bagley wrote: 'As you are aware, AIA did not receive from the state government the assistance it needed to proceed to a complete program of assistance to the farmers of São José do

26. American International Association for Economic and Social Development. p. 11. Collection: Family, Record Group III 4B, Box 01, Folder: AIA – Bolivar Foundation.

27. From Henry Bagley to Martha Dalrymple. Subject: Recollections of AIA in Brazil. p. 04. 5 Oct. 1967. Collection: AIA, Record Group IV IIIB, Box 02, Folder 19.

Rio Pardo'. Thus, 'the work of AIA in Brazil is focusing on technical assistance programs coupled with supervised rural credit, such as ACAR in Minas Gerais and the *Associação Brasileira de Crédito e Assistência Rural* (Brazilian Association of Credit and Rural Assistance, ABCAR)'.[28] Believing that the Rural Association would continue its activities regardless, Bagley continued: 'I communicate in writing what has been known to everyone for some time – the suspension of the direct activities of the AIA in São José do Rio Pardo.'[29] However, the continuity, or lack thereof, of programmes in São José and Santa Rita related to political issues, not just to the initial characteristics of the project, according to Bagley. In reality, the AIA and its programmes would be forced to recognise their control by and dependence upon political groups. Moreover, they also found it difficult to build their legitimacy in the eyes of certain political groups in the state of São Paulo.

Institutional Politics

The AIA's local relations in São Paulo were not those of either unrestricted support or political rejection. In reality, the AIA experienced moments of great local support as well as moments of discredit. In the 1951 municipal elections, for example, the political parties abandoned their local rivalries and put forth a request for agronomist engineer Marcos Pereira, an employee of the AIA, to run for mayor in Santa Rita. He did not accept it, in view of the AIA's principle not to get involved in political parties. In addition, on several occasions, Bagley proposed the creation of a rural extension company in the mould of ACAR. In 1955, for example, he negotiated this proposal with state governor and future President Jânio Quadros, but the negotiations did not reach any agreement.

The appointment of Renato Costa Lima as Secretary of Agriculture for the state of São Paulo in 1953, during the government of Lucas Garcez, was received as 'a great blessing for AIA',[30] as Bagley wrote that year. Costa Lima was the former director of *Avisco*, a producer of nutritionally balanced feed for poultry and, later in the 1960s, become federal Minister of Agriculture in João Goulart's government. The son of farmers, he had managed the Itaiquara plant in Tapiratiba, in the state of São Paulo, during the 1940s. During this period, he

28. De Henry Bagley para Dionysio Guedes Barreto. 3 Aug. 1956. Collection: AIA (closed section), Box 01, Folder: General AIA (including some India papers).

29. Ibid.

30. Third quarterly report to the Board of Directors. (Jul, Sep. 1953). p. 06. Collection: AIA, Record Group IV 3B, Box 15, Folder 132.

met Nelson Rockefeller, who later appointed him as director of the *Empresa de Mecanização Agrícola* (Agricultural Mechanization Company, EMA) – an organisation that worked to incentivise the production and adoption of agricultural machinery, such as tractors.[31] In this sector, US technicians considered Costa Lima the top advisor for IBEC and the companies this agency controlled, such as SASA and EMA itself, as well as one of the promoters of the AIA's work in São José do Rio Pardo in the 1950s. To some extent, Renato Costa Lima had proposed an expansion of the AIA's projects. While reading the 1953 ACAR Yearbook, he wrote to Harry Bagley with the intention of implementing a similar credit and technical assistance programme throughout Brazil.[32] With this in mind, Bagley claimed that Costa Lima had been a supporter of Griffing's techniques for rural improvement.[33] Just as the appointment of Paulo César de Azevedo Antunes to the Secretariat of Health of the State pleased the AIA, Costa Lima's nomination to the Secretariat of Agriculture marked a moment of convergence between the agency and formal positions of political power. An example of these times of political convergence is the agroindustrial fairs organised, for instance in São José in 1953. Shortly after this particular exhibition, Griffing wrote to Costa Lima offering the services of both Marcos Pereira and Lineo Brassoloto to train agronomists in the state of São Paulo, following the AIA's working methods.[34] Another case of the AIA's proximity to politicians is that of state representative Lincoln Feliciano (*Partido Social Democrático* or Social Democratic Party, PSD), then president of the state assembly, who took a letter from John Griffing to the Legislative Assembly. Reading the letter aloud in the session, the representative passed on the message that the agency was offering technical assistance to help control bovine pests using toxaphene in several municipalities of São Paulo state.[35]

Though such attitudes might suggest that the work of the agency enjoyed the unrestricted support of local politicians in different municipalities, relations were complex and nuanced. Initially, the AIA gained legitimacy with

---

31. *Dicionário Histórico Biográfico Brasileiro pós-1930* (Rio de Janeiro: Editora da FGV, 2001).

32. AIA Highlights. 24 June, 7 July 1954. Collection: AIA. Box 02, Folder 17.

33. Third quarterly report to the Board of Directors. (Jul, Sep. 1953). p. 06. Collection: AIA, Record Group IV 3B, Box 15, Folder 132.

34. Third quarterly report to the Board of Directors. (Jul, Sep. 1953). Collection: AIA, Record Group IV 3B, Box 15, Folder 132.

35. American International Association for Economic and Social Development. Fourth quarterly report to the Board of Director. (Oct., Nov., Dec. 1953). Collection: AIA, Record Group IV 3B, Box 15, Folder 132.

farmers and political groups because of work done in cooperation with various state government agencies, but it failed to consolidate itself in the state of São Paulo for mainly political reasons. While in Minas Gerais, ACAR continuously inaugurated local and regional offices, the expansion of the programme was slow and fragile in São Paulo. According to Walter Crawford, the Secretary of Agriculture of São Paulo did not accept the extension system because 'they [the state] had a good structure' already. However, 'Griffing thought that a state program should be done. Then he became intimately connected with our work [in Minas Gerais].'[36] In turn, João Napoleão de Andrade, one of the first representatives of ACAR and president of ABCAR in the second half of the 1950s, attributed the failures to the existence of similar initiatives in São Paulo: 'São Paulo had the Casa da Lavoura [Farming House program] and I thought I had solved the problem with this',[37] he said. Similarly, former agronomist José Calil claims in his memoirs that the greater availability of financial, technical and technological resources to the farmers of São Paulo made it possible not to include the state in AIA's ambitious plan for a national programme. Calil highlighted that State of São Paulo was outside the system – discussed in chapter 10 – as it had its own structure of technical assistance and service provision to farmers, with an assistance network located in municipalities possessing its own headquarters called Farming House.[38] São Paulo state industrialised early compared to the rest of Brazil, and thus developed a much more solid structure of agricultural research than other states. For instance, Adhemar de Barros's administration invested in vocational education for both industry and agriculture,[39] in connection with both the *Escola Superior de Agricultura Luiz de Queiroz* (Luiz de Queiroz College of Agriculture, ESALQ), founded in 1901, and the *Instituto Agronômico de Campinas* (Agronomic Institute of Campinas, IAC), created in 1887. Santa Rita already hosted a local IAC station with lots of pasture experimentation; therefore, pasture and agricultural production was one of the reasons to select this region for the AIA's work. Thus, if the AIA's objective was to build capacity for activities in underdeveloped regions,

36. Walter Lion Crawford, 'Entrevista concedida a Euclides Martins', Belo Horizonte, 10 Dec. 1981, p. 10.

37. João Napoleão de Andrade, 'Entrevista concedida à Romeu Padilha de Figueiredo', *Belo Horizonte*, 11 Nov. 1981. (Projeto 'Registro da Memória Histórica e Técnica da Extensão Rural no Brasil', da Emater-MG), p. 29.

38. José Calil. Rockefeller e o desenvolvimento da agricultura brasileira, INFORMAÇÕES AGRONÔMICAS Nº 88 – Dec.1999.

39. Luiza Cristina Villaméa Cotta, *Adhemar de Barros (1901–1969): a origem do 'rouba, mas faz'* (São Paulo: USP, 2008), p. 45 (M.A. Dissertation in History of Economy).

the choice to set up an office in São Paulo, considered the most economically developed Brazilian state, signalled an apparent contradiction.

As to political negotiations, the early 1950s marked a convergence of the AIA and the São Paulo state government in relation to projects and programmes; by the middle of the decade, on the contrary, a slow rupture between the AIA and the government was already visible.[40] Extending its planning up to 31 December 1956, the agreement would leave the Secretary of Agriculture responsible for projects such as home improvement clubs and trench silos. Likewise, the other secretariats would manage their projects, aiming to expand to other municipalities in the state. In return, the AIA would provide technical guidance for the agricultural activities developed in the two municipalities, among other places. The AIA thus aimed to disseminate and introduce modern techniques such as those demonstrated in Santa Rita and São José into other municipalities[41] and coordinate the activities for a sufficient period of time, until the Secretary of Agriculture could assume responsibility for the continuity of the project. However, on 11 May 1954, Mr Crawford claimed that the state government had not fulfilled its part of the agreement, namely expanding the work done by the AIA to twenty other counties. Crawford expected that the Secretaries of Agriculture would be able to carry on the programme for a period of only two years. Even Nelson Rockefeller's collaborators, such as Renato Costa Lima, created obstacles to the AIA's work, according to João Napoleão Andrade.[42]

Even though the government of São Paulo did not show support for the AIA's wishes, Brazilian members of ACAR and the government of Minas Gerais were 'anxious to continue and expand the work'.[43] This would provide an increase in funding that would allow ten new local offices and one regional office per year to be opened. The AIA's activities in the mid-1950s were increasingly directed to local governments, encouraging them to take over projects

40. From Walter Crawford to Wallace Harrison. Subject: Renewal and extension of the AIA São Paulo agreement. p. 01. 27 May 1954. Collection: Family, Record Group: III 4B, Box 01, Folder 7, AIA Brazil.

41. From Walter Crawford to Wallace Harrison. Subject: Renewal and extension of the AIA São Paulo agreement. p. 01. 27 May 1954. Collection: Family, Record Group: III 4B, Box 01, Folder 7, AIA Brazil..

42. João Napoleão de Andrade, 'Entrevista concedida à Romeu Padilha de Figueiredo', *Belo Horizonte*, 11 Nov. 1981. (Projeto 'Registro da Memória Histórica e Técnica da Extensão Rural no Brasil', da Emater-MG), p. 29.

43. From Walter Crawford to Wallace Harrison. Subject: Renewal and extension of the AIA São Paulo agreement. 27 May 1954. Collection: Family, Record Group: III 4B, Box 01, Folder 7, AIA Brazil, p. 02.

Figure 17. João Napoleão de Andrade (left), Nelson Rockefeller (right), Walter Crawford (back, left) and Santiago Apodaca (back, right), 1956. Rockefeller Archive Center, Series 1 General, 1027 AIA Photograph Collection.

initiated by the agency, especially in São Paulo. Moreover, with the reduction of the budget for 1955/56, the AIA would narrow the focus to activities that could carry out its development objectives. Awaiting approval of the agreement, Renato Costa Lima suggested connecting AIA's operations with the Secretary of Agriculture. However, for the AIA, a new governor's election and the makeover of the legislative assembly cast doubts over the continuity of the project.[44] To highlight the results of its work, the AIA needed adequate political support to demonstrate the real difference between the traditional and the modern. In addition, the programme in Minas Gerais would achieve greater results, resulting in the AIA's divestment from São Paulo projects in 1956.[45]

44. From Henry Bagley to Dick Greenebaum. Subject: AIA in state of São Paulo. 28 Jan. 1955. Collection: Family, Record Group: III 4B, Box: 01, Folder 07, AIA Brazil.

45. From Henry Bagley to Dick Greenebaum. Subject: AIA in state of São Paulo. 28 Jan. 1955. Collection: Family, Record Group: III 4B, Box: 01, Folder 07, AIA Brazil.

Unlike São Paulo's representation as a more economically developed Brazilian state, Minas Gerais symbolised economic stagnation, in spite of its Governor João Pinheiro's best efforts during his tenure (1906–1908) to foster industry at the state level. With the end of World War II, such efforts to articulate agriculture with needed industrial growth returned to the foreground. The Government of Milton Campos (1947–1950) developed activities related to agricultural production and research such as the institution of *Universidade Federal de Viçosa* (University of Viçosa, formerly ESAV), the *Escola Média de Agricultura* (Agricultural College), and others.[46] Another initiative, the *Ensino Agrário Ambulante* (Mobile Agricultural Education), implemented during Milton Campos' government, developed a discreet but efficient contribution, going to the most remote regions of the State, bringing a great quantity of small agricultural implements, technical notions of agriculture and livestock, film education, medicine and health care.[47] Similar activities were developed by ACAR, which, within a short time, had a greater reach than the *Ensino Agrário Ambulante.* Overall ACAR represented how Minas elites felt pressed to industrialise to follow São Paulo's example. I address this subject below.

46. Jack Siqueira, *Planejamento e desenvolvimento em Minas* (Belo Horizonte: Armazém de Ideias, 2001), p. 77–78.

47. Ibid., p.78.

CHAPTER 6.

THE ARCHETYPE OF BRAZILIAN AGRICULTURAL MODERNISATION: THE CREATION OF THE ASSOCIATION OF CREDIT AND RURAL ASSISTANCE OF MINAS GERAIS

A traditional approach may take for granted that agricultural modernisation is exogenous. This argument assumes that it began in Brazil with the agreement between the AIA and the state government of Minas Gerais; here, on the contrary, I demonstrate that processes of agricultural modernisation were initiated in Minas Gerais – with an emphasis on industrialisation – during the first half of the twentieth century. ESAV was home to one of these experiments in the second half of the 1920s. The process of industrialisation, including the pivotal role of the agricultural sector in this process, began during the first decades of the twentieth century. Nelson Rockefeller's proposal was thus not foreign to Minas Gerais' existing political and economic scenario.

Latin American Modernisers: The Balance Between Agriculture and Industry

The intimacy between agriculture and industry is evident in various aspects of Minas Gerais' political tradition. First, Minas Gerais's agrarian tradition reflects the Iberian conception, focusing on the private world, attachment to tradition, hierarchy, religion, family, moderation and labour.[1] These persistent representations, especially in Minas Gerais' rural world, are complemented by other characteristics in the public sphere: 'acceptance of the predominant role in the State in relation to individual initiative, emphasis on cooperation in opposition to competition, aversion to conflict, tendency to resolve disagreements by consensual arrangements, preference for conservation rather than change'.[2] Politicians and intellectuals such as Silviano Brandão, Venceslau Brás and Bias

1. José Murilo de Carvalho, 'Ouro, terra e ferro'. Vozes de Minas, in Ângela de Castro Gomes (ed.), *Minas e os fundamentos do Brasil moderno* (Belo Horizonte: UFMG, 2005), pp. 65–67.

2. Ibid.

Fortes are key symbols of this trend between the second half of the nineteenth century and the first half of the twentieth. The Minas variety of political culture did not see the preservation of the agrarian order as necessarily compatible with industrialisation. However, it was not the agrarian elite or its representatives who introduced agricultural modernisation projects in the state. Another trend – urban and industrial, linked to names like João and Israel Pinheiro and Juscelino Kubitschek – was responsible for initiating and intensifying this process. These politicians utilised conciliation with the agrarian elites to try to implant a model of the state's industrial modernisation.

In the 1930s and 1940s, this idea provided the bedrock for economic decisions. Benedito Valadares, an intervenor appointed by Getúlio Vargas between 1933 and 1945, was responsible for economic policy, beginning the definitive turn of Minas towards industrialisation. After the 1929 crisis, the state saw the need to seek new sources of wealth. Retrospectively, this became the concern of former provincial president João Pinheiro[3] and the Agricultural, Industrial and Commercial Congress of 1903. Valadares had the support of engineer Israel Pinheiro, son of João Pinheiro, within his administration. The search for further resources and development opportunities encompassed two distinct images of the region's economy and of its insertion into the national system. At first, the vision for a highly differentiated economy was predominant, with a strong farming industry grounding a dynamic industrial sector. The idea of productive specialisation gained importance later, when efforts focused on industrial expansion, particularly of the intermediate products sector: these were two distinct projects, but one did not completely exclude the other.[4]

Nevertheless, if Valadares' interventionist government influenced the state's process of industrialisation, it was former Getúlio Vargas opponent and *União Democrática Nacional* (National Democratic Union Party, UDN) state governor Milton Campos who continued it with the Plan of Economic Recovery and Development of Production, launched in 1947. The Milton Campos government's initiative became the first experience of macro-planning on a regional scale in Brazil. This plan's central orientations, mainly the emphasis on the balanced modernisation of industry and agriculture, reflected the UDN model of modernisation. This stood in contrast to the PSD model, implemented next by Juscelino Kubitschek.[5] Despite differences between

3. Ibid., p. 69.

4. Otávio Soares Dulci, *Política e recuperação econômica em Minas Gerais* (Belo Horizonte: UFMG, 1999), p. 38

5. Ibid., p. 78.

Figure 18. Juscelino Kubitschek (left), Harry Bagley (centre) and Walter Crawford (right), 1956. Rockefeller Archive Center, Series 1 General, 1027 AIA Photograph Collection.

UDN and PSD development models, ACAR's creation represented continuity between the government of Milton Campos (UDN, 1947–1950) and Juscelino Kubitschek (PSD, 1951–1955), who nationalised the programme during his presidency (1956–1961). João Napoleão de Andrade, who was responsible for the programme's maintenance, had convinced Governor Juscelino Kubitschek: 'before he made the final decision, he called his party friend, João Napoleão de Andrade, with friends in the United States, to the Palace of Liberty, explaining to him what he thought and requesting that he studied the subject'.[6] During the war, Andrade was in the United States because his family exported rock crystal and, during his stay there, he had the opportunity to get to know the rural extension service and other services of support to agriculture, because, as a farmer in the municipality of Sete Lagoas, he was interested in the subject. Faced with João Napoleão de Andrade's considerations, the story goes, Ku-

6. José Paulo Ribeiro, *A Saga da Extensão Rural em Minas Gerais* (São Paulo: Annablume; Minas Gerais: CPP/Emater, 2000).

bitschek not only continued the ACAR programme, but also fully supported the initiative.[7]

More than an isolated initiative, the permanence of ACAR reconciled two political visions. The Minas Gerais agency demonstrated a conciliatory tone between the two projects: on the one hand, for the Udenistas, the AIA's Minas Gerais programmes represented the modernisation of agriculture and a relationship that could become more entrepreneurial, because rural society would thus increasingly diversify production; on the other hand, for the PSD, these programmes would not transform the agrarian structure. While the extension programme was conceived in relation to small farmers, in the 1960s, large landowners also used extension services. In this context Américo Giannetti provided the most striking contribution to the economic policy of the Milton Campos government; the former was an entrepreneur and, like João Pinheiro, an engineer trained at Escola de Minas de Ouro Preto, as well as founder of the *Federação da Indústria do Estado de Minas Gerais* (Federation of State Industries of Minas Gerais, FIEMG). The formulation of 1947 Plan of Economic Recovery and Development of Production began with the creation of a Technical Council of the UDN during the convention that launched the candidacy of Milton Campos to enter government.[8] As in the Valadares period, Milton Campos's government supported the predominance of basic industries such as steel in conjunction with the agrarian sector.[9] The political action of Milton Campos' government did not signal a break from the industrialising initiatives approached by the PSD. Giannetti himself expressed support for a balance between industrialisation and agriculture in his inaugural address as Secretary of Agriculture in 1947. In this view, industrialisation would enable economic progress, but, in Giannetti's own words, 'this industrial development must be carried out in harmony with that of other production activities, agriculture and livestock, to ensure their economic independence, increase their income and value their work'.[10]

The industrial leadership linked to the FIEMG judged that sales increases in the extractive and manufacturing industries, as well as the agricultural sector, would help these sectors acquire machinery. Giannetti's inauguration speech

7. Ibid., p 101.

8. Dulci, *Política e recuperação em Minas Gerais*, p. 78.

9. de Carvalho, 'Ouro, terra e ferro', pp. 70–71.

10. Ignácio Delgado, 'Independência econômica de Minas Gerais: Imagens do Discurso do Empresariado Mineiro nos anos 40 e 50', *Revista Locus – Revista de História* 1 (1) (1995): 3.

at the Secretariat of Agriculture reflected the rationalisation of agricultural production in the direction supported by business elites, as expressed in a document signed by FIEMG's directors,[11] in 1947, before Nelson Rockefeller and the AIA had even begun their agreement in Minas Gerais. The plan followed the lineaments of Campos' electoral campaign: both industrial and agricultural development, incorporating economic and social aspects. The diagnosis underpinning it considered the region's vulnerability to be associated with particularly disadvantageous geographical and ecological conditions – its enclaved position, without free access to the sea; the dispersion of its economic activities, lacking a centre of gravity; difficult internal communication; and the precariousness of arable land.[12]

To address these challenges, one of the measures introduced by Milton Campos' government was the Itinerant Agricultural Education programme. This consisted of sending multidisciplinary teams to various areas of the state, by rail and road trains, to provide technical and sanitary assistance to communities of small producers. This activity was in line with the 1947 plan, as it sought a solution that would integrate agricultural policy towards economic and technological development, and social policy such as modernisation of rural areas.[13] Already in partnership with the AIA, an agreement signed with Gerais' state government created ACAR on 8 December 1948. Minas Gerais was then deploying an economic strategy of industrialisation and had recently begun projects to modernise agriculture and improve social conditions in rural areas. In other words, the AIA's initiative was not at all strange, given that, on 10 December 1947, Law No. 29 was promulgated, authorising the government of the State of Minas Gerais to issue a State Treasury policy to enable the intensification of agricultural production and the improvement of the economic and social conditions of rural life. Based on this law, the State Government entered into an agreement with the American International Association.[14] The promulgation of this law was not an isolated initative, considering that the state of Minas Gerais had initiated an economic recovery project decades earlier.

---

11. Ibid., p. 4.

12. Dulci, *Política e recuperação econômica em Minas Gerais*, p. 80.

13. Ibid., p. 87.

14. José Alfredo Amaral de Paula, 'Fatos históricos da ACAR, pesquisados pelo Eng. Agr. José Alfredo Amaral de Paula, Coordenador do Projeto Memória da Emater-MG' (Belo Horizonte: EMATER, [s.d]). (unpublished paper), p. 1.

Figure 19. An ACAR Jeep crossing rural areas in Minas Gerais hinterland. Rockefeller Archive Center, Collection 1027 AIA, Series 2, Box 2, Brazil. In its reports and press publications, ACAR suggested the effectiveness of its Jeep automobiles in overcoming the most remote places – the supremacy of technology over wilderness. Rockefeller Archive Center, Series 1 General, 1027 AIA Photograph Collection, Box 2, Folder 31.

While, on the one hand, Minas Gerais would provide the ideal conditions for the implementation of the agreement between the state and AIA, on the other, the agency sought to establish institutions to promote the modernisation of agriculture. Contacts with the state government to discuss the founding of the ACAR began through agronomist Antônio Secundino de São José, former ESAV head and Agroceres founder. Secundino was a classmate of agronomist Paulo Pena de Salvo, who became the first president of the ACAR administrative board. Thus, according to former agronomist José Paulo Ribeiro, AIA and IBEC knew Secundino very well, and Agroceres probably contributed to the first installation in Minas Gerais, since its hybrid corn production unit at that time was located in the city of Ubá.[15] Meanwhile, Nelson Rockefeller, his brothers

15. Ribeiro, *A Saga da Extensão Rural em Minas Gerais*, p 101.
Dulci, *Política e recuperação econômica em Minas Gerais*, p. 58.

David and Lawrence, and John Griffing and other American lawyers were in Rio de Janeiro around 1948. According to Crawford, one of these Americans was close to a banker well connected with the government. Griffing established contact with José Barbosa de Melo Santos, Milton Campos' cousin. From that point, Crawford recalls that it was decided to pursue a programme like ACAR, which would be a supervised credit programme, offering technical expertise on the one hand and, on the other, a line of credit to the small farmer.[16] Crawford was born in Arkansas and started his professional career in the Farm Security Administration, developing similar activities during the New Deal.

Despite the existence of common interests, the agreement did not emerge without resistance. Euclides Gonçalves Martins, who joined ACAR in 1949, reported that the early days of the agency were not frictionless. According to Martins, the North American aluminum exploration company, ALCOA, caused financial problems for the company owned by the Secretary of Agriculture of Minas Gerais, Américo Gianetti: 'There were problems with the Secretary of Agriculture who did not accept our program', because he, 'had a dispute with ALCOA, which was connected to aluminum'. Giannetti 'was annoyed because of this, [we] went there to talk to him and the response we received was that he did not want to talk to Americans. So we were forced to look for the Treasury Department, where José de Magalhães Pinto was'[17] – Magalhães Pinto later became Minas Gerais Governor and, in the early 1960s, was one of the most important conspirators to depose President João Goulart and favour a civil-military dictatorship between 1964 and 1985. However, in Crawford's own recollections from the negotiations, the sacking of the Secretary of Agriculture was expected. In his conversation with Giannetti, along with John Griffing, it was agreed that the former would not be empowered to develop the project as initially planned, with emphasis on credit. When Crawford began to expose ideas, 'shortly afterwards Dr Giannetti's Secretary looked at me and said that this was not his business and that it would be best if we were to speak to Magalhães Pinto'.[18]

The negotiation that shaped the makeover of ACAR's administrative board led to the inclusion of two Brazilian members, two North Americans and one AIA representative. The idea was to start work under the direction of a North American expert. Over time, the Brazilian technicians would take

16. Walter Lion Crawford, *Entrevista concedida a Euclides Martins*, Belo Horizonte, EMATER, 10 Dec. 1981, pp. 5–6.

17. Ibid., p. 9.

18. Ibid., p. 10.

over responsibility for project leadership. The first Executive Director, equivalent to a President of ACAR, was Walter Lion Crawford. Designated by the AIA and accepted by the government of Minas Gerais, he led the agency from 21 December 1948 to 3 May 1953.[19] Paulo Penna de Salvo, an agronomist and agricultural engineer, presided over ACAR's first administrative board. Lawyer and farmer José Barbosa de Melo Santos, cousin of governor Milton Campos, was also part of the first administrative board. The other members were American: Walter Crawford himself, agronomist John Griffing and IBEC lawyer and consultant in Brazil, William H. Alton.[20] Over the first three years, the AIA and the state government of Minas Gerais proposed to invest US $ 225,000 each, totalling US $ 450,000 by 1951, in supervised credit projects. However, the renewal of the agreement would extend no further than 1961, since the Americans were convinced that Brazilian leaders themselves should carry out 'self-improvement'.

In a decade and a half of agreement, the AIA and the ACAR invested the following amounts: between 1949 and 1951, the AIA provided $75,000 annually, and the government of Minas Gerais invested $ 25,000 the first year, $ 75,000 the second and $ 125,000 the final year (see Figure 20). By means of the second technical cooperation agreement, effective between 1952 and 1954, the AIA invested $75,000 in the first year, $60,000 in the second and $45,000 in 1954. The Minas Gerais government, in turn, invested progressively, since the initial contract planned for a gradual increase in the local government's contribution – reaching the same amount of investment as the AIA over three years. In the renewed agreement for the 1955/1956 biennium, the AIA invested a total of $75,000, $45,000 in 1955 and $30,000 in 1956. During this period, the *Escritório Técnico de Agricultura* (Technical Office of Agriculture, ETA) contributed $27,000. So, in the period between 1949 and 1956, the AIA invested $480,000 in technicians and programmes in the state of Minas Gerais via ACAR.[21] In the early 1960s, the contribution of the state government increased to 76 per cent of ACAR's budget.[22] Moreover, ACAR's geographical reach varied from an initial area corresponding to 1.71 per cent

19. Ibid., p. 1.

20. Ribeiro, *A Saga da Extensão Rural em Minas Gerais*, p. 101.
Dulci, *Política e recuperação econômica em Minas Gerais* pp. 241 and 236, respectively.

21. From Walter L. Crawford to the Board of Directors of AIA. Subject: Grant to AIA from Rockefeller Brothers Fund for Brazil Program. 6 Jan. 1956. Collection: Family; Record Group: III 4B; Box: 01; Folder: 7B, AIA Brazil. p. 02.

22. ACAR MINAS GERAIS, *Programa para o ano agrícola 1959/60* (Belo Horizonte, 1962), p. 6.

of the state in 1949/50 to 13.6 per cent in 1958/59. Correspondingly, from fifteen field technicians in 1949/50, the association's staff reached 228 in 1958/59. In ten years, Cr$ 166,414,440 were borrowed and, according to the institution, in 1957, 99.1% of loans were repaid.[23] According to its data, of the CR$ 120,344,640.00 overdue at that time, CR$ 119,515,449.00 had been received.[24]

Year	State of Minas Gerais	AIA
1949	US$25,000	US$75,000
1950	US$75,000	US$75,000
1951	US$125,000	US$75,000
Total	**US$225,000**	**US$225,000**

Figure 20. Origin of resources in the execution of the agreement between the government of Minas Gerais and AIA. Source: ACAR (1960)

These statistics show, in short, that political elites were more willing to accept the programme developed in Minas Gerais than in São Paulo. As I will discuss next, this was not only because of the will of Minas Gerais to recover economically, but also because of the methods and programmes adopted. Initially, the AIA introduced the extension service model to work in the hinterlands of São Paulo through John Griffing and the Brazilian agronomists Marcos Pereira and Lineo Brassoloto. On the other hand, ACAR in Minas Gerais was inspired by the New Deal's Farm Security Administration (FSA) programme of supervised credit in its early years. In 1952, though, ACAR adopted extensionism, which later served as a model for the latter's scaling out nationally.

ACAR's Performance in Minas Gerais: A Synthesis of Supervised Credit and Extension Service

While in São Paulo the extension service predominated in the first years, Minas Gerais adopted supervised credit and assistance programmes. These had their origins in the United States in the 1930s, promoting the creation of the Farm Security Administration. It is therefore important to return to the US historical context and to follow the intense debate on agriculture taking place

23. ACAR MINAS GERAIS, *Relatório 1956/57* (Belo Horizonte, [1957]), p. 5.

24. ACAR MINAS GERAIS, *1959. Dez anos a serviço do povo rural mineiro* (Belo Horizonte, 1959), pp. 13–17.

there at that time. Some of those involved in the AIA and the implementation of the ACAR participated in the creation of credit and assistance programmes in this context. This was the case for James Maddox, who, after working as an assistant administrator for the FSA, joined the AIA. Another example, more directly linked to ACAR, is Walter Crawford, who worked for the FSA in Little Rock, in the United States, until 1943. Robert Hudgens, on the other hand, was an investor who developed a private organisation to provide financial and technical assistance to the landless population as well as to unemployed rural workers in South Carolina in the 1930s. His ideas, wrote historian Darlene Rivas, served as a model to structure the Resettlement Administration (RA), later absorbed by the FSA – which she considers the most ideological agency of the New Deal because FSA agents were notorious for combatting Southern racism and the traditional agricultural establishment.[25] The FSA arose from RA's inability to work with tenants and from the rise of the debate on rural workers in 1935/36 in various segments of US public opinion, such as groups of churches, liberals, socialists, extensionist leaders, politicians.[26]

Roosevelt asked his Secretary of Agriculture, Henry Agard Wallace, to prepare a report on the situation of rural tenants. Wallace and colleague Rexford 'the Red' Tugwell believed that the Natural Resources Committee could provide a report on this situation.[27] Thus, Tugwell organised several Committee Hearings, which acted as a forum where several groups debated and presented their positions on the difficulties facing the agricultural sector in the United States. In Tugwell's conception, every action needed research and analysis; reason would therefore require science, facts, data and education. Action would be revolutionary only if supported by education, which in turn would need to reflect democracy, based on the agreement between means and ends defined through voluntarism and consensus.[28] Following these principles, Tugwell organised the public hearings to gain support for his ideas on direct credit actions.

The organisers of these committees were positioned to listen to the agents who dealt with agricultural issues in the United States. The debates, however, reflected diverse viewpoints, from maintaining the status quo to racist theories. An example of the former was an association – the National Committee

25. Rivas, *Missionary Capitalist*, p. 142.

26. Bernard Sternsher, *Rexford Tugwell and the New Deal* (New Brunswick: Rutgers University Press, 1964), p. 376.

27. Theodore Saloutos, *The American Farmer and the New Deal* (Ames: The Iowa University Press, 1982), pp. 164–65.

28. Sternsher, *Rexford Tugwell and the New Deal*, p. 376.

on Rural Social Planning (NCRSP) – suggesting that tenants should work in community, for, if they became landowners in the South, the United States was in danger of regressing to the use of animal traction.[29] For the second group, however, racial and biological factors could interfere. C.E. Brehm, Director of the Tennessee Extension Service, reflected the common sense of the power structure. For Brehm, there were mental and physical factors in management skills and other qualifications that explained why some became owners and others remained tenants.[30] Rupert B. Vance, from the Institute for Research in Social Science, at the University of North Carolina, argued that if black farmers became owners in areas where they made up seventy to ninety per cent of the population, it would prompt the white population to flee these territories. When these white landlords arrived in the United States, argued Vance, they remained in this territory expecting to stay in dominant positions. Once deprived of these functions, they would rather leave these places to self-govern or to the state government.[31] Mary McLeod Bethune, a representative of black workers in the southern states, argued that 700,000 Blacks in the South of the country needed federal support to become owners or to be included in a land programme.[32] Ms Katherine Bennett, vice-president of the Council of Woman for Home Missions, emphasised the importance of government assuming financial responsibility for migrant workers from the Pacific who were poorly established, underpaid and whose children were prevented from attending school.[33] After this intense public debate, in December 1936, Wallace announced that the USDA incorporated the RA. The following year, with the approval of the Bankhead-Jones Act, RA became part of the FSA, and loan programmes were established, aiming to transform tenants into owners. Even though most of RA's members moved to the FSA, their actions were reoriented: while RA was more in favour of a massive relocation of tenants, the FSA was dedicated to lending, with a greater role over the years in lending credit, until it became the Farmers Home Administration (FmHA) in 1943. All these complex debates, in one way or another, shaped former FSA modernisers such as Hudgens, Maddox and Crawford, now working in Latin America.

In the Brazilian case, one of the greatest obstacles to implementation of ACAR's actions was the definition of its target audience. At a May 1949

29. Saloutos, *The American Farmer and the New Deal*, p. 173.

30. Ibid.

31. Ibid.

32. Ibid., p. 174

33. Ibid.

meeting of ACAR's Board of Directors, Mr Crawford possibly had to take a deep breath. He asked the other members of the board to be patient: 'At all times they remind me that patience is considered the greatest virtue in Brazil and I would like to suggest that those who criticized us exercised in this virtue and gave us enough time'.[34] After all, only six months had passed since the beginning of the Minas Gerais programme. The main difficulty in granting credit to farmers was not exactly lack of resources, but the uneasy definition of a target audience: who would be the beneficiaries? Though the previous decade's North American experience had been successful and well-known, its transposition into the Brazilian context was not simple. When it came to the family type farm, the introduction of the North American model of rural property was ideal. However, the production structure in rural Minas Gerais was somewhat different from that known to programme managers, whether Brazilian or North American:

> We had in mind families who need medical, sanitary, domestic, food preparation, and home improvements. We certainly did not expect to have borrowers who were so well-off that they could afford to keep modern toilets, electric light, and maids in the home. We can see from a survey of farms and households that has been prepared that the applications we are receiving differ considerably from our early conceptions of the kind of family we should be working with.[35]

The ACAR experiment was not successful in the early years. In view of the first reflections and debates within ACAR's Administrative Board, the group had to re-create supervised credit activities, taking into account the complex Brazilian context. In other words, if this association started its work emphasising supervised credit, a modality in which rural credit is associated with educational and social projects, the agricultural modernisers realised that this type of assistance would be very limited.[36] Later on, supervised credit, in ACAR's interpretation, intended to educate by lending money, to facilitate the purchase of modern agricultural inputs: 'This plan details more concretely the real needs of the family'.[37] These

34. ACAR MINAS GERAIS, *Associação de Crédito e Assistência Rural. Relatório do diretor para membros da Junta Administrativa – 1949 a 1953* (Belo Horizonte: ACAR, 1953), p. 5.

35. ACAR MINAS GERAIS, *Associação de Crédito e Assistência Rural. Relatório do diretor para membros da Junta Administrativa – 1949 a 1953* (Belo Horizonte: ACAR, 1953), pp. 6–7.

36. Ribeiro, *A Saga da Extensão Rural em Minas Gerais*, p 101. Dulci, *Política e recuperação econômica em Minas Gerais*, p. 97

37. ACAR MINAS GERAIS, *1959. Dez anos a serviço do povo rural mineiro* (Belo Horizonte, 1959) pp. 39 and 4, respectively.

Figure 21. Various officials of the Caixa Econômica and ACAR witnessing the signing of the first loan agreement with Ms Onofre da Silveira. Walter Lion Crawford is second from the right. Rockefeller Archive Center, Series 1 General, 1027 AIA Photograph Collection, Box 2.

might include buying machinery and tools; acquisition of selected fertilisers and seeds; purchase of water filters or household equipment. As part of the programme, farmers began to receive guidance and lessons from supervisors through individual visits and group meetings.[38] Because of the difficulties faced by ACAR in the first years of the programme, former agronomist José Paulo Ribeiro wrote that the technicians could continue to deploy more extensionist activities by applying methods of extension with individual or group reach. The success of these activities was such that ACAR consolidated itself as an extension service using credit as an instrument for the diffusion of scientific

38. ACAR MINAS GERAIS, *1959. Dez anos a serviço do povo rural mineiro* (Belo Horizonte, 1959), p. 39.

agricultural techniques,[39] especially with the arrival of ACAR's new director, New Mexico extensionist Santiago Apodaca.

The objectives of extensionism and credit, therefore, aligned in ACAR in 1952, when credit became one of the activities of the extension service aiming to educate farmers to use certain agricultural techniques. Therefore, the initial model of supervised rural credit was mixed with the US Extension Service model. This innovation was the result of the joint experience of the US and Brazilian technicians. Finally, the board made adaptations in both credit and extension services, and one of the most important was the continued use of Supervised Rural Credit, now an instrument of the Rural Extension Service educational process.[40] As mentioned, initially the association between the government of Minas Gerais and the AIA came from the Treasury Department and emphasised the credit programme, to the detriment of the Secretariat of Agriculture, which already had a rural education programme. This strategy resulted in the creation of ACAR. However, the actual implementation of the association faced a series of difficulties, forcing alteration of the original plans and resulting in a hybrid programme where supervised credit was intrinsically associated with rural extension. This synthesis was, according to one of those involved, a 'typically Mineira [from Minas Gerais] innovation'.[41] In his book, however, José Paulo Ribeiro did not emphasise other problems that ACAR faced in the early years, such as difficulties in accessing loan money and making the resources of Caixa Econômica do Estado de Minas Gerais available to farmers.[42]

Another issue was the paying back of loans. Contrary to ACAR's expectations, many farmers did not return the amount borrowed.[43] ACAR's bookkeeper Eduardo King Carr produced a list of twenty farmers from four Minas Gerais municipalities, demonstrating that the return on loans was lower than claimed by the agency's propaganda. A similar letter, including fourteen other farmers from six municipalities, was addressed to Augusto Costa, President of Caixa Econômica do Estado de Minas Gerais, on 12 April 1954; this time it was signed by Santiago Apodaca, who replaced Crawford when Crawford was appointed as vice-president of the AIA in Brazil. In other words, the payback

39. Ribeiro, *A Saga da Extensão Rural em Minas Gerais*, p. 101. Dulci, *Política e recuperação econômica em Minas Gerais*, p. 104.

40. Dulci, *Política e recuperação econômica em Minas Gerais*, p. 104.

41. Ibid.

42. De Ivan T. Cajueiro a Walter Crawford. Belo Horizonte, 25 Feb. 1953.

43. Eduardo King Carr (Diretor Interino). Correspondência ao Sr. Augusto Costa (Presidente da Caixa Econômica do Estado). Belo Horizonte, 15 Feb. 1954.

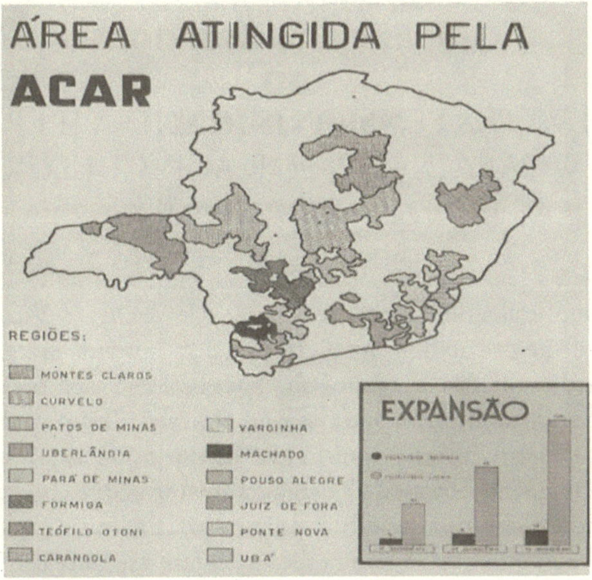

Figure 22. ACAR expansion across Minas Gerais territory in 1964. Source: Revista ACAR. Extensão em Minas Gerais. Belo Horizonte: ACAR, 1964.

of loans made by small farmers during World War II was not repeated in Minas Gerais, generating concern in the early years of ACAR – which responded by obliterating this data from its Yearbook and prioritising a propaganda that did not reflect reality. Despite difficulties, ACAR broadened its scope in the state of Minas Gerais, both in terms of geographical reach and in terms of operational models, linking credit to extensionism. In a context shaped by Point Four's implementation by the US government and new agreements with state governments in Brazil, ACAR's experience began to spread further into the state of Minas Gerais and to other states. The next chapter explores the ACAR experience in detail, discussing how local politics and culture reshaped ACAR programmes.

CHAPTER 7.

TWO EXTENSIONISTS AND A JEEP: NEW PARADIGMS FOR AGRICULTURAL DEVELOPMENT

A workshop evaluation conducted at the University of Viçosa in 1952 changed the orientation of ACAR's strategy towards extension service and supervised credit. As part of the Point Four Program, a partnership linking the United States government and the ETA emerged. This period reflects the increasing popularity of extensionism and its expansion as a model of agricultural development. The model's organisational structure also became more complex, since ACAR grew steadily and aimed to train Brazilian technicians to act. During this period, ACAR and other technical assistance companies such as ETA were forging strong links to local power, including local governments, church representatives and powerful families. As a Canadian anthropologist wrote in the 1950s, the Brazilian countryside, as a rule, was characterised by adhering to paternalistic and authoritarian relations, with power concentrated in the hands of family patriarchs, priests, landowners and political leaders.[1] The task of modernising it would not be easy.

The Complexity of the ACAR Programme: Politics and Culture in Rural Minas Gerais

ACAR tried to reconcile industrialisation with agricultural development while prescribing several changes for the rural world. In the 1950s, with the beginning of extensionist work, the stereotype of the rural dweller was an individual

1. At that time, Latin Americanist social sciences provided descriptions of social reality based on an asymmetrical temporal opposition, fundamental to the legitimisation of modernisation programmes promoted by both national states and private foundations. The work of sociologists and anthropologists like Oberg, but also of Costa Rican sociologist Antonio M. Arce, among others, was based on the premise of social change through agricultural modernisation. Kalervo Oberg, 'Community center project at Chonin, Brazil', in Arthur Niehof (ed.), *A Casebook of Social Change* (Chicago: Aldine Publishing Company, 1966), p. 89. On the connections between social scientists and government in the United States, see Feres Jr., *A história do conceito de Latin America*, ch. 2 and 3.

Figure 23. Contrasting modernisation and tradition. On the left, two ACAR technicians visiting a couple of small farmers for home demonstration and supervised credit orientation. Rockefeller Archive Center, Series 1 General, 1027 AIA Photograph Collection, Box 2.

'retracted and suspicious in nature, isolated in its environment by the lack of means of communication and community interests'. This man 'has lived on the edges of agricultural progress' and ACAR was optimistic, diagnosing the rural environment as cultural and therefore changeable. The agricultural modernisers took the view that, 'by a natural psychological reaction, the farmer does not rush to abandon routine and old-fashioned methods of work' due to the 'lack of orientation and teaching methods applied to rural areas'.[2] With proper methods, 'our man of the countryside' would be more and more 'eager to progress and expand his knowledge'.[3] Hence, the ACAR and the AIA attempted to transform the backward *Mineiro* subject into a South American progressive farmer. Adjusting his working methods and the technologies he

2. ACAR MINAS GERAIS, *1959. Dez anos a serviço do povo rural mineiro* (Belo Horizonte, 1959), p. 1.

3. Ibid., p. 3

employed would be fundamental if rural populations were to achieve these goals. While in the early 1950s credit and technical assistance were the main model of action directed at smallholders, by the end of the decade the objectives were more daring: 'technological education drives progress'.[4] The work of agencies like ACAR showed that it might be possible to achieve ambitious economic and social objectives. Therefore, the term 'progress' came to mean achieving an ideal state, 'a fully developed rural environment inhabited by educated people with a reasonable standard of living',[5] necessitating the elimination of possible obstacles. 'Now', ACAR's report stated, 'increased crop production is achieved', or 'a housewife is satisfied because her children have health and good appearance, or better clothes, previously made by rude unskilful hands that are now agile and painstaking; now a dwelling house is constructed to replace an unworthy *cafua*'.[6]

It would be up to ACAR agents to introduce modern agriculture and domestic economy practices into the countryside, entailing the adoption of equipment and unknown items by farmers. Given that this equipment was not readily available or was considered excessively expensive, ACAR would 'take care of buying [it] from the sources of production, then giving [it] to farmers at cost price'.[7] Principal items on this list were water filters, chemical fertilisers, selected seeds, insecticides, sprays and agricultural machinery. To overcome the effective isolation of rural populations, ACAR sought to introduce attitudes more disposed to developing agriculture by introducing technical and/or technological elements to young people: 'They learn', in this way, 'to produce more efficiently than their parents, mostly clinging to empirical methods of work'.[8] According to ACAR's proposal, it was necessary to advance extension service alongside progress in health and education at universities and schools, to be implemented in partnership with local, state or national governments. In other words, at the macro level, the biggest question was how to overcome political resistance so as to initiate and legitimise the modernising work; at a micro level, the discussion centred on how to lead a process of social change. The person who 'leads the rural families to the modern achievements of science

4. ACAR MINAS GERAIS, *Programa para o ano agrícola 1959/60* (Belo Horizonte, 1962).
5. ACAR MINAS GERAIS, *1959. Dez anos a serviço do povo rural mineiro*, p. 48.
6. Ibid.
7. Ibid., p. 5
8. Ibid., p. 19.

and technology, of research and experimentation, in the field of agriculture and the domestic economy' must be 'empowered' and 'aware of his mission'.[9]

Figure 24. Home demonstration work in Minas Gerais. Rockefeller Archive Center, Series 1 General, 1027 AIA Photograph Collection, Box 2.

ACAR's extensionist work followed the American model. It consisted of two agents, usually an agricultural technician or agronomist and a woman trained in home economics, because of the difficulty of hiring university trained professionals in Brazil. They arrived in their famous Jeep vehicles: 'two extensionists and a Jeep' or 'the man, the girl and the Jeep' was a trope cooked up by Robert Hudgens that encapsulated an extensionist's ideal.

After a successful trial during the Second War, a large number of Jeep vehicles were imported from the United States in the 1950s by the AIA, arriving at the port of Rio de Janeiro and then driven to Belo Horizonte. In turn, each ACAR office had an agricultural supervisor – i.e., an agricultural engineer, veterinarian or agricultural technician – as well as a home economist, who

9. Ibid., p. 2.

travelled to farms in the Jeep, on horseback or on foot.[10] While 'the man and the girl' symbolised the advance of technical knowledge in the rural environment, many extensionists considered the Jeep a symbol of the strength and daring necessary for those involved in Rural Extension in Minas Gerais at that time.[11] As former ACAR director José Paulo Ribeiro stated, the Jeep signified transcending physical barriers, overcoming access and communication difficulties responsible for the isolation of rural families. This vehicle represented the power of conquest, courage, resistance and determination.[12]

Figure 25. The agricultural technician and the home economist – or 'the man and the girl' – tackling how to drive a Jeep Willys. Rockefeller Archive Center, Series 1 General, 1027 AIA Photograph Collection, Box 2.

10. Ribeiro, *A Saga da Extensão Rural em Minas Gerais*, p. 99.

11. Leonardo Gomes Ribeiro, *'Progredir sempre'. Os jovens rurais mineiros nos Clubes 4-S. Saber, Sentir, Servir, Saúde* (Belo Horizonte: Universidade Federal de Minas Gerais, 2013). (MA Dissertation in Education), p. 49.

12. Ribeiro, *A Saga da Extensão Rural em Minas Gerais*, p. 99.

Besides the physical distances, the political and cultural context would also become an obstacle to the advancement of ACAR's modernisers. In his *An Introduction to Brazil*, US anthropologist Charles Wagley characterised the Minas Gerais hinterland as strictly controlled by religion and landowner power: possessing a 'large number of small towns with less than 5,000 people', the state of Minas Gerais in 1950 'had but two cities with over 50,000 inhabitants out of a total of 1,095 urban centers'. Historically, 'many of these small towns and villages owe their origin to grants or *patrimônios* made by landowners to the Church with the express purpose of creating a town devoted to a particular saint'. Finally, mentioning US geographer Preston James, Wagley highlights that mineiros are noted as the most conservative people in Brazil.[13] To this characteristic of religious power over the social order of small communities and municipalities is added the power of local elites based on land ownership. As a result, the rural populations of Minas Gerais – and of Brazil more widely – were labelled as resistant to modernisation, as will be shown.

The model applied throughout the 1950s, and with profound changes in the following decades, faced resistance to its implementation. Although at the state level the AIA had the support of the Minas Gerais government for ACAR's creation, power relations at local levels had different tones as local offices opened throughout Minas Gerais in the 1950s. Initially, the profession of agronomist in Brazil was created with the aim of reflecting an apolitical tone of neutrality – as if this was possible – positioning itself as a professional class united around the modernisation of agriculture as an ideal. Even in the early twentieth century, agronomists' preference was to apply the knowledge considered modern, but not to small properties.[14] In the second half of the twentieth century, this model adjusted to the new needs of production and maintenance of the agrarian structure. Agricultural programmes were thus not simply imported but reformulated models. For instance, extensionist work in the United States relates to the intensification of productive capacity in certain areas, especially small properties suffering from erosion – a very common situation, especially after 1929. The strategists of extensionist ideals in Brazil, however, sought to adapt to the land structure's local conditions – characterised on one side by big farmers and, on the other, by sharecroppers and landless workers.

13. Charles Wagley, *An Introduction to Brazil* (New York: Columbia University Press, 1963).

14. Sonia Regina de Mendonça, *Agronomia e poder no Brasil* (Rio de Janeiro: Vício de Leitura, 1998), p. 30.

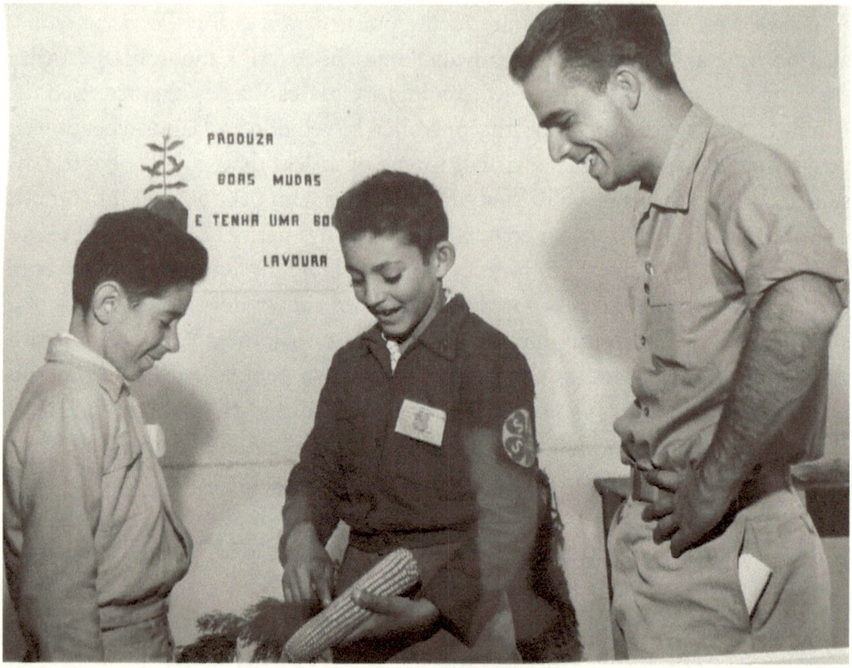

Figure 26. 4-S Clubs in Minas Gerais. The 4-S Clubs are an adaptation of US 4-H Clubs, stimulating projects exclusively intended for rural youth. Rockefeller Archive Center, Series 1 General, 1027 AIA Photograph Collection, Box 2.

It was only in the late 1950s that the notion of agrarian reform was introduced to ACAR, possibly because this discussion was prominent at the national level, especially in the years leading up to the 1964 military coup. In 1961, though, the President of the Republic invited ACAR's 'eminent patricians', together with the former governor and then Senator Milton Campos, to form part of a working commission to evaluate the *Estatuto da Terra* (Land Statute). It would also be mistaken to allege, though, that, during this period, the agency's activity was always complicit with the landowners: this was, in fact, more frequent after 1964, with military control over the ABCAR system. In the 1950s, ACAR set rigid discipline for its technicians, prohibiting political discussion and putting in place specific rules for women: they had to wear trousers, were prohibited from smoking and could not marry. Religious practice was not a rule, but its absence provoked conflicts, as we will see below. The Americans introduced these as control mechanisms: according to psychologist Rita Hilarina Gomes Nelson, 'they were very demanding; they wanted everything to be done right. When we worked, we went to the properties and could not accept lunch or gifts', she explained by way of example.

Rita concluded: 'We could not deal with politics; it was just work.'[15] Another anecdote tells how, in 1951, in the community of Martins Guimarães, the relationship between ACAR and the Catholic Church was positive, with the former enjoying the collaboration of priests. According to an unidentified agronomist, the local population did not accept ACAR because they thought it was a communist project; according to the narrative, ACAR might introduce (communist!) ideas from the United States to the population. Later, the unidentified agronomist claimed that the population had nutrition prejudices, avoiding mixing fruits such as mango with milk. On an ordinary Sunday, with the help of Father Guarino, ACAR made a fruit salad and, after the end of mass, the priest 'forced' the people to eat the fruit salad and drink milk. The people, afraid of the priest, ate the salad without questioning, and ended up liking it and lost their fear of mixing fruits and milk. In the end, the agronomist elaborated optimistically that the 'ignorant' population started to use all sorts of fruits.[16]

On the other hand, there are many examples of conflicts arising from the tense relationship between local politics and ACAR. Threats of eviction, relocation or even removal of the furniture provided by the city hall for ACAR's office were all in the repertoire. In the municipality of Poté, ACAR inaugurated its local office in 1955. Extensionist Odelson Gomes da Silva, better known as Deca, reported: 'for the position of ACAR's office assistant there was a competitive local civil servant exam, and he [Deca] was the only one who passed. As the political opponent of Mayor Omar Afonso, he told him that if he took office, he would take the furniture from ACAR's office.'[17] He wrote that the Mayor, however, did not follow through with his threats. Another example relates to the small municipality of Paraguassú where a rather curious piece was published in a 1959 newspaper. The author was quick to dismiss hearsay about ACAR closing its office in the municipality: 'We can assure that the rumor is absolutely unfounded that ACAR will close its office in this municipality, due to the lack

---

15. José Alfredo Amaral de Paula, *Fatos históricos da ACAR, pesquisados pelo Eng. Agr. José Alfredo Amaral de Paula, Coordenador do Projeto Memória da Emater-MG* (Belo Horizonte: EMATER, [s.d]), (Unpublished paper), p. 26.

16. Projeto Memória, *Fatos pitorescos sobre a ACAR em Lagoa da Prata* [s.d] (unpublished paper).

17. Projeto Memória, *40 anos de extensão rural em Poté. Município: Poté, Minas Gerais* (unpublished paper). José Alberto Motta, ACAR technician, became Mayor of Poté in the following years.

of interest of our authorities and the people in their services'.[18] The situation was considerably tenser, though, in the municipality of Machado, in 1954, when Father Pedro Strabelli heard that the home economist Zélia Rodrigues, who worked in the community, was a Protestant of the Presbyterian Church. In a demonstration of power over this Catholic community, the priest made a complaint to ACAR, asking for her dismissal for not complying with the local religious precepts. According to agronomist Domingos Machado, Father Pedro recognized the good work of Zélia Rodrigues, but he did not admit her presence in the municipality because she was a Presbyterian. Hence, Strabelli asked ACAR to dismiss her and turned the Catholic population against her, creating an unsustainable work atmosphere. To resolve the problem, ACAR transferred Zélia in late March 1954.[19] Even though it avoided dismissing one of its most experienced employees, ACAR needed to respond to local preferences, since in this case it needed the support of the Catholic Church to carry out its activities.

Extensionist Aldo Borges, a colleague of Zélia Rodrigues, ran as a councillor for UDN in the same municipality of Machado, against ACAR's guidelines instructing its agents not to get involved with politics. The extensionist's candidacy caused a true social upheaval, since ACAR was involved in the historical political dispute between two traditional families of the region. According to a contemporary report, this situation became more serious because of the political fight between the UDN and PSD, which became a family fight, dividing the population of the city. On one side was the Mayor, Gustavo Carneiro Dias, brother of the secretary of the local office and head of the UDN. On the opposite side was PSD-sponsored Dr Felicitando Vieira, colleague and friend of the Governor and brother-in-law of the secretary of the local office.[20] The political conservatism of local groups seemed to underlie resistance against ACAR's extensionists. The agency's employees sought ways to survive in the midst of such political conservatism, avoiding political debate with locals. According to extensionist Geraldo Machado, the military police of nearby cities intervened in the conflict to prevent escalation: 'the political climate was unbearable and to maintain public order the Military Police Battalion based in Lavras was transferred to the municipality'. The situation reached such a point that the Regional Supervisor, based in Varginha, could no longer go to

18. *O Paraguassú*, Paraguassú, Minas Gerais, 2 Aug. 1959.

19. José Alfredo Amaral de Paula, *Fatos históricos da ACAR, pesquisados pelo Eng. Agr. José Alfredo Amaral de Paula, Coordenador do Projeto Memória da Emater-MG* (Belo Horizonte: EMATER, [s.d]) (Unpublished paper), p. 25.

20. Ibid., pp. 25–26

Machado.[21] Following the above events, the board dismissed Aldo Borges. But these episodes provoked a series of constraints in the agreement between AIA and the state government. A long discussion on the subject between the Director of the AIA, Walter Crawford, who came from the United States, and the State Governor solved the problem by keeping the office in operation with two new supervisors.[22]

Starting in the mid-1950s, the AIA clearly demonstrated its intention to let Brazilians manage affairs, but conversely perceived that the latter wished the Americans to continue directing the ACAR: 'the Brazilian members of the ACAR Junta refuse to admit to themselves that AIA is ever going to leave the ACAR job to them to do'.[23] The justification for Juscelino Kubitschek and like-minded others was that ACAR, led by the Americans, would stay away from political issues, which would provide an atmosphere of neutrality. In Henry Bagley's perception, 'Juscelino Kubitschek and other Minas leaders have always insisted that the way to keep ACAR strong, and make it stronger, is to leave the actual direction in the hands of AIA which will run ACAR as a technical program, divorced from politics'.[24] However, a group of Brazilians increasingly wanted to take charge. Crawford's replacement, Santiago Apodaca, had a tense relationship with the Brazilian extensionist agent Geraldo Machado due to divergent conceptions of how ACAR should move forward. Due to their conflict, the agency reorganised activities: Apodaca went to ABCAR in 1956 as head of the Technical Department, remaining a member of the Board of Directors, but not in the position of Executive Director, which Crawford from then on occupied. Machado remained as Associate Director of ACAR, but with Crawford and Bagley as direct superiors to whom he had to report before taking any decision.[25] In Walter Crawford's opinion, Machado had proven deficient in executive skills and in the human relations aspects of the job, exemplifying an isolationist tendency among top ACAR technicians with respect to ABCAR, other state programmes and foreign technical guidance.[26]

21. Ibid.

22. Ibid.

23. From Walter Crawford to Louise A. Boyer. Confidential. Brazil Program. 8 Aug. 1958. Collection: Family, Record Group: III 4B, Box: 29, Folder 283.

24. Excerpts from letter of 20 Oct. 1955 from Harry W. Bagley, AIA representative in Brazil. Collection: Family, Record Group: III 4B, Box 01, Folder 07 AIA – Brazil.

25. From Walter Crawford to Louise A. Boyer. Confidential. Brazil Program. 8 Aug. 1958. Collection: Family, Record Group: III 4B, Box: 29, Folder 283, p. 3.

26. Ibid.

In addition to the controversies faced by AIA members in ACAR, issues such as dwindling resources and competition began to challenge the modernising momentum of the Association. This theme will permeate the next chapters.

PART III. LOW-BUDGET IMPERIALISM

CHAPTER 8.

GLOBAL TRIAL IN THE EAST: THE AIA IN THE POINT FOUR ERA

Fourth, we must embark on a bold new program for making the benefits of our scientific advances and industrial progress available for the improvement and growth of underdeveloped areas…

(Harry Truman, Fourth Point of his inauguration address, 20 January 1949)

On the Sunday following Thanksgiving 1948, Christine Hardy Little told husband Benjamin Hardy: 'It's time that we do something to stop the Russians'.[1] Since 1946, the couple had observed the growing influence of Communism. They had encountered and witnessed a 'communist-inspired' strike in the port of Santos, São Paulo state, while returning to the United States. Refusing a job at the US Embassy in Brazil, after working with Frank Jamieson's team, Benjamin Hardy explained to Christine that there were ways to prevent the communists from capturing people's thinking.[2] According to her, Ben Hardy said that he had seen enough in Brazil to convince him that 'the underdeveloped countries could be helped tremendously with agricultural, medical, educational facilities to teach them how to do for themselves what needed to be done'.[3] Later that Sunday, Ben Hardy finally told Christine: 'I've already done it. On Wednesday before Thanksgiving, I sent a memorandum to Francis Russell outlining a foreign aid program.'[4]

During that time, after deciding to found the AIA with his former office mates, Nelson Rockefeller was increasingly sidelined from Harry Truman's government. This became blatant when Truman fired Secretary of State Henry A. Wallace from his role on 20 September 1946. However, as the 1940s ended, a rapprochement occurred between Rockefeller and Truman. During wartime, Frank Jamieson had Benjamin Hardy on his OIAA propaganda team. After the

1. Oral history interview with Christine Hardy Little. Arlington, Virginia (United States), 23 Feb. Available at http://www.trumanlibrary.org/oralhist/littlech.htm, p. 11. Accessed 19 May 2009.
2. Ibid.
3. Ibid. pp. 9 and 11.
4. Ibid.

war, his links to former members of the Office brought him closer to Nelson Rockefeller, and conversations between the two sometimes entertained the prospect of creating an international philanthropic agency.[5] In November 1948, Harry Truman's assistant Clark Clifford, worked on the President's inaugural speech and circulated a memo requesting ideas for a 'democratic manifesto addressed to the peoples of the world, not just to the American people'.[6] Hardy sent a memo to Francis Russell, public relations director, arguing that the President should put in place a great programme to 'capture the imagination of people from other countries', making economic resources and technical assistance available to developing countries. Hardy would not fail to quote in his memo one of Nelson Rockefeller's favourite points: 'Democratic campaign to contain Communism and create a decent life for the peoples of the planet'.[7] According to Cary Reich, Hardy was influenced by Nelson Rockefeller's work, re-signifying the idea of a philanthropic agency as a means to realise a broader programme: 'What Hardy was proposing was, in essence, a reworking of the AIA idea along the more sweeping lines that Rockefeller suggested – with the U.S. government footing the bill', believes Reich. Hardy's memo 'was not scripted by Rockefeller, but it might as well have been, so pervasive was his influence throughout'.[8]

At that time, Undersecretary Robert Lovett replaced the hospitalised Secretary of State General Marshall. Lovett received the memo from Russell and replied to it curtly, stating that the idea would not be appropriate for an inaugural speech. Hardy, however, insisted to George Elsey, another Truman assistant also working on such a speech, handing him a copy of the memo. Later, Clifford and Elsey discussed Hardy's ideas in surprise: 'while we had a speech in search of an idea, Hardy had an idea in search of a speech'.[9] Even with Lovett's continued objections, Clifford and Elsey acted on Hardy's memo, writing a four-point speech, and the proposal for technical cooperation and financial aid would be the fourth topic – the Point Four. 'Hardy's Idea' then won supporters such as Dean Acheson, who would replace Marshall as Secre-

5. Reich, *The Life of Nelson A. Rockefeller*, p. 428.

6. Ibid.

7. Clark Clifford with Richard Holbrooke, *Counsel to the President*. A Memoir (New York: Random House, 1991), p. 249. Reich, *The Life of Nelson A. Rockefeller*, p. 428

8. Reich, *The Life of Nelson A. Rockefeller*, p. 428.

9. Ibid., p. 429; and Clifford with Holbrooke, *Counsel to the President*, p. 250.

tary of State. Most importantly, the idea seemed convincing to Harry Truman himself, who maintained the fourth point in his inaugural address in 1949.[10]

One of the Point Four's most interesting proposals, according to Merle Curti and Kendall Birr's classic book, resembled Nelson Rockefeller's missionary aims years earlier in the Bolivar Foundation days: 'helping people to help themselves'.[11] However, if Point Four grew out of Hardy's memorandum – which, according to Cary Reich, was influenced by Nelson Rockefeller – the AIA's president now saw the technical assistance programme as a way to regain closeness to the government.

Engaging AIA into World History: Drafting Programmatic Content for Underdeveloped Countries

At the end of World War II, as mentioned in chapter 2, Truman fired Rockefeller. By the end of the decade, however, a certain peaceful diplomacy reigned between the President and Rocky, especially with the creation of Point Four. After Truman's speech of 20 January 1949, AIA staff saw the opportunity to participate in international programmes. The Board of AIA at its meeting on 4 March 1949 requested Robert Hudgens and Stacy May to investigate and report to the Board on the potential for carrying out work on Point Four of President Truman's Program and securing the necessary funding. These initial actions led the AIA to seek new projects beyond Brazil and Venezuela; this began the AIA's attempts at global insertion and shows how the agency sought to involve itself internationally in promoting agricultural modernisation, colonisation and cooperatives. On the other hand, due to limited resources, the inefficiency of Point Four – especially in the Eisenhower administration – and competition with other agencies, the AIA model did not achieve its goals satisfactorily.

Although some enthusiasts considered Nelson Rockefeller to be the real influencer in the creation of Point Four, mainly because of his work with AIA and IBEC, the billionaire joined the programme as a distinguished guest. On 30 September 1949, a small note written by an AIA secretary named Rosemary, attached material 'prepared for NAR's testimony on Point Four'. In almost incomprehensible handwriting, the note also indicated that Nelson should talk about many successful AIA and IBEC programmes such as the hoof and mouth

10. Reich, *The Life of Nelson A. Rockefeller*, pp. 429–430.

11. Merle Curti and Kendall Birr, *Prelude to Point Four. American Technical Missions Overseas (1838–1938)* (Madison, Wisconsin: The University of Wisconsin Press, 1954), p. 7.

disease project, the scientific importance of spraying and seed improvement programmes. Moreover, the handwritten note suggested explaining more about SAPS, Santa Rita 'through [agronomist Miguel] Bechara and other state leaders [which] affect trends in the whole state', a laboratory and training center for the Minas Gerais programme and 'outlet for humanitarian impact of IBEC'. With this in mind, a speech was prepared for interlocutors eager to hear about the budget and statistics, wherein Nelson Rockefeller could reinforce his theories that associations like the AIA would have a low relative cost compared to state programmes and at the same time have a great impact on local society. The programmes developed by staff living in Venezuela until 1949 – Turrialba Training Program in Costa Rica, Nutrition Information Program, Community Services Program and Investigative Program – cost $2,522,587, while the Home Demonstration and Community Services programs cost a total of $573,000. In sum, adding the operating costs of the New York office, AIA invested a total of $3,095,587 in its programmes. This notion of spending a little to change the lives of thousands would provide an effective argument to consolidate the AIA and the IBEC models for international policies connected to Point Four.[12]

Approved by the US Congress in June 1950, Harry Truman signed the Act for International Development, translating into government action the ideas contained in his inaugural address. That year, finally, Truman appointed Nelson Rockefeller as Chairman of the Advisory Board for International Development, the agency responsible for implementing the Point Four Program. In 1950, Robert Hudgens addressed a letter to the US Department of State concerning proposed Point Four projects and to the Economic Cooperation Administration (ECA) concerning an Italian Emigration study – entitled 'Emigration Study and Point Four Proposals'. Regarding the Point Four topic, they proposed cooperative projects as an agreement with expenses to be covered by the AIA; ECA, for its part, would provide recruitment, transportation and home leave expenses to support projects to stimulate Italian emigration to Latin America or Middle East to cooperate in rural development activities. Years earlier, in 1947, Ken Kadow had been enthusiastic about attracting qualified immigrants to Venezuela. In his opinion, 'the particular difficulty in Venezuela would be to obtain the necessary Venezuelan technical personnel'. He felt, according to minutes of an informal meeting with Nelson Rockefeller, 'that there and in any country, the secret of success would be to hook in, one way or the other, with colonization'. In this way, Kadow considered it would be possible 'to obtain

12. NAR's testimony on Point Four. Collection Family, Record Group IIIB, Box 1, Folder AIA General, 1946-1958, n. 2.

cheap foreign talent that is looking for a personal opportunity', mentioning that the Dutch government had offered Dee Jackson the services of 35,000 tropical farming experts from Indonesia. Finally, 'the Danish government had made an offer also'.[13] Returning to 1950, J.W. Hisle did not encourage Hudgens to go ahead: in 1948, the Board of Directors took the position that AIA would not deliver personnel to foreign countries for jointly undertaken projects at the expense of the Association.[14] With these decisions having been made by the Board of Directors, settlement initiatives would be increasingly outwith the AIA's focus.

Even if the Board of Directors did not consolidate the colonisation projects, the importance of Nelson Rockefeller to the new diplomatic programme advanced, at least with regard to the recognition of the AIA in the international context. At Truman's suggestion, Rockefeller, in accepting the appointment to the Advisory Board, did not give up his position in the AIA because Truman felt that in many ways its work covered important areas for implementing the Point Four concept: 'It is the feeling of Mr. Rockefeller and his associates that his work in this organization and his advisory board services to the government are complementary'.[15] Very optimistically, Robert Hudgens indicated that the AIA's work could yield many good results in the near future: 'We recognize that the programs in Venezuela and Brazil have not revolutionized the living habits of the people of those countries, but we feel that the process by which this will be accomplished is already apparent.' This view was based on 'the pattern that has been set and … the enthusiasm by which the respective governments and private contributors are supporting the continuation of AIA activities'.[16]

In the early 1950s, Robert Hudgens took over from Ken Kadow as the AIA's chief ideologue. Hudgens demonstrated a magnificent awareness of the early Cold War context, noting the role of private agencies and ultimately US diplomacy in building a new world order. Kadow's yeoman model had been giving way to Hudgens' globalised farmer model, advancing what these US technicians considered obstacles to modernisation: language, customs and race. 'It is our purpose to demonstrate a plan by which private philanthropy and

13. Minutes of Informal Meeting in Nelson A. Rockefeller's Office. Tuesday, 17 Dec. at 11:00 A.A. New York, 3 Jan. 1947. Collection Family, Record Group III 4B, Box 1, Folder AIA-Bolivar Foundation.

14. From J.W. Hisle to Robert Hudgens. 'Emigration Study and Point Four Proposals'. New York, 18 Oct. 1950. Collection AIA (closed section), Box 2.

15. From Robert Hudgens to Chester C. Davis. New York, 12 Jan. 1951.

16. Ibid.

private business can perform dynamic and coordinated functions in this field', stated Hudgens in 1951, 'undertaking demonstrations and exploring activities that government agencies are not equipped to undertake'.[17] Hudgens' awareness of making history in this new post-1945 world is stated concisely in his own words: 'In this period of world history' it was, he believed, 'more important than ever before that private enterprise should demonstrate its ingenuity, its willingness, and its ability to furnish leadership and effective administration adequate to the demands of our responsibility'.[18] Therefore, even if post-1945 modernisers like Hudgens adjusted their agendas and models of performance, the sense of mission remained almost intact.

In its communication with Chester Charles Davis (1887–1975), former Secretary of Agriculture and then Associate Director at the Ford Foundation (1951–1953), the AIA displayed a singular approach to international development. Hudgens noted that the AIA had competition in the struggle to rebuild what he called underdeveloped countries:

> In its broad objectives of trying to develop improved patterns of international relations between developed and underdeveloped countries, AIA is, of course, similar to many other agencies, both public and private. Its methods of operation, however, are unique among privately financed, non-profit organizations, and have many features that have not yet been undertaken by governmental or United Nations agencies. In this period of growing interest in the under-developed areas of the world, the methods and experiences of AIA's action programs in Venezuela and Brazil constitute important demonstrations that can be expanded and repeated in other areas by other agencies.[19]

In a seminal insight, Hudgens concluded his reasoning by seeking to demonstrate that the AIA had a different approach from other public development and modernisation programmes: 'AIA is convinced that it has arrived at a pattern which is repeatable in Latin American countries, and can be adapted to other under-developed areas of the world.'[20] After five years of experience, its ideologues were convinced that the march of science and technology could overcome the obstacles of language, race and customs, not only in Latin America, but throughout the underdeveloped world. Hudgens pointed out two ways to put these ideas into practice: the first suggestion was for the United Fruit Company to explore financing a region-wide rural development programme

17. Ibid.

18. Ibid.

19. Ibid.

20. Ibid.

in the six Central American republics. Secondly, the AIA should discuss the 'possibility of initiating and managing a programme of rural development with Point Four funds in the São Francisco Valley of Brazil'.[21]

Neither idea ever got off the drawing board. However, AIA operations in Brazil and Venezuela were 'coming to be viewed as laboratory tests by the technical assistance agencies of this government and of the United Nations', Robert Hudgens stated enthusiastically in May 1950. In his letter to Nelson Rockefeller, the AIA director affirmed that the United Nations could duplicate some of the Latin American projects in other countries. Hudgens thus pushed to Rockefeller the 'real need' for 'extending our present pilot-plant operations into several other Latin American countries for further testing and modification in Latin America' and, in addition, the need to test out and adapt 'to the problems of other underdeveloped areas of the world, such as, Southeast Asia, Africa and the Near East'.[22] In the same letter, after trying to convince Rockefeller to spread the AIA's programmes to the Global South, Hudgens analysed the weakness that similar programmes faced: 'the absence of a backlog of technicians who are both trained in their specialty and conditioned to the requirements of the areas in which they operate'. In his analysis, technicians from the United States, Canada and Western Europe had problems with fluency in the necessary foreign languages. Moreover, they had a 'lack of knowledge of the history, customs, social institutions, politics and geography of the countries to which they are assigned'. Finally, technicians had a 'lack of appreciation of the relationship between the application of their technical knowledge and the spread of democratic ideas'.[23]

Hudgens believed that AIA would be on another level, demonstrating the effectiveness of the Association in this newly opened field: 'During its four and one-half years of experience AIA has developed an efficient administrative package of technical assistance to agriculture which can be quickly duplicated in other underdeveloped areas of the world'. As examples, he mentioned a programme of agricultural credit and extension education, an agricultural research programme, and 'a program for training agricultural technicians of the cooperating country in methods of effectively working with farm people'.[24]

21. Ibid.

22. From Robert Hudgens to Nelson Rockefeller. Proposed Expansion of AIA Activities. New York, 14 May 1951. Collection AIA, Box 2, Folder 14.

23. Ibid.

24. Five Year Program Proposal for Brazil, Peru, and One Country in the Middle East. Collection Family, Record Group III 4B, Box 1, Folder 7 AIA – Brazil.

Other AIA directors and technicians shared Hudgens' analysis, especially Walter Lion Crawford. These modernisers sought to convince politicians to turn these ideas into practice: 'The Southern Presbyterian Church has indicated its desire to initiate a small-scale program of technical assistance in agricultural and home improvement in connection with several of its rural mission groups in Brazil'. Crawford continued: 'It has asked what, if any, assistance AIA might be in a position to render to such a program. Similar requests may be received from other religious and private groups.'[25] Finally, during 1949 and 1950, Mr and Mrs James Monahan of Readers' Digest visited Brazil and Venezuela – 'confidentially' – to research a book concerning IBEC and AIA as it related to Point Four.[26]

With the creation of Point Four, the AIA found a favourable international political context. It first indicated its intentions to reach countries outside Latin America in 1946, when the Association started a project with China: in the fall of 1946, the AIA agreed to grant $100,000 to the American-Chinese Committee of the Mass Education Movement, Inc. It aimed to support its proposal to produce, adapt and distribute audio-visual materials such as motion pictures, filmstrips, still pictures and posters as part of its mass education movement in China. The AIA conditioned the grant upon a contribution for the same purpose of $90,000 by United China Relief, best known as United Service to China – which was a cooperative association of development agencies active in China during the Second World War and the immediate post-war era. In addition, the American motion picture industry provided 200 million Chinese dollars from their blocked accounts in China. However, before the motion picture industry could make its contribution available, the value of the Chinese dollar depreciated to such an extent as to make the programme impossible to accomplish. So, 'meetings were held with Dr Y.C. James Yen as a result of which Dr Yen was informed that, as and when the programme as originally contemplated became practical, he could call again upon the AIA for its assistance'[27].

Further complicating matters was the outbreak of the Chinese Revolution in 1949, which put a stop to any kind of educational programmes run

25. From Walter L. Crawford to the Board of Directors of AIA. New York, 3 Dec. 1953. Collection AIA, Box 2, Folder 14.

26. From Nelson Rockefeller to T. Quartim Barbosa. Confidential. New York, 27 July 1949. Collection Family, Record Group III 4B, Box 1, Folder 6 AIA-Barbosa, T. Q.

27. American International Association for Economic and Social Development. Annual Report, 1947. Collection AIA, Record Group IV 3B, Box 1, Folder 2, p. 5.

by private American agencies. Foreign policy attention turned strongly toward Asia, with involvement in the Korean and Vietnam wars in the first half of the 1950s. Agencies like the AIA, therefore, gravitated around these international policy movements, trying to insert themselves into battlefields against the advance of communism in Asia. On 1 June 1951, Nelson Rockefeller heard some suggestions for a project on South Asia. In 1955, Rocky expected to raise up to $4 million to 'break the back of India's food production problem and constant famine', designating $2 million for a Well Drilling project. The AIA technicians realised that there were extensive subsoil water reserves in India 'which are not being tapped for agricultural purposes today because of the lack of equipment and foreign exchange'. The programme aimed to involve careful geological work, strategically located wells for agricultural irrigation and the development of local cooperation for the use of the water, subsequently visualising general agricultural development. Then, a special service organisation would set up in cooperation with the Indian government, private Indian business groups and the AIA: the Indian government would contribute money and services, selling the wells and pumps on credit to local group. With the rupees thus realised, the Ford Foundation would cover local expenses in dollars. In sum, the technicians expected it might be favourable to get various United States communities to 'adopt' an Indian village community cooperative development around one of the wells'.[28]

As noted above, the AIA developed plans connecting with the Ford Foundation's interest in community development plans. Robert Hudgens held a meeting with Ford representatives Chester Davis, Mrs Davis and Howard Tolley. According to the AIA moderniser, the Ford Foundation wanted to know about specific types of programmes; and he took India as an example, explaining the three major programmes of well drilling, land clearing and overhead irrigation, experimentation and demonstration. Hudgens outlined how, with an intensive programme in these three areas and experimental work in insecticides, fungicides and weed killers along with fertilisers, the Ford Foundation could break the back of the famine in India. In the end, 'they liked this idea very much and wanted then to know how they could go about it'.[29]

The AIA also contemplated expanding its activities in the early 1950s and focused for a short moment on Central America, trying to approach United

28. Memo of Conversations. Ford Foundation on Wednesday evening, 16 May. New York, 21 May 1951. Collection Family, Record Group III 4B, Box 3, Folder 23 – AIA Ford Foundation.

29. Ibid.

Fruit, the World Bank and the Rockefeller Foundation for agricultural credit.[30] However, the AIA's interests focused on the new direction of US foreign policy in Asia and the Middle East, while consolidating programmes in Brazil and Venezuela. In Pakistan, the programme was intended 'not to antagonize them through a feeling that India is being favored and Pakistan neglected'. In Burma and Indonesia, the AIA aimed to increase food production for export to depressed areas in Asia: 'Political and psychological impact of major importance – confidence in and friendship for West', were highlighted in the report of an AIA and Ford Foundation meeting. Robert Hudgens demonstrated his preferences for expanding the AIA's work toward Asia, in conjunction with the Ford Foundation – and its funding: 'the most important places to work at the present time were India, the Near East and Indonesia' and 'our group would be very interested in working in those areas'. Finally, Hudgens stated: 'but … frankly we didn't have the funds to go outside the present countries in which we were now operating'.[31]

A substantial change occurred, however, in subsequent years. On 17 February 1953, Nelson Rockefeller wrote a sort of letter of recommendation of the services offered by Hudgens' new venture. The copy of this letter addressed to Arthur T. Proudfit of Creole Petroleum Corporation, Richard C. McCurdy of Shell Caribbean Petroleum Company and Hoyt Sherman of Mene Grande Oil Company, explained, 'Mr Hudgens and several other members of the New York staff of AIA left that organization to form a new agency know as International Development Services, Inc'. According to Rockefeller,

> They propose to make the services of this agency available under contract to groups and organizations here in the United States for operations abroad. They thus hope to expand their field of service and to spread their overhead. All of us here are most interested in this new undertaking of Pete Hudgens and his associates. They should be able to render a very valuable service based on their knowledge and experience. The AIA has entered into an experimental contract with the new organization for managerial services related to the CBR program among others for the current year.[32]

30. From Nelson Rockefeller [to John E. Lookwood]. Plan for review of AIA. New York, 10 Oct. 1950. Collection Family, Record Group III 4B, Box 1, Folder AIA – General.

31. Memo of Conversations. Ford Foundation on Wednesday evening, 16 May. New York, 21 May 1951. Collection Family, Record Group III 4B, Box 3, Folder 23 – AIA Ford Foundation.

32. From Nelson Rockefeller to Arthur T. Proudfit. New York, 2 Mar. 1953. Collection AIA, Box 2, Folder 14.

Wallace K. Harrison became AIA president in 1953, while Walter Crawford became Acting Director. The AIA, Ford Foundation and India joint programme continued through the early 1950s; in 1954, President of Washington State Trade Fair, Griffith Way, spent three months touring the Far East, inspecting the AIA-Cooperative League work in India. According to him, Rockefeller Foundation representative Thomas Keehn's work with the Indian Cooperative Union 'seemed to me to go to the very heart of some of the problems which are so difficult for the Indian to solve at this time'. Finally, Way enthusiastically stated:

> I was so impressed by your activities and by those of your representative that I wanted you to know how pleased I was to find such a program being conducted through private means. There can be little question that the private programs of your Association and of the Ford Foundation in its work on small cottage industries are substantially improving conditions in India.[33]

Walter Crawford arrived in India for conferences with Government officials and with the leaders of the Cooperative Movement on 25 January 1955.[34] Again, the strategy sought to bring private groups from the United States closer to Indian communities. The AIA discussed two additional plans: one for the development of social welfare projects between India and America; the other recommending a cultural exchange programme between the two countries. For the first time, however (at least in a document available to researchers) an AIA report mentioned the word 'communist'. It described – probably – Walter Crawford's comments on the Communist Party strategy in Kerala, a state located in the South of the country, concerning on education and land reform:

> In the field of higher education, the Communist Party is playing it straight at the moment. Mr. John Mathai, respected citizen, former Finance Minister of India, businessman and educator, has been made the first Vice Chancellor of the newly established Kerala University. He has been given a free hand, according to his own statement. His name obviously adds prestige not only to the University but to the Government and the Communist Party … The land reform measures, which are now being proposed, exclude the large estates – tea, rubber and coconut. In this respect, Communists have exactly reversed the order followed by the Chinese. In Kerala the land reform program is directed at the medium sized farmers and land owners. Naturally, the tenants and small farmers will be pleased and the large estate owners have been neutralized because for the time

33. American International Association. Highlights. New York, 27 Dec. 1954.

34. American International Association. Highlights. New York, 1 June 1955. Collection AIA, Box 2, Folder 14.

> being at least they have been excluded from the land reform program. Therefore, the medium sized landowners and farmers are nicely squeezed in the middle.[35]

The narrative aimed at uncovering the strategies of the Communist Party and the legitimacy that some of its characters possessed within the Kerala community. Communist movements in India began around the 1920s and, at a time of rising tension in Asia, the AIA observer sought possible cracks in the land reform actions. In this context, the AIA could more easily insert itself through cooperative programmes, as it attempted to do in states outside the control of the communists. Finally, in September 1955, the AIA and the Cooperative League of the US extended a year-to-year basis agreement, spending $ 403,000 in 1958. While the costs were borne by the League, the AIA provided technical assistance to the project. In 1957, the project worked on supervised credit, educating cooperative members and knowledge exchange through study abroad. Again, the Indian case showed that practically 'no loans have been defaulted' and small amounts of supervised credit reached 1,000 farmers that year, promoting 'an average increase of 20 per cent over non-borrowers' production, according to an AIA report. In addition, the group of modernising agencies explored seed and fertiliser experiments among the cooperative farmers.[36]

These few AIA-engineered projects outside Latin America that attempted to consolidate modernisation and development faced resistance in Asia. The nascent Cold War political context created both opportunities and obstacles for the actions of modernising groups such as the AIA. The Rockefeller philanthropic agency represented a vanguard performance in Latin America; leaving the continent, the AIA tried to gravitate around a more complex solar system, competing with hundreds of agencies emerging from Point Four – including International Development Services, Inc., founded by former AIA director Robert Hudgens. The AIA's efforts to broaden its territorial base, however, faced problems such as lack of funding and interest from politicians and similar foundations in the US itself. It is possible to argue that missionary, imperialistic or arrogance-based ideals – as demonstrated by Robert Hudgens' rhetoric – drove attempts to bring the West and East closer together amid growing tension between the US and Korea and Vietnam, and observation and containment of communism. Ultimately, they were also attempts to secure funding and power, to pay staff salaries and promote community development programmes. Finally, if one considers the AIA a representative agency of US imperialism, its

35. A Few Comments on Communist Party Strategy in Kerala. Collection Family, Box 1, Folder General AIA (include some India papers).

36. AIA Report, 1957.

experience in the East demonstrated the difficulty of practising imperialism without financial backing.

For different reasons, the IRI Research Institute finally achieved the dream of expansion to other Latin American countries and continents advocated by the AIA, in later decades with the financial support of the Alliance for Progress. I will discuss part of this history – when IRI merged into the AIA – in the next chapter.

CHAPTER 9.

SCIENCE HAS NO BORDERS: THE IRI RESEARCH INSTITUTE AND THE AIA

Between September and November 1953, Fritz W. Went, a Dutch researcher living in the United States, conducted an experiment at the California Institute of Technology. There, coffee seeds of the varieties Red Bourbon (*C. arabica L. var. red bourbon*), Semperflorens (*C. arabica L. var. semperflorens K.M.C.*), Caturra (*C. arabica L. var. caturra K.M.C.*), and Mundo Novo (*C. arabica cv. 'Mundo Novo'*) germinated in a greenhouse maintained at an average temperature of 30 degrees Celsius during the day and 23 degrees during the night. In this experiment, the seeds from Brazil developed faster than expected and, in about eight months, the most vigorous plants began to form their first lateral shoots. Placed under a considerable number of experimental conditions, with variations in temperature during the day/night and in lighting, all plants received at least eight hours of natural light. At night, Went placed most plants in darkness at different temperature levels, but in four treatments they received an additional eight hours of artificial light. As a result, they grew under a sixteen-hour photoperiod. In two other treatments, the plants received natural light for twelve or thirteen hours, but, in the last four to five hours, were given light combined with night temperature, i.e. close to 23 degrees. According to the researcher, the growth of all the plants was satisfactory.[1] As mentioned earlier, the research, funded by the IRI Research Institute and conducted by Went over fifteen years, resulted in the publication of the influential book entitled *The Experimental Control of Plant Growth* (1957).[2]

Although the diffusion and exchange of experiments did not exactly represent a novelty in terms of coffee production, a traditional type of cultivation predominated in Brazil despite initiatives by governmental actors, institutions, researchers and producers to increase production. Nevertheless,

1. F. W. Went. IRI Coffee studies at California Institute of Technology. Part I. Report on coffee Research in Earhart carried out for Ibec Research Institute. Oct. 1954. Rockefeller Archive Center. Collection IRI, Record Group 3.1, Box 476, Folder 2898.

2. F.W. Went, *The Experimental Control of Plant Growth. With Special Reference to the Earhart Plant Research Laboratory at the California Institute of Technology*. With contributions by W.C. Ashby (New York: Ronald Press Co., 1957).

during the Cold War, efforts intensified between private institutions and governments to develop experiments and knowledge on the technical repertoire. In 1950, Nelson Rockefeller established the IBEC Research Institute 'to carry out agricultural research in various parts of the world, but principally in the tropics and subtropics'. Originally created as an IBEC research arm, the IRI had financial support from Nelson Rockefeller, the Rockefeller Brothers Fund and individual members of the Rockefeller family, such as David Rockefeller, as well as several industrial groups. In terms of the local projects, the IRI received technical assistance support, use of equipment and facilities from the IAC, Cambuhy S.A. and Ubatuba S.A., and others in Brazil contributed the use of land, labour and facilities for the field phases of the work. According to an IRI report, its programmes concentrated on crops and agricultural problems, nationalising a rice programme in Venezuela in 1954 and then concentrating its activities in Brazil, chiefly in coffee and pasture improvement.[3] The AIA incorporated the IRI between 1957 and 1963 for organisational reasons. Beyond its experimental research, both the IBEC and the AIA had financial and philanthropic interests in it, respectively.

The history of the IRI involves an important paradox: once the advance of the agricultural frontier towards the west of the state of São Paulo and the north of Paraná promoted the clearing of new strips of forest, the promotion of intensive cultivation became one of the main objectives of Brazilian and foreign researchers. Through the recuperation of infertile soils, the mechanisation of harvesting, the intensive study of micronutrients and selection of the most suitable plants for the environment, consistent and influential experimentation with coffee growing techniques in Brazil took place. Over the course of a decade of research, the researchers and farmers involved proved that producing coffee through deforestation continued to be more profitable. In summary, throughout the 1950s and early 1960s, the application of rationalism to agricultural techniques did not overcome traditional cultivation, based on the devastation of forests.

Early Years: Attempts to Modernise the Brazilian Coffee Industry

The IRI based its technical beliefs on the adapting models trialled in other regions of the globe, such as pineapple plantations in Hawaii and fruit cultivation

3. Jerome Harrington and Bill Sorenson, *O desenvolvimento das terras de cerrado do Brasil: a experiência do IRI* (São Paulo: Agronômica Ceres/Instituto de Pesquisas IRI, 2004), p. 5.

in California; it even reviewed the English colonial experience in East Africa and that of the Dutch in Indonesia.[4] After transferring the rice project to the Venezuelan government, the IRI conducted its Coffee Tillage programmes with support from a state public institution, the Agronomic Institute of Campinas, and from large private farms in the Matão region of São Paulo state. Many other projects gravitated around the Coffee Tillage programme, such as the adaptation of grasses for animal feed, the application of herbicides to combat weeds, and the planting of cotton, among others. On certain points, the research areas converged, since weed control was of interest for coffee cultivation and harvesting; and research on the lack of nutrients in coffee plantation soils could also serve as a reference for cotton cultivation.[5]

Figure 27. Exhausted coffee plantations in the state of São Paulo. Rockefeller Archive Center. Record Group 3.1, IRI Research Institute.

4. Alfredo Scheide Lopes and Luiz Roberto Guimarães Guilherme, 'Fertilidade do solo e produtividade agrícola', in Roberto Ferreira Novaes et al., *Fertilidade do solo* (Viçosa: Sociedade Brasileira de Ciência do Solo, 2007), pp. 25–26.

5. Harrington and Sorenson, *O desenvolvimento das terras de cerrado do Brasil*, p. 3.

Figure 28. Restored coffee plantations following the IRI fertilisation paradigm. Rockefeller Archive Center. Record Group 3.1, IRI Research Institute.

Between 1950 and 1963, its activities went through two distinct phases: first, recognition of a site's natural resources and, second, the conducting of field experiments. According to the US experts, inadequate practices in coffee farming limited soil fertility, mainly due to the non-adoption of techniques and technologies already known in other countries. Coffee cultivation, as a historical construct, resulted from anthropic choices, devastating the forests proportionally to the profits obtained. Environmental historian Warren Dean emphasises how coffee-growing elites expanded their plantations in Southeastern Brazil without taking into consideration agricultural knowledge developed in foreign lands. Dean also states that such groups sought to attract foreign capital to transform barren land into wealth and power, idealising the planting of coffee in virgin forests because it required little additional investment of capital and labour.[6] The techniques of slashing and burning the forest, intermittent planting without

6. Warren Dean, *A ferro e fogo. A história e a devastação da Mata Atlântica* (São Paulo: Companhia das Letras, 1997), pp. 183 and 194, respectively.

replacement of nutrients and cultivating plants of different origins and aligned in the most disastrous way possible,[7] created a model that entered the twentieth century without substantial changes. Even after the Second World War, the traditional system of coffee production in Brazil continued to follow the same steps as before: cutting down the forest, burning the wood and planting crops in the deforested areas. Coffee farmers exploited the natural fertility of the soil for twenty or thirty years; productivity then usually declined below the point of interest, leading the farmers to abandon these areas and release them for pasture and cattle ranching.[8]

In their 1951 (first) Brazilian report, IRI experts observed that the coffee farms were in a lamentable situation: erosion had taken over the plantations near the municipality of Matão:

> We have visited the regions of Santa Rita; of São José do Rio Pardo; of Jaú and the Paraíba Valley where prosperity built on endless stretches of successful coffee culture sparked the economic well-being of the nation. We saw the scarred landscape where the last vestiges of that culture attest the abuse suffered by the land. Trees were planted straight up and down on steep hillsides where the naked land eroded strongly with every successive rainy seasons. The yields of these trees depleted the resources of nutrients and organic matter with which a generous nature had bestowed them, in amounts ample to withstand abuse for nearly 100 years. The nutrients were not replaced: generally no fertilization was practiced. Mining of the soil was pushed to a point where only the dried and rotting stumps of the Grand Fazendas marked the dissolution of prosperity in the area. Now there are thousands of square miles from which the destructive culture of coffee has receded. Out of these same areas the populace is migrating in caravans of trucks, much as our own people were driven from the nation's 'dust bowl' by a generation of ill-advised farmers.[9]

The IRI expert concluded that farmers did not adequately replace soil nutrients.[10] With the soil challenged by the abuses inflicted on nature over a century, they proposed an efficient antidote: the complete technification of coffee production in the state of São Paulo. In the early 1950s, the IRI signed a technical cooperation agreement with the IAC, taking advantage of the laboratories and expertise of the Brazilian researchers. To structure the programme, IRI/

7. Ibid., p. 200.

8. Alfredo Scheide Lopes and Luiz Roberto Guimarães Guilherme, 'Fertilidade do solo e produtividade agrícola', in Roberto Ferreira Novaes et al., *Fertilidade do solo* (Viçosa: Sociedade Brasileira de Ciência do Solo, 2007), pp. 25–26.

9. IBEC Research Institute, *Progress Report: Brazil Operations,* 1 June 1951, p. 2.

10. Ibid., p. 3

IAC jointly created four departments: the coffee processing and horticulture departments, headed respectively by Paul Teeter and James Medcalf; the agricultural chemistry department and the plant chemistry laboratory, headed by Lawrence Quinn and Wreal Lott. The choice of the *Cambuhy* farm facilitated the experimentation process, as there were plots of various ages and on different types of soils, and readily available information regarding the yields of the various plots as well as data on fertilisers used, frost damage, production costs, prices attained and other variables.[11] The technical team developed another section of the research in Campinas with the help of the IAC. Meteorological information was studied, at the same time as Lott helped the IAC to set up the first laboratory for leaf analysis in Latin America. In this laboratory, scientists analysed coffee leaves for thirteen mineral elements essential for plant growth.[12] In sum, the economic interest involved in the industrial production of coffee sought to standardise the entire process, from the seed to the processed bean, by way of the variety to be used, the planting process, harvesting and storage, and all sort of procedures involved in the search for a flavour that would conquer international markets.[13]

In one section, an IRI report highlights the importance of coffee standards, virtually unknown in Brazil.

> Coffee is processed to modify it along certain desired lines. Coffee differing in composition when harvested must be processed to achieve a more homogeneous condition for marketing or for subsequent use. In designing new processing methods, it is essential to know the composition of incoming lots and measure, relative to the important constituents, the effects of variables imposed during experimental operations. Facilities do not currently exist to allow such studies. Coffee is consumed as a stimulant and because of flavor. Both of these characteristics are dependent on chemical composition. Many new varieties of coffee are being developed, many new cultural techniques are being tested. These factors alter composition -- having substantial effect on processing requirements and ultimate quality potentials. There are no facilities or competent staff in Brazil to deal with such absolutely fundamental problems.[14]

11. Lopes and Guilherme, 'Fertilidade do solo e produtividade agrícola', pp. 25–26.
12. Ibid.
13. Development of methods to improve and to exploit improved moisture relationships. Rockefeller Archive Center, Collection IRI, Record Group 3.1, Box 475, Folder 2894, p. C-3.
14. Ibid.

The starting gun for experiments came from New York, at a meeting of the IRI Board of Directors. Though the initial auspices of the institute revolved around the production of instant coffee, the board cancelled all investigations and investments in this direction on 15 January 1953. This strategy would allow the concentration of financial resources on other processing aspects not explored by other corporations, such as General Foods or Standard Brands. This new situation favoured the exchange of scientific knowledge to conduct a critical examination of the coffee production system, as technicians were able to travel abroad.[15] This examination pointed out that coffee processing methods had not been scientifically developed in this system.[16] According to a report presented to the IRI by one of its consultants in the state of São Paulo, a barely rational 'natural method' of grain processing predominated. The technicians' criticism emphasised that the whole cherry was dried before the skins and pulp were removed. The process they proposed instead would follow most of the stages used in other countries: removing the pulp first (depulping); then removing the peel; fermenting the seeds to break the mucilage layer; and then washing to remove processing residues. Drying would then follow, producing a superior coffee.[17] The consultants considered theirs a superior method because of a constant limiting factor in Brazilian coffee production: the labour shortage. This scarcity dictated the adoption of a specific harvesting method, known as stripping. In this method, the fruits remain on the coffee tree until only a small percentage is still green. The vast majority of the fruit passes through the ripening stage and is partially dry. A first harvest from each bush is then possible. Theoretically, the worker runs his closed hands along the coffee branches, from the inside to the outside of each branch, knocking the cherries onto tarps spread out at the foot of the coffee trees. The result of this harvesting method is a mixture of fruit, leaves, twigs and dust, separated only when the fruit is thrown into the air using a sieve.[18] The consultants pointed out that the harvesting practised in other parts of the world consisted of picking the fruit when ripe. In this way, each bush would need to be harvested several times during a season. The first

15. IRI Minutes of the Board of Trustees Meeting. 15 Jan. 1953. Rockefeller Archive Center, Collection IRI, Record Group 3.1, Box 475, Folder 2893.

16. Development of methods to improve and to exploit improved moisture relationships. Rockefeller Archive Center, Collection IRI, Record Group 3.1, Box 475, Folder 2894, p. C-3.

17. Ibid.

18. Ibid.

option, long established in Brazil, would have a much higher cost than the second because of greater number of labourers needed.[19]

Another determining factor in *derriça* (threshing) was the workers' education level, as well as the customs and traditions of the rural populations performing this task. Coffee farmers employed seasonal and untrained migrants. The consultants argued, moreover, that poor supervision by poorly educated people, combined with poor diet and lack of incentives, resulted in apathetic workers. Farm managers were unwilling to adopt new procedures, especially complicated ones. Experts noted that managers underestimated the potential of workers, as, in many cases, improved diets, good living conditions and job training could lead to increased productivity.[20] Additionally, the report suggested that Brazilian farmers and technicians should focus research on a specific bean, the *Mundo Novo*, already developed by IAC researchers in collaboration with local producers. Considered a gift from nature, this hybrid grain emerged from successive empirical experiments undertaken without defined criteria over decades. According to some, this lack of rational criteria in coffee production fortuitously resulted in a bean that presented the best results in terms of flavour and quality. According to an article published by the IAC team, agronomist Carlos Arnaldo Krug selected coffee cherries from several trees based on characteristics such as vegetative aspect, existing productivity and, finally, probable production in the following year.

The *Mundo Novo* coffee progenies, previously known generically as Sumatra and derived from plants selected in Urupês and Jaú municipalities, indicated that these beans were of the red Bourbon type and were probably recombinations of a primitive cross between Sumatra and Bourbon coffee.[21] The most productive progenies of *Mundo Novo* coffee were multiplied so that soon their seeds could be supplied to the farmers who had shown so much interest in this coffee.[22]

The research developed by the IAC in 1944 gained a boost with the arrival of the IRI. After the publication of the article by Krug and Carvalho, Fritz Went used the *Mundo Novo* variety in his experiments. While Went experimented, the creation of the Brazilian Coffee Institute in 1952 gave a new impulse to coffee production. The experiments carried out by the IAC,

19. Ibid.

20. Ibid.

21. A. Carvalho et al., 'Melhoramento do cafeeiro. IV - Café Mundo Novo', *Bragantia* 12 (4-6) (1952): 126–27.

22. Ibid.

agronomic research institutes and local farmers quickly spread *Mundo Novo* coffee among producers. The IRI gradually gave more attention to this bean, to the detriment of old varieties; in 1958, the institute concluded that its bean provided a better product.[23]

As historian Stuart McCook points out, 'In Brazil, technification programs were initially based on the Mundo Novo cultivar, a high-yielding tall arabica developed by the IAC', and breeders 'also developed a dwarf arabica cultivar that they named Caturra'. Both high-yielding coffee cultivars figured at the heart of the technified system – and then adapted to local conditions in other countries. While Caturra's short stature allowed denser planting and therefore improved yield and facilitated harvesting, it 'did not do well in Brazil, but it did prosper in the wetter environments along the Cordillera, where it became the basis for technified coffee production'. The IRI experiments related to coffee farming did not prosper; and McCook pointed out a second problem: 'Although these dwarf cultivars were highly productive, they were still based on pure arabicas, so they remained susceptible to the coffee rust' in the following decades.[24]

Fertilisers also came under study in the Coffee Tillage programme. During the mid-1950s, experiments based on NPK fertilisers revealed a good response to nitrogen, which encouraged the institute's experts. Initial calculations showed that, with the application of NPK, it would be possible to increase profit on average by $100 per arroba compared to traditional planting and harvesting. Researchers triangulated data from the use of mulching, cover crops or clean cultivation techniques. The first presented a higher yield than the others. During the first three years of research, the small experiments gradually reached a larger scale. Experts sought to cross-reference data: cultivation using mulching techniques, cover crops or clean cultivation carried out on clay, purple soil or soils with greater acidity. Foliage analysis of coffee trees and cotton plants sought to recognise the potential or deficiency of the thirteen micronutrients and their response to fertilisers.[25]

The preliminary results of an experiment about the nutritional status of coffee plantation in São Paulo and Paraná indicated zinc deficiencies. With this experiment, IRI advanced nutritional knowledge of the plants, revealing

23. IBEC Research Institute, *IRI-Brazil. Progress Report to Trustees,* Dec. 1958. Rockefeller Archive Center. Collection IRI, Record Group 3.1, Box 477, Folder 2904, p. 1.

24. Stuart McCook, *Coffee is Not Forever. A Global History of the Coffee Leaf Rust* (Athens, Ohio: Ohio University Press, 2019), p. 160.

25. IBEC Research Institute, *Report to the Trustees, 1956–1957*. Rockefeller Archive Center. Collection: IRI. Record Group: 3.1 Box: 477 Folder: 2903 Nov. 1950 to Dec. 1956 IBEC Research Institute Report Nov. 1950 to Dec. 1956, p. 6.

that the soils of several regions were deficient in several micronutrients.[26] Correcting certain natural aspects could thus mitigate nutritional deficiencies and increase productivity. Some of the experiments guided by the control plot contained a sample of the crop from the seeds, plants or techniques generally used in the local or regional area. From the initial plot, scientists conducted further experiments with each of the micronutrients, with each type of soil and with different fertilisers and other chemicals. In a region of soils with high manganese content, for example, its almost toxic level knocked the vigour out of the plants; not even the application of Chelate spray was able to correct plant growth. On the other hand, the introduction of nitrogen in coffee plantations generated a profit of around fifty per cent higher compared to other areas. In the experiment applying NPK fertilisers at various levels and combinations, the best response came from young plants (averaging five years old) on sandy and clay soil in the Matão region. By 1957, fertilised plots produced 321 per cent more than the control plot.[27]

However, as the 1950s ended, the techniques and technologies presented by IRI did not convince farmers to adopt them on a large scale. Nor did they convince the Rockefeller Brothers Fund to continue funding the Coffee Tillage programme. Nevertheless, during the experiments, it became increasingly clear that a technology based on NPK, lime and micronutrients could increase agricultural production on acidic soils, especially on the characteristic *Cerrado* savanna soils in the state of São Paulo. Even if such a formula did not bring enough significant results to encourage Brazilian farmers to abandon extensive deforestation in favour of intensive cultivation, the experiment influenced several others, both in Brazil and elsewhere. IRI experts from the US produced a panacea aimed at adapting cultivation, harvesting and processing practices in a global context, as we will see below.

The Panacea: NPK Fertilisers, Lime and Micronutrients for Acid Soils

Fritz Went's research on Brazilian coffee varieties, conducted at the request of the IRI, is only a first example of exchanges in agricultural research during the post-war period. The IRI facilitated the adoption of technical procedures known in other countries, or chose to create others. As an example, another consultant from the University of California, Sherman Leonard, in his consultancy for IRI, systematised the evaluation systems developed from Went's experience. The

26. Ibid.

27. Ibid.

systems sought to adjust coffee research by standardising processing methods. He proposed that farmers adopt rational methods instead of the natural ones known on the farms in the West of São Paulo: he advised variable-by-variable experimentation during the development of horticultural practices to improve the coffee's flavour. This was what the experts expected based on researchers' experience with fruit in California. Years earlier, researchers had measured the influence of insecticide use, soil fumigants, field techniques, size, maturity and processing methods on flavour. The research showed that the influence of insecticides and fumigants resulted in a very different flavour from products then on the market. Sherman Leonard suggested that coffee harvesting and processing practices should follow the pattern set by canned olives and pears, using these techniques to improve flavour through the application of chemical processes.[28] The 1954 data indicated a significant improvement in average drying through preliminary separation of harvested grain by variety and by size. Subsequently, it was necessary to increase the average dehydration temperature.[29] One of the solutions attempted was the introduction of mechanical harvesting and separation, still only incipient in Brazil at that time.

Brown University's coffee processing specialist, H. Elliott Foote, based on 1954 harvest data, carried out another technique suggested by the IRI consultants, still related to the bean drying experiments. Foote had worked for seven years with Standard Brands Corporation. IRI then invited him for a month-long visit to watch and mentor Paul Teeter's work on coffee growing and processing methods. He achieved significant water loss – up to 100 times faster – by drying the beans in ripe cherry form. Based on the improvement of the *terreiro* method,[30] Foote also suggested application of heat from sources other than the sun, the improvement of coffee handling methods and a comparative study of drying costs between the terrace method and mechanical methods.[31]

28. From Sherman Leonard to Jerome Harrington. São Paulo, 2 de maio de 1955. Rockefeller Archive Center, Collection IRI, Record Group 3.1, Box 476, Folder 2899.

29. Paul Teeter and Paul Leonard, *Coffee processing research for 1955*. IBEC Research Institute: Matão, May 1955, p. 2. Rockefeller Archive Center. Collection IRI, Record Group 3.1, Box 476, Folder 2900.

30. Reni Saath, Microscopia eletrônica de varredura do endosperma do café (*Coffea arabica L.)* durante o processo de secagem (Lavras: Universidade Federal de Lavras, 2007. Dissertação de Mestrado em Engenharia de Agrícola), p. 12. (M.A. Dissertation in Agricultural Engineering)

31. H. Elliott Foote. A study of the drying of coffee on the terreiro. São Paulo: IRI, setembro de 1954. Rockefeller Archive Center, Collection IRI, Record Group 3.1, Box 476,

Ultimately, though, the huge expense of the six-year experiment without satisfactory progress towards addressing Rockefeller's concerns about combatting world hunger led the Rockefeller Brothers Fund to reduce funding and its interest in the IRI. They wanted more concrete results.

Coincidentally or not, research following the completion of the IRI project in the early 1960s linked the decline in coffee production with increasing soil acidification. This is a complex technical process involving the replacement of the basic cations (Ca, Mg and K) with aluminum, causing aluminum toxicity and nutritional disturbances.[32] The previously discussed coffee experiments revealed the nutritional problems hindering the increase in production. Around 1955, with the arrival of American agronomist Andrew Colin McClung (1923–2015), coffee experiments gradually redirected their focus to soil acidity problems. In 1959, IRI technicians published in the journal *Bragantia* a first paper on the use of *Cerrado* areas for large-scale agriculture.[33] This paper, based largely on the survey and analysis of soil acidification data, indicated that the findings from experiments initiated in the Coffee Tillage programme were applicable to other regions with agricultural potential.

Direct and indirect results of this report were felt most in the 1960s, as we will see in Chapter 11. For the moment, the main observation is how a national extension service programme was taking shape and had profound impacts on the consolidation of a large-scale agricultural model.

Folder 2897.

32. Harrington and Sorenson, *O desenvolvimento das terras de cerrado do Brasil*, p. 8.

33. Luis Martins de Freitas, Andrew Colin McClung and Wreal Lott, *Field Studies on Fertility Problems of Two Campos Cerrados, 1958–1959* (New York: Ibec Research Institute, 1960).

CHAPTER 10.

A NATIONAL ACAR: THE ASSOCIAÇÃO BRASILEIRA DE CRÉDITO E ASSISTÊNCIA RURAL

What about creating a national ACAR, with these big funds that I now have available?
(Attributed to Juscelino Kubitschek, Brazilian President)

[We] never had so much cooperation from the Brazilian side
(Attributed to Ralph Hansen, US co-director of ETA)

Getúlio Vargas' second government aimed at an expansion project for ACAR. However, it would not be until Juscelino Kubitschek's election as president that negotiations for consolidation of a national system of extension service more directly connected to the Brazilian state would become effective. On 21 June 1956, Kubitschek signed ABCAR's creation act designed to coordinate the Brazilian Extension Service System; it fostered the maintenance of extensionist principles and encouraged the emergence of other associations.[1] The AIA enjoyed advantages in participating in ABCAR; on 26 September 1955, Walter Crawford and Henry Bagley sent Louise Boyer and Frank Jamieson a pitch for what they proudly named 'Brazilian ACAR'.[2] If, for the Americans, ABCAR meant the expansion and consolidation of the project started in Minas Gerais in 1948, for Juscelino Kubitschek it signified a concrete step in his plan to rationalise Brazilian agriculture.[3] The President argued that many farmers were opposed to the introduction of rational methods of cultivation.[4] Furthermore, he considered that the improvement of agricultural processes would be predicated on an adequate education for rural populations and the improvement of the technical knowledge of farmers and supervisors. State intervention would mean persuasion, convincing and material demonstration.[5] Clearly, when the

1. Ribeiro, *A Saga da Extensão Rural em Minas Gerais*, p. 107.
2. Excerpts from letter of 20 Oct. 1955 from Harry W. Bagley, AIA representative in Brazil. Collection: Family, Record Group: III 4B, Box 01, Folder 07 AIA – Brazil. p. 2.
3. Juscelino Kubitschek de Oliveira, 'Mensagem ao Congresso Nacional', Rio de Janeiro, 1956, p. 293–94.
4. Ibid.
5. Ibid.

federal government nationalised the programme, the *Mineira* experience of combining credit and technical assistance with extension served as a model.

Negotiations around the establishment of an integrated extension service system began in 1955 with a presentation of the advantages of a national ACAR to the AIA. On 27 February 1956, Henry Bagley commented that he was approached by Brazilian First Lady Sarah Kubitschek, who asked whether the AIA could make a donation to the volunteer social service programme, so that the 'Pioneers' who provided social and medical assistance in poor areas of Rio de Janeiro could be expanded to the rest of the country. According to Bagley, the request, backed up by Juscelino Kubitschek himself, was realistic because Nelson's son Roddy Rockefeller had already donated $ 5,000. Thus, 'it would be a good idea to use the money for a medical unit. We believe it will not only be a gift, but we will also make friends who are at the top'.[6] During the conversation with Kubitscheck, after Walter Crawford began describing the AIA's expansion, the president asked: 'What about creating a national ACAR, with these big funds that I now have available?'[7] Bagley's response was hesitant: 'Our first reaction is that this is not wise to try at this point. We only promised Kubitschek that we would study and he promised the most complete cooperation.'[8] However, that same year, efforts of both the federal government and the AIA, along with those of other associations and agencies, converged to result in the foundation of ABCAR. The Brazilian Rural Confederation, the ETA, the AIA and the Banco do Brasil all participated in the foundation. This arrangement, though, was not without conflicts.

At the local level, the member agencies involved in the creation of ABCAR dealt with strong institutional power that hindered the adoption of new relationships, but work processes functioned differently at the national level. Still in 1951, the AIA proposed extending its work to the southern state of Rio Grande do Sul with the creation of *Associação Sulina de Crédito e Assistência Rural* (Southern Association for Credit and Rural Assistance, ASCAR). However, due to resource scarcity, the project did not go forward at that time.[9] In 1953, the expansion of the CAR system to other states started, following ACAR's guidelines. State governors from the Northeast created the *Associação*

6. From Henry Bagley to Francis A. Jamieson. Collection: Family; Record Group: III 4B; Box: 01; Folder: AIA – General, 1946–1958 2(A).

7. Ibid.

8. Ibid.

9. Excerpts from letter of 20 Oct. 1955 from Harry W. Bagley, AIA representative in Brazil. Collection: Family, Record Group: III 4B, Box 01, Folder 07 AIA – Brazil, p. 2.

Nordestina de Crédito e Assistência Rural (Northeastern Association for Credit and Rural Assistance, ANCAR), on 16 February 1954. It would expand the same action model into the Brazilian Northeast, including Bahia, Pernambuco, Paraíba, Rio Grande do Norte, Ceará and Sergipe states. The consolidation of ABCAR in the Brazilian Northeast, starting in the arid region known as the *Polígono das Secas* or Drylands Region, led to the decentralisation of ANCAR's programmes, transforming them into several state ventures:

Associação Nordestina de Crédito e Assistência Rural do Ceará (ANCARCE)

Associação Nordestina de Crédito e Assistência Rural do Rio Grande do Norte (ANCAR – RN)

Associação Nordestina de Crédito e Assistência Rural da Paraíba (ANCARPA)

Associação Nordestina de Crédito e Assistência Rural de Pernambuco (ANCARPE)

Associação Nordestina de Crédito e Assistência Rural do Sergipe (ANCARSE)

Associação Nordestina de Crédito e Assistência Rural da Bahia (ANCARBA)

1948	ACAR-MG
1954	ANCAR (CE, PE, BA)
1955	ASCAR-RS, ANCAR (RN, PB)
1956	ABCAR, ACARESC
1958	ACAR-RJ
1957	ACAR-ES
1959	ACAR-GO, ACARPA 1
1962	transformation of ANCAR state programs into autonomous associations, the first in SE
1963	ANCARs: autonomies of RN, AL, MA & BA
1964	ANCARs: autonomies of PE. PB & CE
1965	ACAR-Pará, ACAR-MT
1966	ANCAR-PI, ACAR-AM
1967	ACAR-DF
1968	ACAR-AC
1971	ACAR-RO
1972	ACAR-RR
1974	ACAR-AP

Figure 29. Expansion of the Brazilian System of Extension Service (1948–1974). Elaborated by Leonardo Ribeiro Gomes.

Irineu Cabral, Director of Bank of Nordeste do Brasil, created in 1952, was charged with conducting negotiations between the Northeastern states.

These projects also had access to funds from *Banco do Brasil* and technical assistance from the AIA.[10] In other words, the AIA and its most important Brazilian experiences to date were integral to the expansion plan.

During this period, other states began negotiating with the AIA to carry out similar projects. The states of Rio de Janeiro, São Paulo and Espírito Santo initiated a dialogue with the agency during Vargas's government. ABCAR's existence would only make sense if similar agencies were to emerge in other Brazilian states. Even though the second Vargas government prompted an expansion project, the actual negotiations for the consolidation of a national system of rural extension more directly connected to the Brazilian state only became effective with Juscelino Kubitschek's election as president. Even though the government established an antagonistic relationship with the AIA, it also contributed to the expansion of agencies such as the ETA, due to the technical cooperation between Brazil and the United States through Point Four. An agreement signed on 26 June 1953 between the federal governments of the United States and Brazil created the ETA – an official Brazilian institution subordinated to the Ministry of Agriculture. The ETA had Brazilian and US co-directors. The office developed projects in agriculture and natural resources in partnership with other organisations, and Brazilian technicians developed activities alongside US specialists to combine different organisational techniques.[11]

However, before ETA even emerged, the first contacts between the AIA/ACAR and Point Four representatives aimed to expand the Supervised Credit and Technical Assistance to Agriculture and Home Economics programme. The AIA/ACAR proposal suggested at that time investing US$ 250,000 in the Institute of Inter-American Affairs (IIAA) 'because of the urgent need to increase agricultural production and improve the standard of living of rural populations in Brazil'.[12] On 22 August 1951, Juscelino Kubitschek, then Governor of Minas Gerais, wrote to Ari Torres, stating that 'the great success' of ACAR 'fully justifies an expansion of the program'. He recommended 'that funds from the Technical Assistance Program (Point Four) be used to facilitate the expansion of services already started' in Minas Gerais.[13]

---

10. On ANCAR, see Luiz Goes Vieira, *Extensão rural. Origem, evolução, conceituação, filosofia, princípios*, (Recife: Universidade Federal de Pernambuco, 1988).

11. Ribeiro, *A Saga da Extensão Rural em Minas Gerais*, p. 106.

12. De Walter Crawford e Eugene P. Campbell a Ari Torres e Melvin Dohan. 9 Oct. 1951. (EMATER; Pr. 08, Cx. 55, Doc.14).

13. De Juscelino Kubitschek a Ari Torres. Belo Horizonte, 22 Aug. 1951. (EMATER; Pr. 08, Cx. 55, Doc.14).

A National ACAR

Initiatives such as this, aiming to expand technical assistance programmes, made the AIA and its representatives particularly optimistic when Juscelino Kubitschek, a few years later, became President of the Republic. 'As governor, Juscelino Kubitschek told us that he would like to sign an agreement with the AIA to continue ACAR for fifty years', said Bagley.[14] Starting in the mid-1950s, several states' governments sketched out a performance projection for projects similar to ACAR in various parts of Brazil. In 1955, the state government of Espírito Santo formalised a request for the AIA to carry out a technical cooperation programme similar to ACAR; however, ABCAR, the state government and the *Centro Comercial de Café*, a coffee-centred commercial organisation, carried out the consolidation of ACARES in 1956. A year earlier, the governor of Rio de Janeiro, Amaral Peixoto, had requested the same. ACAR-RJ started its activities in 1958. Likewise, the Technical Office in Agriculture's projects, ETA 15 and 17, prompted the creation of extension service agencies in Paraná and Santa Catarina, respectively. Later, these programmes changed their names to *Associação de Crédito e Assistência Rural do Paraná* (Association for Credit and Rural Assistance of Paraná, ACARPA) and the *Associação de Crédito e Assistência Rural de Santa Catarina* (Association for Credit and Rural Assistance of Santa Catarina, ACARESC). These programmes were not directly involved with the AIA.

In São Paulo state, in 1956, Jayme de Almeida Pinto, then Secretary of Agriculture, restated Governor Jânio Quadros' desire to restart planning a project similar to ACAR. To this end, the secretary organised a meeting with several agencies. The newly created São Paulo Rural Social Service Agency, under the responsibility of the federal government, invited ABCAR to a strategic planning meeting where, according to Bagley, 'there were no dissonant voices'.[15] However, no agreement was reached during the meeting involving ABCAR, AIA, *Serviço Social Rural* (Rural Social Service), *Fundação de Amparo à Pesquisa do Estado de São Paulo* (São Paulo State Research Support Foundation), *Sociedade Rural Brasileira* (Brazilian Rural Society), *Banco do Estado de São Paulo* (Bank of São Paulo), *União das Cooperativas* (Union of Cooperatives), *Bolsa de Mercadorias* (Commodities Exchange,) *Bolsa de Cereais* (Grain Exchange), *Federação das Indústrias* (Federation of Industries), *Associação Comercial* (Comercial Association), the *Cooperativa de Cotia* (Cotia Cooperative) and the *Comissão de*

14. Excerpts from letter of 20 Oct. 1955 from Henry W. Bagley, AIA representative in Brazil. Collection: Family, Record Group: III 4B, Box 01, Folder 07 AIA – Brazil.

15. From [Henry Bagley] to Walter Crawford. 12 Oct. 1956. Collection: Family, Record Group: III 4B, Box: 01, Folder 07 B, AIA – Brazil.

Agricultura da Assembléia Legislativa (Agriculture Committee of the Legislative Assembly). They scheduled a new meeting to continue the negotiations. The US and Brazilian technicians chose the ACAR model as a main reference. The São Paulo representatives planned to create the *Paulista* Association of Assistance and Rural Credit (APCAR) 'following the ACAR standard and based on its success, starting small and expanding after sufficient experience'.[16] Governor Jânio Quadros had sent the AIA's study outlining creation of an ACAR in São Paulo to the Secretary of Agriculture and its partner organisations. The governor, according to Crawford, favoured implementing the project. However, almost unanimously, the secretariat opposed it, shelving the creation of APCAR.[17]

After the implementation of Point Four's downstream projects, such as ETA, relations became more complex. Several agencies sought to legitimise themselves as actors in the organisation of new associations in other Brazilian states and a national association. Technical cooperation sometimes gained connotations of rivalry: 'In my conversations with the American ETA team, I think they are hopefully waiting for our response if AIA will be in the five ACAR programs, now including Rio Grande do Sul', wrote Santiago Apodaca to Walter Crawford in October 1955. Apodaca was correct in limiting his optimism about ETA, like the American co-director Snyder, since he (Apodaca) saw relations with the Brazilian co-director, Alberto Ribeiro de Oliveira Motta Filho, differently. Apodaca would say in the same document addressed to Crawford: 'My impression is that Motta is trying to go fast in expanding ACAR model programs in other states and making many commitments. It scares me that he does not know or even realize what it takes to make these programs work.'[18]

Although Motta was not opposed to the nationalisation of ACAR, Apodaca considered the latter a real problem for consolidation of ABCAR in the way AIA had intended. In May 1956, Jimmy Apodaca wrote to Walter Crawford stating that negotiations for the creation of ABCAR advanced but could not be included in the federal government's budget that year. João Napoleão explained that he had met with the group that assisted him in the elaboration of the ABCAR projects and Motta. This group suggested the inclusion of the ETA funds, both in Brazilian currency (Cruzeiro) and in US dollars, which did

16. Study of the possibilities of the creation in the State of São Paulo of a program of technical assistance and supervised credit, p. 2. Collection: Family, Record Group: III 4B, Box: 01, Folder 07 AIA – Brazil.

17. From Walter Crawford to Louise A. Boyer. Rio de Janeiro, 9 Mar. 1956. Collection: Family, Record Group: III 4B, Box: 01, Folder 07 B, AIA – Brazil.

18. From Santiago Apodaca to Walter Crawford. 4 Oct. 1955. Collection: Family, Record Group: III 4B, Box 01, Folder 07 AIA – Brazil.

not please Motta.[19] However, the conflicts between Motta, the AIA/ACAR and defenders of this proposal intensified when the working group excluded the AIA/ACAR. According to Bagley, ETA's co-director said that 'they presented a completely stupid formula, we tore it to pieces and wrote a new one, and it was approved'. Bagley was surprised by this answer and asked Motta, 'approved by whom?' Then, still by Bagley's account, Motta said only 'just approved', leaving the meeting afterwards.[20] What is more, according to João Napoleão de Andrade, 'now, we had difficulties with the Secretary of Finance, I had difficulty with the staff of the Ministry of Agriculture; there was a large group at the Ministry of Agriculture, contrary to ABCAR and ACAR'.[21] According to Walter Crawford, an agreement between Motta and Rio Grande do Sul's Secretary of Agriculture, Bento Pires Dias, would support ETA's employee.[22] When Ralph Hansen became the American co-director of ETA in 1956, the situation became even more complicated for the AIA, since its critics claimed that the binational office had little to offer.[23] Henry Bagley wrote to Francis Jamieson on 29 February 1956, explaining his conversation with Juscelino Kubitschek. The latter had said initially that the AIA did not need to inject more money, then went back and spoke of a 'small contribution'.[24] After meeting Kubitschek, Crawford and Bagley met with Jimmy Apodaca and Aleta McDowell, and the proposal for a new programme met with a lack of enthusiasm. With so many state agencies emerging in that context, many driven by ETA, a federal ACAR would be too expensive, probably inefficient and subject to political pressure,[25] said Bagley, referring to what he understood as a tumultuous period in Brazilian political life. However, after visiting some new agencies, Bagley presented a statute to Juscelino Kubitschek in April 1956.

19. Excerpt – Letter 15 May 1956 from Santiago D. Apodaca to Walter L. Crawford. Collection: Family, Record Group: III 4B, Box: 01, Folder 07 B, AIA – Brazil.

20. From Harry Bagley to Walter Crawford. Bahia, 15 May 1956. Collection: Family, Record Group: III 4B, Box: 01, Folder 07 B, AIA – Brazil.

21. João Napoleão de Andrade, 'Entrevista concedida à Romeu Padilha de Figueiredo', Belo Horizonte, 11 Nov. 1981. (Projeto 'Registro da Memória Histórica e Técnica da Extensão Rural no Brasil', da Emater-MG), p. 31.

22. From Walter Crawford to Louise A. Boyer. Rio de Janeiro, 9 Mar. 1956. Collection: Family, Record Group: III 4B, Box: 01, Folder 07 B, AIA – Brazil.

23. Ibid.

24. From Henry Bagley to Francis A. Jamieson. Confidential. 29 Feb. 1956. Collection: Family, Record Group: III 4B, Box: 01, Folder 07 B, AIA – Brazil.

25. From Henry Bagley to Francis A. Jamieson. Confidential. 29 Feb. 1956. Collection: Family, Record Group: III 4B, Box: 01, Folder 07 B, AIA – Brazil.

João Napoleão de Andrade and Walter Crawford outlined the statute of what was to become ABCAR, with the assistance of Henry Bagley and João Gonçalves de Sousa – a friend of the Ministry of Agriculture – and presented it to Juscelino Kubitschek in a letter dated 23 April 1956. Kubitschek discussed the idea of expanding ACAR during Nelson Rockefeller's visit to Brazil in 1956.[26] The new agency aimed to organise existing state programmes and encourage the programmes in states that did not yet have them.[27] Still, according to João Napoleão, 'Juscelino requested a meeting at the Palace of Catete [Presidential Palace in Rio de Janeiro] expecting to elaborate ABCAR'S statute.[28] Once this was done, ABCAR was created and the minutes were taken, in a meeting that everyone attended, including the AIA, and were signed at the Palace of Catete – everyone tried to hide it, I do not know if because of the situation of Juscelino'.[29] It was clear that the way to solve the conflicts was to request Motta's demotion. According to João Napoleão de Andrade, the imperative tone of

26. Translation of letter, which accompanied draft of national ACAR statutes. Collection: Family, Record Group: III 4B, Box: 01, Folder 07 AIA – Brazil.

27. João Napoleão de Andrade, 'Entrevista concedida à Romeu Padilha de Figueiredo', *Belo Horizonte*, 11 Nov. 1981, 22–23. João Napoleão de Andrade narrated the process as follows: 'He (Motta) was against us at that time – just say this: in a meeting we had at the ETA [office], João Gonçalves, Irineu (Cabral), all the staff were there and we insisted on the formation of ABCAR, and Motta didn't want it. He wanted an organisation more or less linked to the ETA or the Ministry of Agriculture, that would not be appropriate to do business as we wanted to do, and there was a time when he was reluctant. I said; 'on behalf of the President of the Republic, I want to tell you that ABCAR has to be founded, in the shape we propose. This is definitive, so let's work towards that. He stared, seeing me speaking on behalf of the President of the Republic. Then I told Juscelino and he told me that he had done very well'.

28. João Napoleão de Andrade, 'Entrevista concedida à Romeu Padilha de Figueiredo', Belo Horizonte, 11 Nov. 1981. (Projeto 'Registro da Memória Histórica e Técnica da Extensão Rural no Brasil', da Emater-MG), p. 22–23.

29. Ibid. João Napoleão said: 'Mas você vai [saber] a verdade aqui, agora'. At this point, the interview is interrupted and the tape recorder turned off in order for the fact to be narrated. Everything leads one to believe that there is a connection with Colby and Dennet: 'Kubitschek had just survived a coup attempt and was desperately trying to assure American investors of his good intentions towards them – particularly Standard Oil and US Steel, whose employees were said to have participated in the conspiracy. The inspiration for this conspiracy, it was said, was the election of the left-leaning Vice-President João Goulart, who had been Vargas' Minister of Labor until conservative generals forced him out. Kubitschek was anxious to avoid similar luck by demonstrating that his administration would not follow Vargas' nationalist direction.' Colby and Dennet, *Thy Will be Done.*

the request achieved this objective.[30] Hence, according to João Napoleão de Andrade himself, the AIA/ACAR's and its representatives' influence improved relations between the US, the Minas Gerais and ETA agencies: 'the conditions and relations in ETA could not be better. [Alberto Martins] Torres, a substitute for Motta, is well connected with all Americans or Brazilians', Crawford wrote to Lawrence Levy on 10 February 1957. Even Ralph Hansen, in turn, 'stated that he never had so much cooperation from the Brazilian side'.[31]

Motta's departure from ETA would not ultimately resolve the tensions and political disputes over development projects in Brazil. Studying the correspondence and memoranda exchanged between AIA staff in New York and São Paulo or Minas Gerais demonstrates an ever-growing tension over the association's direction, which was also true for IRI. The founding of ABCAR would turn AIA's tacit dream of nationalising a major project into reality. Nevertheless, internal tensions and political timing caused other institutions such as ETA to embrace ABCAR's project. Already by the late 1950s, for various reasons, the AIA was beginning its slow process of collapse, as we will see in the next chapter.

30. João Napoleão de Andrade, 'Entrevista concedida à Romeu Padilha de Figueiredo', Belo Horizonte, 11 Nov. 1981. (Projeto 'Registro da Memória Histórica e Técnica da Extensão Rural no Brasil', da Emater-MG), p. 34. Finally, Andrade speaks: 'Talk to the President [of the Republic] and tell him that the Brazilian element, in the Technical Office of Agriculture, is against us, does not support us and creates every difficulty, and I absolutely need that man to be demoted and to put one of our elements there. Sete Câmara [then sub-chief of the Civil Cabinet of the Presidency] talked with the President of the Republic and came back with an envelope with his handwriting on it: Alberto Martins Torres. Sete Câmara then said [that] the President told you to take steps to have [this] other one demoted and this one appointed to the place'.

31. From Walter Lion Crawford to Lawrence Levy. 10 Feb. 1957. Collection: AIA, Box 01, Folder 14.

CHAPTER 11.

'A QUIET BUT EFFECTIVE REVOLUTION': NEW PROJECTS AND PROGRAMMES IN THE EARLY ALLIANCE FOR PROGRESS ERA

> *The students are not only carrying out their practice teaching in the rural communities, but are actually organizing football (soccer) teams and choral singing groups. These activities and others like them are creating a completely new spirit of interdependence and cooperation between what is locally called 'las fuerzas vivas' (the live forces), of the urban center, and the rural back country*
>
> (Ernst E. Maes, AIA Director, December 1963).

In 1960 Chile was hit by a destructive earthquake; Ernst E. Maes, an AIA representative in Venezuela, visited the country while the Rockefeller Brothers Fund decided to provide some assistance. On the advice of a consultant, Dr Galo Plaza, formerly president of Ecuador, the Fund agreed to specify that its aid should be used by Chile for the construction of rural schools and, later, the general improvement of rural education in the devastated area. This decision was communicated in a letter of intent sent by Mr Laurence J. Rockefeller, President of the Fund, to don Jorge Alessandri, then President of Chile; the letter of intent also stated that the AIA would represent the Fund in negotiating an appropriate agreement for a programme.[1] After the preliminary exchange of letters between the Fund and the Government of Chile, the AIA carried out a series of discussions with working level personnel of the Chilean Development Corporation (CORFO), the coordination agency, and a special technical committee appointed for the purpose by the Ministry of Education. During these discussions, Chilean educators considered the technical development aspects of the proposed programme more important than school construction; moreover, it would be necessary to set up a special organisation to operate the programme, closely related to the Ministry, but with considerable independence to allow for experimentation. The AIA representative prepared the draft of a written agreement that was to provide the basis for the programme, and included the

1. Ernst Maes, 'Plan Victoria: An Experiment in Rural Education in Chile' (New York, 1967). Collection: American International Association for Economic and Social Development (AIA) records. 1949-1968. p. 1.

Figure 30. Map of Chile.

following points: 'The program would be carried out in the Department of Victoria within the devastated area in the south, and having a Rural Normal School, which was to be designated as "experimental" by the Ministry of Education'. In addition, a Special Commission for Rural Education was created to carry out the program, connected to Corfo, the administrative agency and made up of a representative of each of the parties in the agreement. Finally, the AIA would make available to the Special Commission the sum of $450,000 to be spent for construction of model rural schools and for the technical development of rural education.[2]

The communities surrounding Victoria, located in the south-central region of Chile, served as an important laboratory of experiments – and disputes – during the Cold War. As Vasconcelos has shown, there were three urban agrarian reform projects in dispute in the region: technocratic modernisation, Christian Democratic structural agrarian reform, and finally the agrarian revolution of the Chilean road to socialism. In a moment of growing tension throughout Latin America around agrarian disputes, the AIA's activities were marked by a relative silence on private land tenure: as in Brazil, the Association's reports concealed fundamental data for any successful modernisation project at the time: in 1955, only seven per cent of the Chilean population controlled 78 per cent of the agricultural area.[3] The technocratic modernisation plan, therefore, advanced on 'Americanist' pillars, as opposed to 'Iberian' means of organisation, emphasising that with community organisation and cooperation – rather than by revolution or structural agrarian reform – modern precepts of life and education would be achieved by Latin American populations, as we shall see below.

A 'New Spirit of Interdependence and Cooperation': Victoria and Nuble Plans

In the late 1950s, several variables contributed to AIA programmes not being accepted by local elites or, in some cases, not bringing results deemed desirable by the Association. First was the departure of Nelson Rockefeller during his term as governor of New York. At the same time, a context eager for developmental policies convinced some of the Latin American elites to launch their own programmes. In 1958, Brazilian President Juscelino Kubitschek proposed

2. Ibid.

3. Joana Salém Vasconcelos, *'O lápis é mais pesado que a enxada': reforma agrária no Chile e pedagogias camponesas para transformação econômica (1955–1973)* (São Paulo: USP, Ph.D. Diss. in Economic History, 2020), p. 11.

the Pan-American Operation (PAO) that, added to the fears caused by the 1959 Cuban Revolution in the capitalist world, drew attention to the geopolitics of the region and its modernising claims. In September 1960, the conclusions and recommendations of studies on the PAO proposals were presented in Bogotá during the Inter-American Economic Conference. Afterwards, a special fund was created and the Inter-American Development Bank (IDB) made available funds for land reform, housing, education and sanitation projects. The following year, early in John Kennedy's administration, the United States and 22 other nations of the hemisphere signed the Punta del Este Declaration. Theoretically, local governments would provide their development plans and most of the resources, while the United States would provide the rest through the United States Agency for International Development (USAID) – by the end of that decade, some local governments were sponsoring up to ninety per cent of their own projects.[4]

Therefore, as historian Loureiro has shown, there is a certain consensus about the origin of the Alliance for Progress: the 1959 revolution and Cuba's subsequent entry into the Soviet orbit of influence (1960) stimulated or accelerated a plan to combat what US governmental and intellectuals used to consider the structural causes of communism.[5] Moreover, McCook, Andrade and others argue, contrary to the simplistic imposed modernisation approach, that Latin American elites developed cooperative programmes aimed at modernising agricultural research even before WWII.[6] Therefore, as demonstrated by Point Four, there was a certain confluence between the United States' foreign policy and the Latin American elites' desire for modernisation and development. Besides this aspect, it is important to note that the Bogotá conference strongly opposed the original precepts of the AIA and IBEC. In the early 1960s, therefore, economists and politicians from both the North and South of the continent indirectly challenged the thesis that private capital by itself would enable economic growth in Latin America; it would be necessary, from this new perspective, to support national development plans involving public investment.[7]

To a certain extent, AIA's idea of starting a small programme like ACAR and then nationalising came to seem quite modest in the face of the financial

4. Dalrymple, *The AIA story*, p. 191.

5. Loureiro, *A Aliança para o Progresso e o Governo João Goulart*, p. 20.

6. Stuart McCook, *States of Nature: Science, Agriculture and Environment in the Spanish Caribbean (1760-1940)* (Austin: Texas University Press, 2000).

7. See Loureiro, *A Aliança para o Progresso e o Governo João Goulart.*

Figure 31. Proposed Latin America AIA programme, 1960–1965.

contributions made available in the following years by USAID. Although it did not totally abandon its principle of carrying out small experiments that could become a model of development for the hemisphere, in the face of USAID resources, the AIA practically ceased to be a vanguard in Latin America and became a relatively small association seeking contracts to maintain the employment of its employees while trying to place itself as a reformist think tank: a low-budget imperialism. In effect, the AIA ceased to be an innovative association, directed by one of the most powerful American business leaders and an inducer of development ideals, to become effectively a fundraising office for USAID and other sources – although very influential, a species of think tank addressing specific themes. In the late 1950s, for example, then Brazilian Ambassador in

Washington Walther Moreira Salles and officials from IRI – part of the AIA at that time – tried, on behalf of Nelson Rockefeller, to convince Brazilian President Juscelino Kubitschek to create a research centre exclusively focused on the study and adaptation of animal breeds for the tropics. The Rockefellers and the Moreira Salles had, at the time, over thirty years of corporate business experience related, mainly through the American Coffee Corporation, to the production and export of coffee. In 1956, Moreira Salles and Nelson Rockefeller partnered in the venture of Fazenda Bodoquena, a 400,000-hectare estate in the state of Mato Grosso do Sul, in the far west of Brazil, near the border with Paraguay and Bolivia – which expanded, in a way, the IRI work carried out in Fazenda Cambuhy, in which Moreira Salles was a forty per cent shareholder.[8] However, even the influential Moreira Salles' presence did not convince the Brazilians, and the Tropical Institute project was shelved.[9]

At this time, Crawford and Camp's interests were moving toward expansion beyond Venezuela and Brazil – and the small experiences of cooperation in other countries – so they re-established a relationship that had been dormant since 1947 with the Inter-American Institute of Agricultural Sciences in Turrialba, Costa Rica. In the early 1960s, IAIAS was expecting a financial contribution from the International Cooperation Administration (ICA), the agency that in a way gave rise to AID, for extension work services, favouring a cooperation agreement with AIA for a mass communication programme. Signed in 1958, the agreement became known as the Inter-American Popular Information Program (PIIP, in Spanish) and agricultural communications specialist Schuyler Bradt became AIA's representative in Costa Rica. In the following years, programmes working with rural youth were organised through new agreements between AIA and IAIAS, based on the North American 4-H Clubs model. Communication programmes and work with rural youth were joined by continued cooperation in the training of technicians through scholarships, and finally, in 1962, a Rural Development programme was initiated through cooperation between AIA, CBR, and the IAIAS. Louis Heaton of the Venezuelan office became the AIA representative for the programme and approved a USAID loan to the Agricultural Bank of Venezuela to provide supervised credit. Between 1962 and 1966, 7,377 loans were made, with 81 per cent repayment.[10]

The AIA office in Venezuela was also able to expand its operations through Ernst Maes, via a contract with the Chilean government for an ambitious rural

8. See Colby and Dennet, *Thy Will Be Done.*

9. da Silva, *De agricultor a farmer.*

10. Dalrymple, *The AIA Story*, p. 164.

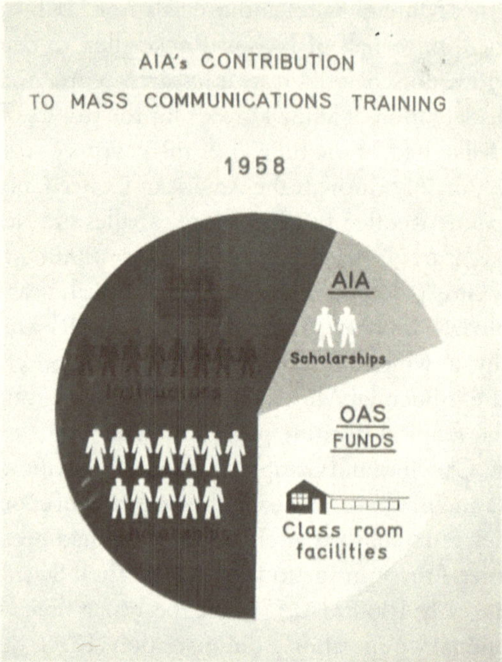

Figure 32. AIA's contribution to mass communications training, 1958.

education plan. The Victoria Plan draft agreement was submitted for approval to the Ministry of Education, CORFO and AIA, which in turn submitted it to Rockefeller Brothers Fund. It was approved and signed by the three parties on 21 December 1961.

Among the Chilean personnel involved were Enrique Salinas, the Executive Secretary of the Commission, together with Don Domingo Valenzuela. These two key collaborators served as a liaison between the AIA, the politicians and the local population in order to fight against the environment, the local people's traditional way of life and poverty, as highlighted by the AIA personnel:

> At that time of the year, it rains there almost constantly, it is always cold and the grey clouds hang low. The roads become almost impossible to motor vehicles, and the rural communities, never very conspicuous, seem to disappear into dripping landscape. The children of those communities, most of them ragged and barefooted, and protected from the cold only by a poncho, walk up to 4 miles to school – when they have one available. These schools are almost always

> dark, dirty, unheated wood buildings with an always inadequate number of dilapidated benches crowded into small rooms. The children sit there shivering, passively listening to lessons having virtually no relationship to their life at home. The teacher, usually a normal school graduate but even so inadequately trained for working in this environment, tries for a year or two after he graduates to apply a program in accordance with some of the theory he has been taught. The lack of teaching materials or of supervision and help, however, gradually defeat him and force him to lapse into a deadly rote learning system of teaching.[11]

Although scholars have analysed the influence of the United States during the Cold War through the lens of anti-communism, not all the activities of these agencies resulted from combating a possible Sovietisation of Latin America. The tradition versus modernity binary, as well as the operations of foundations such as Ford and Rockefeller, predate the Cold War; since the late nineteenth century the principles of European-style science, as well as a wide range of habits and customs, were ethnocentrically amalgamated in a great diversity of local societies. And although the fight against tradition adapted smoothly to the anti-communist agenda, communism being associated with poverty and lack of opportunities existing in a liberal and capitalist world, in a way it still echoed in AIA's ideology a perception of static communities, where time refused to move on: in the Chilean region of Victoria, especially in rural areas, 'the communities should be poor and having limited political or other influences, so that their prospects of obtaining a school from other sources was minimal'. For the American experts such as Maes, in an anachronistic and ethnocentric way, the typology of the communities resembled 'a semi-feudal social organization' in ranchos or 'fundos', 'in which a number of families live on and are more or less attached to the land, as dependents of the owner'.[12]

> The agriculture practiced is very extensive and of very low productivity, so that the poverty of the majority of the families living on these farms could be said to be inherent and built into the antiquated system. There are also areas of medium sized, family operated, land holdings, with only periodic use of outside labor. These are what could be considered the middle-class communities of rural Victoria, and relatively the most prosperous. There are also some areas where small holdings have been distributed in the past and where, for the most part, the settlers have found it impossible to make a living off the land, and have become part-time laborers on the larger farms. At the bottom of the rural social pyramid, there are dozen or so Araucano Indian 'reducciones' or reservations, where the people are poorest, and where the agriculture practiced

11. Maes, Plan Victoria, p. 5.

12. Ibid., pp. 5–7.

> in the fragmented holdings is of a subsistence type. Finally, there are a few villages made up largely of wage workers and part-time farmers.[13]

With the involvement of Salinas, the Special Commission selected eight areas of operation: Colo and California, located in areas of large farms; Rosario and San Gregorio, located in areas of medium sized, family operated farms; Las Cardas, Las Lilas and Coihueco, located on Indian reservations; and finally Quino, considered by the experts as 'a typical rural village'. Within the ideology of the AIA and its Chilean collaborators, the community had organised itself, with the assistance of Salinas and some of his collaborators from the Victoria Rural Formal School. This means that, unlike an Iberian tradition where the state organises society, Americanist enthusiasts encouraged rural teachers to discuss and decide on even the material used to build the schools in specific workshops:

> the most common material in the area is of course lumber, and at first it had seemed logical to use this material. However, it was pointed out that if wood stoves are used for heating, the only economic way of providing spare heat in that area, fire is a constant hazard, and an extremely large number of wooden schools burned each year. Furthermore, wood buildings had to be maintained and painted every year in that area of heavy rains, and long experience had convinced the teachers that the Ministry would never provide funds for adequate maintenance in its normal permanent budget. The most persuasive argument was that it would be very inappropriate for a plaque indicating the Rockefeller Brothers Fund contribution to be placed upon an unworthy structure. The teachers' building committee recommended that the buildings be of reinforced concrete frames with brick fill for the walls, and that the construction be earthquake proof of the best quality. The commission accepted these recommendations, and the plan of work for 1962 so instructed Salinas. Unfortunately, there were no workers in the area who knew about concrete construction, and it was soon found that there are only a few isolated deposits of sand and gravel in the Department of Victoria. Another basic problem was to develop a type of organization for the construction jobs that would not use basic contractors, but instead would create local school buildings committees as the sponsors of the project. In effect this made it necessary for the Plan Victoria organization itself to administer the funds and materials and organize the works crews on the various construction projects.[14]

The solution found was, as Martha Dalrymple later summarised, to 'lead to other projects in which neighbors worked together democratically on a com-

13. Ibid.

14. Ibid.

mon project in a way reminiscent of the North American frontier tradition',[15] exemplifying the frontier myth of collective labour by training 200 workers, and using benevolent donations of sand and gravel from several communities: 'It resulted in this organization of complicated cooperative activities, such as entire communities hauling sand by truck, oxcart, wheelbarrow, and even by sack to the site of the building'.[16] With the programme's proclaimed success in organising and training all from manual labourers to teachers, the AIA would conquer its main target in the following months: to finance the extension of a Plan Victoria type programme to another area of Chile. The Plan Nuble was developed in the Nuble province by the same Special Commission under an agreement that was signed by the Ministry of Education, CORFO and AID, and AIA's continued participation was made possible by an AID contract for technical assistance. The Plan Nuble programme, involving the construction of six schools, in effect continued Plan Victoria until late in 1956 and included technical development in addition to its school construction component.

Finally, although AIA considered its participation in the Victoria and Nuble plans successful in terms of forming a spirit of community cooperation, Ernst E. Maes considered the main progress of the projects to be in combating illiteracy – in a clear reference back to the Bolivar Foundation's early goals. At the time, educational indicators showed 'the drop-out rate for the rural schools … estimated to be 84%'; in other words 'of every 100 children who enter the first grade of a rural elementary school, only 16 finish the sixth grade', approaching the low educational indicators of Bolivia, Venezuela, Colombia and other Latin American countries. The AIA considered there to be three groups of problems leading to this situation: those involving historic, economic, social structure and political situations and developments within which the educational systems functioned; those involving the inadequacy of the resources the society provides for education, especially at the elementary level; and finally, those involving the inefficient use presently being made of the inadequate resources.[17] AIA's experience at both levels would represent advances and create models for the work of US foundations in the southern hemisphere. First, the analysis of the problems of rural education and the development of the idea of a post-graduate practical teacher training centre, were considered another significant result of Plan Victoria. The reason, according to Ernst E. Maes,

15. Dalrymple, *The AIA Story*, p. 180.

16. Ibid.

17. Ibid., p. 11.

> is that together they delimited a strategic area where a relatively small-scale program could have significant impact of the quality of a national rural education system. This could be of interest to U.S. foundations, which tend to shy away from programs in elementary or secondary education in Latin America, simply because the fields appear too massive, and too low on the educational pyramid, to be significantly affected by small scale projects. Because of this possibility, this contribution of Plan Victoria needs some elaboration.[18]

According to Maes, Plan Victoria demonstrated that the drop-out rate could be drastically reduced if the rural school programme were made more functional by adding attractive practical courses at the level of the 4th, 5th and 6th grades. Not only did this affect the drop-out rate after the crucial 3rd grade, but it also had an immediate impact on all the other elements of the rural school programme, including the teaching of the basic core subjects at every grade. In addition, Maes considered that the Plan demonstrated it was not necessary to attempt to reform the entire elementary programme of the existing system of teacher training to bring about significant improvement: 'This can be done merely by developing sound methods for teaching the practical subjects, an element of the rural school program that is now usually neglected'.[19] In this perspective, the analysis of the problems of rural education clearly indicated that the 'basic reforms demonstrated there could be put into effect gradually, on a national scale, with relatively few trained teachers using inexpensive equipment'.[20] According to him, the reason in any country for a drop-out rate of over eighty per cent is that the number of children at the level of 4th, 5th, and 6th grades is relatively small; so, at the initial stage, a correspondingly small programme can significantly affect the entire national system.

Finally, critically, an evaluation of Plan Victoria would involve differentiated planning if it were to be made suitable for other countries: 'In terms of a foundation program in this field in another country, therefore, the basic agreement should from the beginning make the organization of a postgraduate practical teacher training center a primary objective'. So, in 1966, the pedagogic and financial contributions amounted to eighteen community organisations; eighteen school buildings, models of their kind; the training of 110 rural school teachers; eighteen workshops for manual training; fully equipped workshops for vocational education in the Victoria normal schools; six vehicles for supervisory work and services; techniques in group dynamics;

18. Ibid.
19. Ibid.
20. Ibid., p 16.

collaboration and training workshops for foreign and national teachers and, finally, expanding this experience to all the training schools for rural teachers in Chile. In summary, the AIA experience in Chile sought to take up some of the original aspects of its Latin American programmes, such as the notion of community work and combatting illiteracy. In addition, the model found in the Chilean case of small experiments adaptable to national situations carried hope for expansion to the rest of Latin America, while another part of the Association conceived future projects, as we will see below.

A Think Tank for the Hinterlands

> *This could be a land reform program developed in a democratic tradition that would answer the 'commune' system of the Red Chinese and would dwarf the 'virgin lands' development program of the Soviet Union.*
>
> (John Camp to Nelson Rockefeller, referring to the Campos Cerrados programme)

John Camp's affirmation about the Central Brazilian plateaus and their agricultural potential would produce – as we have seen through the agreement between AIA and IAIAS –the concept of rural development as a way to oppose the discourse of agrarian reform, then in vogue in the vocabulary of the Latin American Left-Wing. The AIA did not abandon the concept of agrarian reform, since this was an agenda in countries like Brazil, Chile and Venezuela, but by bringing the concept of rural development closer to colonisation, the AIA's approach sought to differentiate itself from the models of communist China and the Soviet Union, but also from the Latin American political left. In the last years of the Association, three projects stood out in this direction, although with differing levels of success: the Jaíba, Central Plateau and Campos projects.

The first would be implemented in a state-owned area of approximately one million acres near the São Francisco River Valley in the state of Minas Gerais, as proposed by Robert Hudgens in 1951 (see chapter 8). Initially, Walter Crawford prepared a settlement project for 1,000 families in the semi-arid region, funded in part by the state; the remainder would be financed by the Inter-American Development Bank. The initial stimulus came from a report prepared by Crawford in 1961, entitled 'Agriculture in Brazil.[21] Based on

21. Walter Lion Crawford, *Agriculture in Brazil; a Report* (New York: AIA, 1961).

reports and proposals written by Brazilian technicians,[22] Crawford's writings portray the situation of Brazilian agriculture and rural areas from the point of view, above all, of experts interested in overcoming backwardness and tradition, whose project is the technification of agriculture and the rationalisation of labour. The diagnosis conceived by Crawford was realisable through bilateral cooperation projects between Brazil and the United States – and driven by local governments – with subsequent regional and national impact on Brazilian agricultural production.

His main thesis revolved around the idea that the pressure of growing demographics required farming and colonisation of new underdeveloped lands, mainly in the semiarid Northeast and the Cerrados of Central Brazil – emulating Frederick Jackson Turner's notion of a social escape valve. Of the Northeast, Crawford stated that 'the most important problem to overcome is that of a depressed and unstable agriculture. Drought, outmoded farming methods and the prevalence of under sized, subsistence units are major factors.' Moreover, 'irrigation will not cure all the ills of the region. It can never be used on more than a minor fraction of the area and exaggeration of its possibilities tends to obscure a more important agricultural solution, better dry-land farming.' Finally, 'resources can support at acceptable economic and social standards, indicating that re-settlement of large numbers in more favorable areas of Brazil should be given high priority'.[23]

The then governor of Minas Gerais, Magalhães Pinto (1961–1965), and the then Secretary of Agriculture, Industry, Commerce and Labor under Magalhães Pinto and former president of ACAR, Paulo Penna de Salvo, upon hearing Walter Crawford's thesis, were convinced that a project in the semi-arid region of Minas Gerais was possible. In the following years, both contacted Crawford to elaborate a project of colonisation and agricultural modernisation – an extensive report entitled Plan for Colonization of Jaíba. This was not the first time that a development project had been designed for the region: a related colonisation plan was conceived during Juscelino Kubitschek's term as governor of Minas Gerais in 1952. The project was the responsibility of the National Development Institute for Irrigation and Colonization (INIC) and, after three years, was considered unviable due to the supposed isolation of the region, lack of transportation and lack of technical assistance. In the mid-1960s, the military dictatorship also prepared a survey of the irrigable potential of the

22. Marcos Pereira, Jefferson Rangel and Plínio Luppi, *Crédito Rural Supervisionado no Brasil* (Rio de Janeiro: ABCAR, 1961).

23. Crawford, *Agriculture in Brazil*, pp. 36–37.

São Francisco River Basin in Minas Gerais, in cooperation with the Bureau of Reclamation, part of the US Department of the Interior for the management of water resources. These studies indicated the existence of 100,000 ha of arable land in the region of Mata de Jaíba. With the civil-military coup of 1964, Magalhães Pinto shelved Crawford's project, already well advanced in its topographical and economic surveys. At the same time, Paulo de Salvo created the Colonization Program of the State of Minas Gerais, approved by the IBD.

This beginning was fundamental for the new governor Israel Pinheiro (1966–1971), who in 1966, through the Fundação Rural Mineira de Colonização e Desenvolvimento Agrário (Minas Gerais Rural Colonisation and Agrarian Development Foundation, RURALMINAS), ordered the reformulation and expansion of the old Colonization Center of Rio Verde Grande and the implementation of a pilot irrigation project over an initial area of 5,680 hectares.[24]

In *Agriculture in Brazil*, Crawford also considered other regions problematic for agriculture and in need of more attention from governments and bilateral cooperation programmes with the United States. In general, the entire Northeast region should receive investment and effective settlement and agricultural modernisation programmes; as a way of corroborating his argument, the report produced by Crawford on behalf of the AIA attached a special report by Ted Szulk for the *New York Times* dated 31 October 1960, entitled 'Northeast Brazil poverty breeds threat of a revolt'. With a strong anti-communist intonation, the text by the then *New York Times* Latin America correspondent stated: 'the makings of a revolutionary situation are increasingly apparent across the vastness of the poverty-stricken and drought-plagued Brazilian Northeast'. Adopting a discourse contrary to the recent rise of Fidel Castro in Cuba, the reporter opines that 'the misery is exploited by the Leftist influences in the overcrowded cities', and explores the connections of the Peasants' League – a movement to demand agrarian reform, led by the then deputy in Pernambuco, Francisco Julião – with communist China. And, in a way, this revolutionary 'ferment', as Szulk termed the protests of poor peasants in the region, became a pressing concern especially for Magalhães Pinto, not only in the ideology of development, but in the political-institutional sense. Elected on a conservative platform, which paradoxically had also included support for state agrarian reform, Magalhães Pinto came to defend solutions similar to those projected by AIA, ACAR and ABCAR, centred on agropastoral modernisation and, later, colonisation. Although today Minas Gerais is part of the Southeast region of Brazil – considered the most developed part of the country – the extreme

24. *Correio da Manhã* [newspaper], Rio de Janeiro, 7 March 1968, p. 12.

north of the state is generally associated environmentally and socially with the Northeast in terms of poverty and scarcity of natural resources, especially water. Therefore, colonisation would be a conciliatory way to maintain the interests of the latifundia while a mass of poor workers could be taken advantage of in pilot projects such as Jaíba, considered a *terra devoluta* – untitled land that became state property. In addition, this strategy was intended to enable anti-communism policies, for which the then governor of Minas Gerais became one of the most fervent enthusiasts and then one of the main instigators of the civil-military coup initiated on 31 March 1964 – initiating a 21-year dictatorship in the country.

Crawford's report also looked at the old settlement area in the Southeast – in the states of Espírito Santo, Rio de Janeiro and São Paulo – and the area of European colonisation in the states of Santa Catarina and Rio Grande do Sul; finally, Crawford's major concern was the plateaus of Central Brazil, an extensive area composed mostly of grasslands, savannas and forests: 'Of all those suggested, one solution – the opening up of new agricultural lands in West-Central Brazil for settlement by a large number of farmers now poorly situated in other areas – stands out as one of the most feasible and promising', stated Crawford. Emulating again a Turnerian conception of free land west of the original settlement nuclei, the author considered that 'Brazil is particularly fortunate to have such a large area of immediately available land'. If Rockefeller's initial interest was centred in Amazonia because of the strategy of latex production during World War II, Crawford strategically changed the axis of the modernising imaginary to an area of almost two million square kilometres, (23 per cent of the Brazilian territory). In his argument, he demonstrated, using data from the Brazilian Institute of Geography and Statistics, that the region had an estimated population of 2,365,000, only four per cent of the national total, with a density of less than one inhabitant per square kilometre in the northern portions – where the state of Tocantins is now located – varying to approximately five inhabitants in the southern part of Goiás. In 1950, there were 79,750 *fazendas* in the region, representing only 3.8 per cent of the total number in Brazil. But, on the other hand, Crawford saw great possibilities for agricultural development and colonisation in these savannas and grasslands: 'The average Brazilian farmer, and many technicians, believe these soils unsuitable for anything except the most extensive pastoral use. If the soils are left in their natural state, this is true, except for the very best grade' of the small forests known as *Cerradões*.[25]

25. Crawford, *Agriculture in Brazil*, p. 65.

In 1961, therefore, in light of the fertilisation experiments conducted by the IRI – remember that between 1957 and 1963 the IRI was incorporated into the AIA – Crawford wrote a brief genealogy of fertility studies: 'Until quite recently no conclusive research on the fertility problems of these soils had been done, and therefore the few attempts that had been made to use them, mostly with little or no corrective measures being taken, had resulted in failure'. The AIA report suggests two major policies: the first is devoted entirely to the Cerrados and was inspired by New Deal programmes, such as the aforementioned Resettlement Administration, Farm Security Administration and Farmers Home Administration. Thus, Crawford recommends 'the opening up of the West-Central area through the establishment of a regional land authority to encourage, facilitate, guide and assist voluntary settlement by rural people from congested and depleted areas'. The second measure is general, but with emphasis on the Northeast, dialoguing with what would later become the Jaíba project or the Central Plateau: 'through research, area planning, consolidation of small units and extension education [to concentrate] on improving efficiency of agriculture, introduction of new technology and the development and conservation of land and water resources'.[26]

Based on empirical research and experiences of technical cooperation with local governments, the AIA of the early 1960s did not have sufficient funding to compete with the growing number of other programmes, but it positioned itself as a true think tank, spreading recommendations about what it considered fundamental for agricultural modernisation and, consequently, a society based on values shared by the Association – which we will discuss again below. And as a way to try to consolidate an expansion, in 1963, IRI signed an agreement with the United States Agency of International Development, resulting in new studies and projects. In May 1963, Eric Eustace Williams, the Prime Minister of Trinidad and Tobago, met with the Board of Texaco Inc. and the President of Chase Manhattan Bank. Following the meeting, Williams announced the inauguration of the Better Village Program. According to Walter Crawford, 'the resulting Better Village Program was intended to nationalize the peasant/village culture' and 'Williams aspired to build the nation of Trinidad and Tobago upon villages, not in reserves'. According to Tsuji, cultural engineering of a new nation is connected to the post-Enlightenment idea of *social telesis* in which technology and education can direct the evolution of society – very close to the aims of the AIA. Williams, on the other hand, conceived Trinidad as a non-Western postcolonial society, where 'the major sources for cultural

26. Ibid.

engineering are traditional folk cultures'. Tsuji understands that Williams presumed villages to be collectives of 'naturally distinguished' peasants; these groups 'had become modern without being Western by liberating themselves from the hegemonic colonial culture of their own conscious motions'. Finally, 'reflecting the apparent economic equality among peasants, he assumed that the interactions between distinct cultural origins would have produced a unique cultural form through interculturation, neither assimilation nor acculturation'.[27]

Despite Williams' beliefs, the group worked in a technocratic manner, reiterating technical ideals as fundamental to the success of the Village Program. A committee was appointed, composed of representatives from various ministries and the above companies; and it was agreed that Chase would provide the services of a technical consultant to the Committee, during a period of one to two months, to suggest a specific plan of action with priorities for things to be done. Thus, the services of the AIA in the persons of John Camp, then its Executive Vice President, and Walter Crawford, developed a report with recommendations such as grants in aid, or contracts to conduct research and studies in agriculture, in addition to short-term training grants for study abroad, particularly in agricultural extension and credit.

Moreover, Crawford highlighted the importance of locally conducted in-service training courses in credit, extension, home economics, rural youth clubs and communications. According to the author, 'these courses should be held for persons presently employed in agriculture and for training a new type of village level extension worker'. Then, foreign trained specialists could be engaged as instructors: the group planned a training centre for such workers in cooperation with the College of Agriculture, Village of Centeno, or the East Caribbean Farm Institute, conducting, in cooperation with government entities, a pilot extension, home economics, rural youth club, and supervised credit programme. This programme might be started in part of one county or, perhaps better, in a few selected villages located in various parts of the islands. All the results of available research should be put to use in the pilot programme by specially trained personnel and method and result demonstration techniques should be used to the maximum.[28] In addition to recommendations for agriculture, the report's emphasis on fisheries, community organisation and facilities – health centres, roads, film libraries, housing or village councils, for

27. Teruyuki Tsuji, 'Villaging the nation: The politics of making ourselves in postcolonial Trinidad', *Callaloo* 31 (4) (2008): 1148–74, at 1157.

28. Walter Crawford, *Report on Village Improvement and Rural Economic Development in Trinidad and Tobago* (New York: AIA, 1963), pp. 12–13

example – and, finally, the organisation and operation of a village improvement and rural economic development programme, would require a five-year contract supported by both public and private corporations, amounting to a total of five million British West Indies dollars.

Thus, the AIA dialogued with rulers interested in a decolonial future for their emerging nations, while, as we saw earlier, Chase Bank and David Rockefeller viewed rising nationalism with reservations. This did not prevent imperial actors like Chase and anti-imperial actors like Williams from forging alliances around the development ideal. Also, at this point in global history, new experiments in social engineering were joining the TVA and the New Deal programmes. Williams would have been inspired by Nkrumah's Village Model, while other examples from post-colonial Africa presented themselves as valid, and in many cases non-Westernised, development options. The cases of Tanzania and Ethiopia, as studied by James Scott, presented a need to build manipulable units, unlike the colonial past. As summarised by Tsuji, 'the native political elites mobilized the occupants of stateless spaces in their anti-colonial struggle'. After independence, 'they typically undertook a comprehensive rural (re)settlement program in order to transform these autonomous social, political, and economic spaces into controllable "state spaces"'.[29] The growth of technical cooperation through USAID assisted in these aims – but the role of private enterprises was fundamental for state goals.

Also in 1963, Walter Crawford edited a report deepening the discussion about the Central Brazilian plateaus, which he had viewed with enthusiasm two years earlier. The fundamental change in this new report is that the 'Survey of the Agricultural Potential of the Central Plateau of Brazil' presented by AIA resulted from a contract with USAID at the request of the Brazilian government. A multidisciplinary team was formed to study 750,000 square kilometres across the states of Minas Gerais, Goiás and Mato Grosso, including Crawford and geographer William M. Denevan (University of California, contracted by AIA), Brazilian Oswaldo Alvarenga (Representative of the Ministry of Agriculture), research agronomist James L. Haynes da USAID-Northeast Brazil), rural economist J.K. McDermott from Purdue, the crops and soil specialist Clayton L. Schroeder and soil specialist Herbert Williamson, both from USAID-Brazil agricultural division. The group presented individual studies coordinated by AIA, and right from the start concluded that 'physical resources are adequate to support development, that strong economic forces exist favoring it and that the

29. Tsuji, 'Villaging the nation', 1149.

area can absorb appreciable number of new people from more populated areas'.[30] An important detail is Schroeder's indication that the Ceres Agricultural Settlement, a colonisation and settlement programme founded during the Getúlio Vargas government in order to attract national migrants to the Central Plateau of Brazil in the Cerrados region, should be studied in detail with the objective of serving as a reference for new experiences. In his view, the government should stimulate private groups or individuals, owners of agricultural areas, to divide the land and sell it to settlers as long as the government played a role in providing schools and roads, among other infrastructure actions.[31] Finally, in general, for this venture to succeed, it would be necessary to considerably increase sources of fertilisers, reconnaissance surveys of soils, vegetation and water resources, agricultural research on limiting fertility factors, and training and demonstration activities.[32]

Other projects were drafted during this period: at the request of the Ministry of Agriculture during the Paraguayan dictatorship (1954–1989), there was interest in colonisation programmes; Crawford also facilitated student exchanges from Paraguay to Brazil.[33] Finally, in 1964, Walter Crawford was invited by farmer Edmundo Barbosa, head of the Antunes Foundation, to analyse how sugarcane producers could recover the productivity of their areas located in the Parnaíba delta, considering that the farms had been established in the region for 300 years. After a brief study, Crawford suggested that the farmers should diversify production by attending to regional bases, and above all build a milk cooperative in the Campos and São João da Barra region.[34] In his memoirs later collected by Martha Dalrymple, Crawford associates the situation of certain Brazilian regions with his time in Arkansas, during his work for the Farm Security Administration: 'Physically and psychologically Eastern Arkansas during the '30s and Campos today are very much alike', he opined; 'they look alike – black soil, lots of mud, bad roads, sad little shacks for homes, even sadder little shacks for schools, little or no health or sanitation services'. The reasons for this would not be centred on the race aspect; the similarity lay, besides the environment, in the monoculture production model: 'And both with a one-crop economy – cotton in Arkansas and sugar cane in Campos'.

30. Crawford, *Agriculture in Brazil*, p. 1.

31. Ibid., p. 21.

32. Ibid., p. 1.

33. Dalrymple, *The AIA Story*, p. 165.

34. Ibid., p. 171.

Some of the results of the Campos programme will be discussed later, but at this point it is worth thinking how the notion of temporality exposed in Crawford's thought connects with the emerging Modernisation Theory, expressed mainly in the thought of Walt Whitman Rostow, especially in the vision of progress. For Crawford, Arkansas' past was overcome through the model of supervised credit, rationalisation of agricultural production and infrastructure. Campos was, according to Rostow's model, in a 'backward' stage in relation to the Northern Hemisphere, but, with this model, it could achieve similar results: 'Arkansas has changed and I have hope that Campos will also',[35] he affirmed, demonstrating a certain connection with the Enlightenment and Positivist imaginary, more involved with the idea of progress than, for example, the original IRI report of 1951, where the archetype of the Dust Bowl dominated perceptions. In short, while in the 1950s the lands devastated by centuries of exploitative agriculture in São Paulo were almost synchronic with the US Midwest of Depression times, and represented decline, the imaginary consolidated at the end of the decade placed the Arkansas and Campos environments diachronically; the problems of Arkansas lie in the past, while solving the problems of Campos lies in the future.

If I have concentrated my discussion in this chapter so far on a genealogy of the most important programmes developed and carried out by AIA staff in the early 1960s, it is worth asking: although different, what are the similarities, differences and consequences of these projects proposed in the early 1960s for the Association, for its partners and, above all, for the regions affected? Firstly, it is necessary to clarify, these reports are preliminary surveys on specific subjects that, until then, were unfamiliar to the government and business elites. Therefore, it was not a matter of a simple imposition of exogenous programmes upon local populations, but of recommendations for the exploitation of natural matters and manpower training from a perspective considered modern, rational and, therefore, decisive for the social and economic integration of certain regions or countries into post-war capitalism. Much more than theoretical suppositions, I believe that it is necessary to demonstrate how these ideals – which, as I stated in the introduction, resignified some of the old imperialist ideologies with a certain notion of benevolence or philanthropy – were consolidated to a greater or lesser extent on the foundations of these reports and their recommendations. So, for example, in the case of Chile, the Victoria and Nuble plans were an

35. Ibid.

innovation of the approach later followed, in some aspects, by the educational policy of USAID.[36]

Crawford's report on the Cerrados (1963) was not necessarily groundbreaking: years earlier a commission headed by the Brazilian Institute for Geography and Statistics had already demonstrated how Brazil found itself at an agricultural crossroads where either it must intensify the recovery of the Eastern areas devastated by more than 300 years of exploitative agriculture or advance over the Cerrados.[37] On the other hand, Crawford's report resulted in a consortium of four Land-Grant Colleges (Wisconsin, Illinois, Indiana and Michigan) cooperating with the DNPEA. This consortium was to coordinate development projects; however, no agreement was reached and the project was shelved. But, in different ways, the civil-military dictatorship dramatically exploited the Cerrados' agricultural potential in the following decades, through agreements with USAID, which, around 1964, started working with the DNPEA/Ministry of Agriculture in order to promote research and technical assistance in eight different ecological regions of Brazil – including the Central Plateaus. As a result, years later, farmers would be stimulated to adopt NPK fertilisers, lime and micronutrients, consolidating the fundamental paradigm for large-scale agricultural expansion in the Brazilian Cerrado.[38] The dictatorship adopted this paradigm established by the studies of the Portuguese agronomist Luís Martins de Freitas and the American experts Andrew Colin McClung and Wreal Lott, which, as discussed earlier, resulted from a shifting of the Coffee Tillage programme developed by the IRI to gradually give space to this savanna experiment. In terms of soil ecology, the reclamation experiments on land devastated by coffee plantations in the interior of São Paulo state found similar results to the fertility studies in Cerrado regions. In 1961, the IRI published a bulletin reporting on its experiments with cotton, corn and soybeans in Cerrado soils in the state of São Paulo.[39] In subsequent years, with the dictatorship's growing interest in exploring agriculture in the area, the work of McClung – who left the IRI to work with the Rockefeller Foundation, largely due to the lack of governmental interest in his studies and the decrease

36. Vasconcelos, *'O lápis é mais pesado que a enxada'.*

37. Dalrymple, *The AIA Story*, p. 171.

38. de Freitas, McClung and Lott, *Field Studies on Fertility Problems.*

39. Andrew Colin McClung, Luis Martins de Freitas, D.S. Mikkelsen and Wreal Lott, *Cotton Fertilization in Campo Cerrado Soils of the State of São Paulo, Brazil* (New York, IBEC Research Institute, 1961).

in resources from the Rockefeller Brothers Fund – became a reference, though more in academic than in practical terms, at least until the early 1970s.

In institutional terms, on the other hand, this period marked a consolidation in the creation of organisations focused on the exploration of low agricultural productivity regions, among them the Cerrado. In 1967, the aforementioned agreement between the Brazilian government and USAID expanded the Cerrados research started by IRI to several regions in Brazil, as part of the Programa Nacional de Fertilidade dos Solos (National Program for Soil Fertility), with support from AIA affiliated ABCAR and the Serviço Nacional de Extensão Rural (National Rural Extension Service).[40] The IRI – which became independent from any formal Rockefeller connection in 1963 – also embarked on a new phase of internationalisation, signing new agreements provided by technical training programmes and the development of agricultural projects. Within a strong collection of experimental research and technical reports, two projects in particular sought to adapt IRI's experiences to other regions of the planet.

The first took place in Indonesia: though Java Island had a population of approximately 95 million, its situation contrasted with those of other islands such as Sumatra, Kalimantan, Sulawesi, and Iryan Jaya, with sparse populations and small-scale agriculture. Large transmigration projects were underway, seeking to remove 2.5 million people from Java between 1979 and 1984 to other islands because of population pressures. The famine was underway, compounded by the construction of dams and other large projects that flooded or expropriated areas traditionally occupied by approximately 12,000 families.[41] The TropSoils programme, created in collaboration with the Bogor Centre for Soils Research, University of Hawaii, and North Carolina State University, sought to increase local food productivity in Indonesia. At the programme's first seminar, held in Bogor on 1 March 1980, 55 specialists from various institutions discussed soil acidity problems, highlighting experiences in the Brazilian Cerrado.[42] According to former IRI Director Jerome Harrington, the project in Indonesia demonstrated how technology developed in the Cerrados areas of Brazil could be transferred to other tropical and subtropical regions of the world with similar

---

40. Harrington and Sorenson, *O desenvolvimento das terras de cerrado do Brasil*, p. 29.

41. Michael K. Wade et al., 'Overcoming soil fertility constraints in a transmigration area of Indonesia', *TropSoils Bulletin*, no 88-01, Raleigh, North Carolina State University, Dec. 1988.

42. P. A. Sanchez and S.W. Buol, *Trip Report to Indonesia and Sri Lanka by Soil Management CRSP Planning Team* (Bogor; Indonesia, February 18-March 5, 1980), p. 13.

soil acidity problems.[43] More specifically, IRI joined the TropSoils project and provided support in Sulawesi, Indonesia, involving soybean and cotton crops, combining limestone, NPK fertilisers and micronutrients as had been done in Brazil.[44] Since the mid-1970s, other producers have achieved more satisfactory results with soybean, corn and sorghum productivity, due to new genetic improvement techniques; however, IRI's Soil Fertility project was recognised in 2006 by Norman Borlaug, who nominated McClung – along with two Brazilians, former minister Alysson Paulinelli and researcher Edson Lobato – for the World Food Prize. Paulinelli, in his speech, acknowledged that when he headed the Ministry of Agriculture in the early 1970s, he had access to the reports produced by IRI; the creation of Embrapa in 1972 was a way to remake soil fertility experiments on a broader scale, consolidated with the creation of a specific Embrapa unit in the Cerrados in 1975.[45]

IRI experts also cooperated in a second soil project during the 1990s under an agreement between the United States Agency of International Development and the Salvadoran Coffee Research Foundation (PROCAFE), aiming to revitalise the coffee industry in El Salvador. The technical cooperation aimed at increasing productivity, with an emphasis on small producers.[46] The IRI received similar responses to the ones achieved in Indonesia with the use of lime, NPK fertilisers, and micronutrients[47] in a project coordinated by plant nutrition specialist Marcos Pavan. Jerome Harrington highlighted that this project demonstrated that soil technology transfer from one location to another is possible, with important positive impacts on the production of food and other agricultural products in many developing countries.[48]

---

43. Harrington and Sorenson, 'O desenvolvimento das terras de cerrado do Brasil'.
44. Ibid.
45. 'Starting in 1975, the federal government established a set of efforts to accelerate development in the states of Goiás, Minas Gerais, Mato Grosso and in the Federal District. Programs for financing production were created, such as the Polocentro (Program for Development of the Midwest Region), which included construction of roads, schools, silos and warehouses, agricultural research, technical assistance and rural extension, financing for the incorporation of new areas into the production process and the use of limestone and phosphate. Besides credit for investments, costing and commercialisation, minimum prices and agricultural insurance were established'. https://www.embrapa.br/cerrados/historia
46. United States Agency for International Development Mission to El Salvador. Action Memorandum for the Mission Director. *Project Assistance Completion Report of the 'Coffee Technology Transfer' Project n. 519-0362*, 16 Oct. 1998, p. 2.
47. Harrington and Sorenson, 'O desenvolvimento das terras de cerrado do Brasil', p. 40.
48. Harrington and Sorenson, 'O desenvolvimento das terras de cerrado do Brasil', p. 40.

As regards the Campos Project, in the state of Rio de Janeiro, many activities were carried out in the years following the AIA report; in 1967, the Norte-Fluminense Foundation (FUNDENOR) was organised for the rationalisation of the economy of the wider area, which created the Rural Development Office (EDR) in Campos. The EDR structured the Central Dairy Cooperative (Coperleite), a feed mill and a poultry slaughterhouse with funds from the Inter-American Development Bank; and Italian experts were hired by OAS to diversify production into pineapples, poultry, small fruits, pigs, soybeans and cassava[49]. EDR was absorbed by FUNDENOR itself, which again requested from the OAS the sum of $600,000 dollars for land use studies in 1970. Besides this first initiative, the Antunes Foundation was still in contact with the AIA to make possible a manganese exploration project, also through the foundation of a Development Institute, but this time in the state of Amapá, on the dividing line between the North and South hemispheres. To those on manganese deposits were also added experiments in fishery, crop and livestock production, forestry and mining.[50]

To a greater or lesser degree, the Association's reports were adapted by regional and national governments – however, projects like Central Plateau or Campos have not held true to Crawford's propositions, for example. In this percolation, the agency succeeded in its initial objectives of encouraging development programmes that would become national, and the last years of the AIA are paradoxically demonstrated in the ABCAR example.

AIA, ACAR and ABCAR: Final Years

Finally, the AIA started to detach itself from both the ACAR and the ABCAR, although it continued to exert influence over the ABCAR until 1968.[51] In 1960, the consortium agreed to reduce supervised credit for ABCAR-organised programmes. That year, the AIA stated that they understood the difficulty in Federal and State Governments contributing financially. While AIA had contributed $10,000 in August, the plan to open new offices in the state did not reach completion in September: ACAR opened only one office. The lack of resources would soon prompt technicians to leave the programme.[52] From the outset, the AIA's goal was to start a project in Brazil and withdraw when Brazilian

49. Dalrymple, *The AIA Story*, p. 171.

50. Ibid.

51. Ribeiro, *A Saga da Extensão Rural em Minas Gerais*, p. 116.

52. Ibid., p. 3.

technicians were ready to perform the work unsupervised. The objective was to introduce technical cooperation and, after its ideals were adopted, 'get out' of the country.[53] However, this was not the only reason behind the non-renewal of cooperation agreements after 1961. Even if, at that time, a project initiated by the AIA could be considered consolidated, the agreements were not being carried out in the agency's desired way – with governments delaying the transfer of funds, for example. In addition, ABCAR's incorporation process as well as the regional reach of ACAR and other agencies prompted a more complex negotiation process, involving other agents at the local level – the Church, the oligarchies – or at the national level, such as Motta and ABCAR. In the early 1960s, the AIA was not the only agency carrying out this kind of work and thus faced competition for both its legitimacy and its funding.

During the commemorations of ACAR's tenth anniversary in 1959, Walter Crawford's watchful eye analysed whether the Brazilian politicians' speeches referred to the AIA. João Napoleão cited the foundation and Nelson Rockefeller's name. However, he did it in the first paragraph of his speech while adjusting the microphone, and for this reason, the audience did not hear him. The speech of the former governor of Ceará and then President of *Banco do Nordeste*, Raul Barbosa, 'was poorly organized and had no purpose', according to Crawford.[54] Mário Meneghetti, the Minister of Agriculture, communicated 'purely political propaganda for the PTB labor party',[55] while the Governor of Minas Gerais, Bias Fortes, even though he was giving a political speech, praised ACAR and stated that the contract with the AIA would be renewed.[56] Crawford also reported that rumours were circulating that governor Bias Fortes would not continue cooperating with the ACAR/AIA agreement.[57] In this context, Crawford saw the antagonistic relations between the agencies dedicated to the development of Brazilian agriculture as an opportunity to legitimise the AIA.[58] However, the difficult scenario and the growing interest in other projects caused the AIA to

53. Dalrymple, *The AIA Story*.

54. 'Raul Barbosa's speech was poorly organized and had no purpose', no original. From Walter L. Crawford to Louise Boyer, Berent Friele and Lawrence H. Levy. Memorandum. Subject: Report on Brazil program. 13 Sept., 1959. Collection: Family, Record Group: III 4B, Box: 29, Folder: 283. p. 03.

55. From Walter L. Crawford to Louise Boyer, Berent Friele and Lawrence H. Levy. Memorandum. Subject: Report on Brazil program.13 Sept. 1959. Collection: Family, Record Group: III 4B, Box: 29, Folder: 283. p. 3.

56. Ibid.

57. Ibid., pp. 3–4

58. Ibid., p. 4

declare that its contribution to the development of Brazilian agriculture was complete in 1961, and that it would thereafter be incumbent upon Brazilians themselves to carry out this task.[59] Besides the Chilean-Brazilian experience connected to USAID, the AIA and the IRI spent much energy researching the agricultural potential of the upland savannas in Brazil. More than ever, this programme evolved into a great number of national and international partnerships, which lasted for more than four decades. While Nelson Rockefeller or scholars have highlighted the importance of AIA in terms of the politics of post-war international development, when the IRI merged with the AIA between 1957 and 1963, it laid the foundations for the most dramatic environmental change, still ongoing. Nelson Rockefeller died before the Cerrado programme boosted hundreds of colonisation projects, fruit industry, cattle breeding and fattening, and high technological corn, soy, cotton and maize plantations. The NPK project stimulated the frontier advance westward in early 1960s; later, USAID, Embrapa, the World Bank, Japan International Cooperation Agency (JICA) and others carried out the job of modernisation.[60]

The decline of the AIA was interrelated with its difficulties in finding funding commitments, even though the association was never intended to be a permanent Association. Though the budgets of the AIA or the IRI seem high, many documents from both agencies show that the so-called 'backward' Latin American governments hosted for years a visitor that reproduced what it criticised: a high payroll commitment and lavish spending, as opposed to 'rational' use of money. For instance, in 1956, Robert Russell wrote to David Rockefeller about his conversations to raise funds for experimental research with business organisations. 'The returns are now in from practically all the request for funds for Brazil made by IRI last fall', he wrote, concluding that 'the situation … is very discouraging'.[61] While part of the AIA, the IRI tried desperately to use its alleged political capital to convince Juscelino Kubitschek, and later Jânio Quadros, of the importance of building a tropical agriculture and cattle ranching research centre, with the participation of Walther Moreira Salles, former ambassador and partner of Nelson Rockefeller in the Bodoqueña Farm.

59. Ibid., p. 4

60. From Robert Russell to David Rockefeller. 19 Jan. 1956. Rockefeller Archive Center, Collection IRI, Record Group 3.1, Box 477, Folder 2902.

61. From Robert Russell. IBEC Research Institute. Fund-raising activities by Robert P. Russell. [New York], 19 Oct. 1956. Rockefeller Archive Center, Collection IRI, Record Group 3.1, Box 477, Folder 2902

In a long message, Robert Russell summarised the difficulties of convincing US and international agencies such the FAO to support projects: 'As of the time of the discussions in Rome, as well as in Rio it was apparent that there was little hope of securing any FAO or Point Four support' in the field of coffee research. 'No decisions could be made, according to the Rome FAO Director (Dr Phillips), until after the arrival of Dr Krug sometime in August'.[62] Coincidentally or not, the FAO office invited former IAC Dr Carlos Arnaldo Krug – an IRI partner during the Coffee Tillage programme, discussed in Chapter 9 – to work in its tropical field crops department, in Rome. If the contact with Krug seemed to be an advantage, on the other hand, the Brazilian researcher shifted his investigations from coffee to cocoa: 'there is little hope of securing his assistance in gaining funds for IRI's coffee research',[63] stated Russell. Multiple other documents paint a similar picture. Besides the low-budget (neo) imperialist desire to shape the world in the image of the US, Point Four and Alliance for Progress brought to the battlefield of international development a fantastic number of new players. Agencies such as ETA, FAO, Hudgen's International Development Co., in addition to the local players, had also unfolded hundreds of projects clamouring for instant funding: in no time at all, every disgruntled employee who was money also became a possible new competitor for USAID contracts.

According to its proponents, a quiet but effective revolution was already under way,[64] and therefore the work of the AIA would no longer be necessary. On the other hand, when Latin Americans took control over programmes, they also took control over social memory, obscuring the (dis)encounters between Rockefeller-connected US experts and agricultural modernisation in Latin America. The Great Agro-Acceleration of the early 1970s was made effective by the Alliance for Progress with the wave of dictatorships that plagued Latin America in the period; with their disappearance, the Alliance for Progress was also practically forgotten and its results strongly questioned by democratic groups between the 1980s and 2010 – when a new wave of coups began in the region.

62. Ibid.

63. Ibid.

64. Dalrymple, *The AIA Story*, p. 190.

CONCLUSION: MODERNISATION AND DEVELOPMENT AS POLYSEMOUS NOTIONS

If Nelson Rockefeller and his allies planned a brave new world for Latin America, on the ground, confrontations and encounters reshaped the original programmes, causing imperialists not to emerge unscathed from the battlefield of modernisation and development in the Global South. In its relatively short history, the agency had a decisive impact not only on Latin America, but also on US foreign policy itself in subsequent decades. Therefore, I consider the AIA as a milestone for understanding topics such as the relationship between the United States and Latin America and the role of private US agencies in the construction of the post-1945 world. Moreover, in order to develop these modernisation programmes, the oil companies provided money for the adaptation of programmes such as the Extension Service and, finally, the ideology of modernisation and development – and the newly clothed old ideologies of Manifest Destiny, Frontier and Progressivism. Each of these issues, in its specificity or combined in the general context, offers an important framework for understanding entanglements between micro and macro scale world events in the period of the Great Acceleration – when the principles of the Industrial Revolution expanded into diverse areas, including agricultural production, dramatically changing the planet. Even with its moderate contributions to the achievement of global transformations, the genealogy of the great agricultural transformations in the Global South can be linked intrinsically to the ideals of the Rockefeller Foundation, the Ford Foundation and the AIA.

Aiming to explore this complex subject, my study strikes new ground compared to the existing literature on the AIA. That literature has approached the role of Nelson Rockefeller and the AIA in Brazil and Venezuela based on solid archival research. However, previous works examined the figure of Nelson Rockefeller and adopted a top-down approach, emphasising his role as a politician, entrepreneur or decision-maker. In fact, one cannot mention AIA, IBEC or IRI without highlighting the biography of the American multimillionaire. Although this book also emphasised Rockefeller's role in the constitution of a practically new world during and after World War II, his centrality as actor shifted to different levels; Nelson Rockefeller was not identical with the AIA. That is why, at the international level, I highlighted the role of social actors like Kenneth Kadow in elaborating the agency and proposing programmes; although briefly, Henry Wallace or even the other founders of the AIA made important contributions to the development of a modernisation agenda for Latin America – according to their own ideals. On a national level, important characters such as Romulo Betancourt in Venezuela and a number of Brazilian politicians deserve attention, with their nuanced approach to the work of the AIA. In a very general way, the aforementioned AIA and US and Latin America bibliography based its assumptions on straightforward acceptance of the international aid proposed by these foundations and associations, both on a national and on local level. Especially in Brazil, I observed that there was strong resistance to the work of the AIA and its partners, such as ACAR. So this book contributes in two ways: while the literature on peasant resistance in Latin America deals very appropriately with organised movements struggling against capitalist modernisation, I demonstrate that not all resistance has come from the political left-wing. The weight of local communities, within what we generally describe as 'tradition', had a great impact both on the implementation of programmes and on their reorientation or abandonment by modernising agents. The second point is that the national states were very interested in these programmes despite sometimes treating Nelson Rockefeller and the AIA as almost a joke: 'This was an American thing', agronomist José Paulo Ribeiro told me in a distant tone during an informal 2006 conversation at Emater/MG, the institution that evolved directly from ACAR. The ACAR became an important agricultural development model for Brazilians after the Americans' departure, mainly with the creation of ABCAR and later with the research and rural extension network created by the civil-military dictatorship. ACAR, however, evokes a romantic past rather than an institution that provided the theoretical and technical bases for the modernisation of Brazilian agriculture in the following decades.

Several social actors were fundamental in this story, prompting me to avoid simple interpretations of Nelson Rockefeller as a capitalist missionary, a missionary of science, a philanthropist or an imperialist, and to refrain from trying to understand the AIA through the lens of his initial intentions. In fact, the Protestant, philanthropic, liberal, capitalist and democratic ideals conceived by Rockefeller were tributaries to the philosophical underpinnings of his own time and relationships that he established with other agents. This entanglement of ideals served as an instrument of negotiation with Latin American and United States governments. In other words, capitalism and philanthropic rhetoric did not always fulfil expectations, as when communicating with Romulo Betancourt, for example. The Venezuelan leader's Marxist background called into question the business arguments used by the Americans – the usual left-wing contestation of capitalism comes together with the idea that philanthropy is nothing more than smoke and mirrors, eclipsing the true motives of action: the exercise of domination. Therefore, these different configurations attributed to Rockefeller – Protestantism, philanthropy, liberalism, capitalism and democracy – were viewed with distrust by many Latin American politicians and farmers. Actually, Latin America had more or less its own development agenda. This had been built since the end of the nineteenth century, seeking to contain global fluctuations in the price of commodities or to connect central governments to regions considered distant from processes of occupation and industrialisation.

Modernisation and development therefore absorbed local aspects, such as access to land in Venezuela and the maintenance of the latifundia in Brazil. This reality demonstrates that the ideology of modernisation foresaw the need for gradual steps in the transition from a society considered traditional to an industrial one, in the manner of the United States. However, modernisation gradually also meant adoption of practices and programmes considered traditional, such as the trench silo and its uses in the hinterlands of the state of São Paulo. Therefore, when white men in the Global North desiring to expand a business empire encountered a reality that they knew little about, a series of changes occurred and their initial purposes had to adapt to the dynamics of the South. The AIA as an idea or project, in short, did not endure for more than a decade; and the programme practised had little to do with the Yeoman vision highlighted by Kadow. In addition, a fundamental conclusion of this work is that not only did local culture and traditions impose modifications on exogenous programmes, but they also modified the experience of private agencies in Latin America, forcing remodelling of their initially planned actions and, in turn, remodelling the imaginary and actions of politicians, entrepreneurs and decision-makers. As historians and social scientists, we need to focus on more examples of the experiences of the Global North in Latin America, Asia and Africa. We also need to explore how these experiences influenced the empire itself. This is because the bibliography that addresses both the AIA and various other colonial, imperial, or postcolonial experiences is largely interested in how the Global North shaped the actions of the Global South. We need to recognise the contradiction in this interpretive process – that we obliterate how modernising agents, imperialist or otherwise, modified themselves and other regions in countless ways.

Latin Americans, in their own way, adapted the modernisation programmes that AIA proposed while disrupting the formulation and consolidation of foreign policy programmes of global reach. In addition, we can ask, in an exercise of historical imagination, whether if Betancourt, Vargas and the Latin American left had not imposed conditions on American diplomacy or agencies like the AIA and the Rockefeller Foundation, there would have been programmes like Point Four or the Alliance for Progress? Did the experience in Latin America – as well as in Africa or Asia – impose changes in the order of discourse and the budgets of the empire itself, even if the latter sought to consolidate its domination? From this study, it is clear that the agents of modernisation developed a perception that it would be possible to create a model of socio-cultural change adjustable throughout the underdeveloped world with some minor changes. When Robert Hudgens, from his Rockefeller Plaza office, made this statement less than a decade after the Nazis' genocidal policy ended, it was observed by modernisers that even businessmen were inclined to accept that the notion of culture should take precedence over that of race. The exercise of neocolonial or neoimperial domination, in this sense, was to be based in other kinds of strategy: bringing more and more Global South populations into agricultural modernisation projects through supervised credit, with the aim of creating an elite of capitalist farmers. In fact, Hudgens' ideal seems to be nothing more than a daydream of Yeoman expansion: in the following decades, peasant organisations and their ideals of autonomy in the face of capitalism only grew in Latin America and the entire Global South. Institutions like the World Bank and large corporations that entrenched a movement of land concentration and subordination of small farmers to large banks, deepening exclusion, poverty and violence in rural areas, embraced agricultural modernisation. Thus, if we recognise in the proliferation of brutal dictatorships in Latin America the political element that engendered this violent process of conservative modernisation, we find in US foreign policy and in actors like Nelson Rockefeller its main guardians since the 1960s. Throughout his life, Nelson Rockefeller was thus not only a missionary of philanthropy, science or capitalism, a skilful negotiator who interacted with both the left and the right, but also an important supporter of dictatorships that tortured and killed thousands of people.

I reached these conclusions by innovating in primary source research. I and other researchers who have addressed the AIA's trajectory have accessed the Rockefeller Archive Center documents, located in Tarrytown, New York. The beautiful collection of documents made available by the institution– which also provides grants for researchers to explore its collections – has provided much of the information in virtually all the books written about the AIA; and historians have read this information looking for different issues, increasing the complexity of reflections on the importance of the agency. On the other hand, historians are currently debating how the layout of documents, their ordering, the concealment or otherwise of certain memos or notes, can affect the results of research. In short, the information used by researchers to build their analysis, in this case, follows both the narrative elaborated by the archivists – in chronological order, creating folders about the different institutions such as AIA, IBEC and IRI – and by Martha Dalrymple, who explored the AIA archives as early as the 1960s and collected the memories of Hudgens, Bagley and others. However, although I also chose to follow certain chronologies and clues provided by the RAC, I searched for other libraries and archive sources that would point me in other directions; in view of the classical bibliography on the AIA, I chose to include other voices involved in the process. In the primary source research that I conducted in the Emater library of Minas Gerais in 2006, I found official documents and, in addition, I collected a series of reports from the late 1990s, published in celebration of the 50th anniversary of ACAR. In these interviews or simple accounts, typed, the oldest technicians of the institution wrote anecdotes, 'curious facts', aiming to highlight the simplicity of the working conditions at the beginning of ACAR, contrasting with the modern Emater. From the point of view of agricultural technicians and agronomists, we find narratives about the rural environment of Minas Gerais and the mismatches between technical knowledge and tradition. Although this information has informed only a small part of this book, because I did not find similar sources on Venezuela, SAPS, or other programmes, it has helped me understand how the programmes were resized to meet local objectives or even abandoned, and supported my theorising about bottom-up relationships, the advances and setbacks, and the impact on American technical thinking.

Another aspect is that studies on AIA, ACAR, CBR, CIDEA and others provide new implications for the history of science and technology. First, because the Latin American technology ideal was not exactly the same as those of European and North American counterparts in the period. If, as Michael Adas claims, Europeans abandoned the ideals of progress and their relations with technology after the First World War while these continued to be embraced in the United States, the situation in Latin America was at a crossroads. While Marxist critics were wary of the technological advances achieved by capitalist society, which promised better living conditions through adoption of the industrial mode of production, advocates of capitalism understood European and American models as a means to rid the world of communism. Important intellectuals like the Brazilian philosopher Álvaro Vieira Pinto (1909–1987), criticising Marxist orthodoxy, observed the need for Latin Americans to appropriate and subvert technology through autonomous development projects. Technology, in this sense, should be made to serve the objectives of creating better living conditions for peasants and the urban working classes. With this basis, new questions arise, such as how technology, technical and scientific knowledge are reconceived, how materials were transformed into resources and, above all, how the AIA influenced the transformation of the Latin American environment.

Finally, I think that a further research agenda should include the classic insight provided by historian Deborah Fitzgerald. In her 1986 article, Fitzgerald showed how historians somehow abandoned the analysis of the green revolution, leaving the field to economic analysis alone.[1] Historians, in other words, often write their work based on narratives of successes and failures provided by scholars from other fields. Regarding these agricultural modernisation programmes, economists and agronomists often either exalt or criticise their models. Historiography, in my opinion, should follow other paths, considering failure, abandonment and conflict to be elements equally as important as the direct influence of an agency like the AIA. So, I would like to finish this book with a question: after reading it, do you really agree that the march of science and technology overcame the obstacles of language, race and customs? To what extent have the different worlds amalgamated? After all, in his nomination speech in 1974, Nelson summarised the problems assailing his venture in Latin America, saying of IBEC – and here AIA and IRI are included: 'I lost a great deal of money in the early days in this corporation. This was because many of the experiences of this country were not translatable directly into the other countries'.

Five decades after Rockefeller's reflections, neither governments nor private global institutions have yet learned the most superficial lessons about adaptability of development projects created in the Northern Hemisphere. Similarly, it seems that the same actors have not learned the deeper lessons that development and modernisation *per se* still involve hierarchies and domination, even if accompanied by concepts such as sustainability.

1. Deborah Fitzgerald, 'Exporting American Agriculture: The Rockefeller Foundation in Mexico, 1943–53', *Social Studies of Science* 16 (3) (1986): 457–83.

APPENDIX

Timeline of the AIA

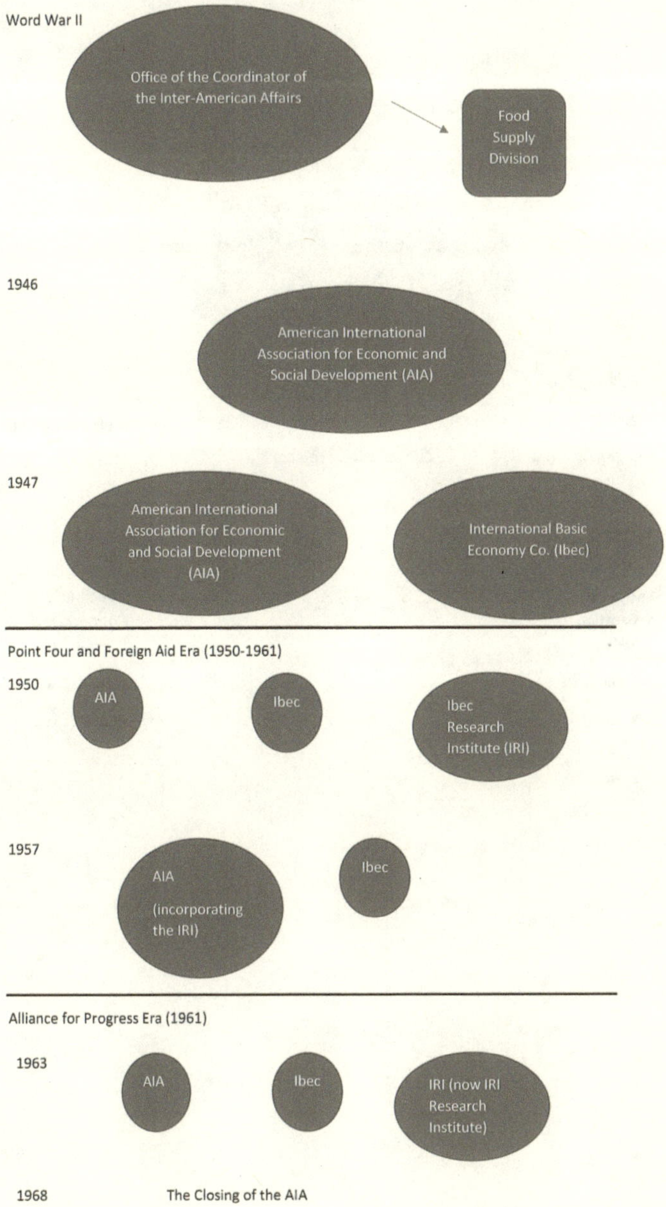

Spider Organogram of the AIA

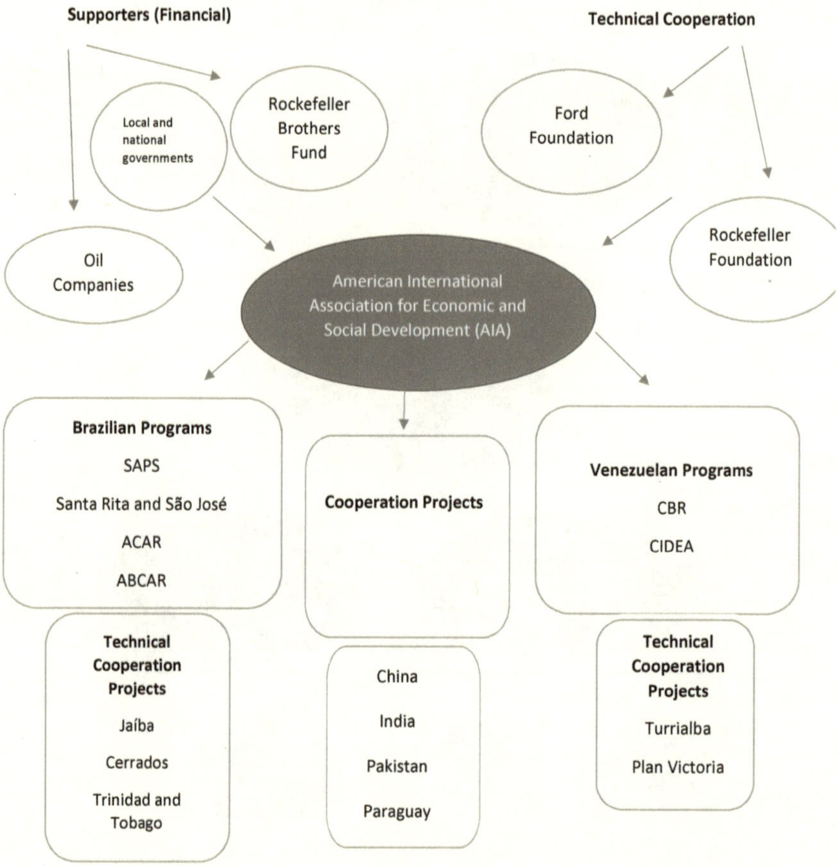

BIBLIOGRAPHY

Adas, Michael. 2003. 'Modernization theory and the American revival of the scientific and technological standards of social achievement and human worth'. In David Engerman, Nils Gilman, Mark Haefele and Michael Latham, Michael (eds). *Staging Growth. Modernization, Development, and the Global Cold War*. Amherst: University of Massachusetts Press.

Arnal, Yollanda Texera. 2014. 'Extranjeros en el Ministerio de Agricultura y Cría de Venezuela. 1936–1958'. *Bitácora-e Revista Electrónica Latinoamericana de Estudios Sociales, Históricos y Culturales de la Ciencia y la Tecnología*, n 2.

Azevedo, Cecília. 2008. *Em nome da América: os Corpos de Paz no Brasil (1961–1981)*. Rio de Janeiro: Alameda.

Bethel, Leslie. 1992. 'Introduction. The postwar conjuncture in Latin America: democracy, labor, and the left'. In Leslie Bethel and Ian Roxborough (eds). *Latin American between the Second World War and Cold War, 1944–1948*. New York: Cambridge University Press, 1992.

Beçak, Peggy. 2007. *Evolução das relações comerciais Brasil – Estados Unidos de 1945 a 1995: no contexto da política externa e dos 'interesses nacionais'*. Ph.D. Dissertation in History of Economy, University of São Paulo.

Benedict, Murray. 1953. *Farm Policies of the United States, 1790–1950: A Study of Their Origins and Development*. New York: Twentieth Century Fund.

Biasillo, Roberta and Claito Marcio da Silva. 2019. 'Cultivating arid soils in Libya and Brazil during World War II: The two-fold war between colonial and neo-colonial experiences'. *Global Environment* 12 (1).

Campos, André Luiz Vieira de. 2006. *Políticas internacionais de saúde na Era Vargas: o Serviço Especial de Saúde Pública, 1942–1960*. Rio de Janeiro: Editora Fiocruz.

Carvalho, José Murilo de. 2005. '"Ouro, terra e ferro". Vozes de Minas'. In Ângela de Castro Gomes (ed.) *Minas e os fundamentos do Brasil moderno*. Belo Horizonte: UFMG.

Clifford, Clark with Richard Holbrooke. 1991. *Counsel to the President. A Memoir*. New York: Random House.

Cobbs, Elizabeth. 1988. *Good Work at a Profit. Private Development and United States – Brazil Relation (1945–1960)*. Ph.D. Dissertation in History, Standford.

Colby, Gerard and Charlotte Dennet. 2017. *Thy Will Be Done: The Conquest of the Amazon: Nelson Rockefeller and Evangelism in the Age of Oil*. New York: Open Road Media.

Coronil, Fernando. 1998. 'Foreword'. In Joseph Gilbert, Catherine Legrandand Ricardo Salvatore (eds). 1998. *Close Encounters of Empire: Writing the Cultural History of U.S.-Latin America Relations*. Durham: Duke University Press.

Cotta, Luiza Cristina Villaméa. 2008. *Adhemar de Barros (1901–1969): a origem do 'rouba, mas faz'*. M.A. Dissertation in History of Economy, University of São Paulo.

Cueto, Marcos (ed.) 1994. *Missionaries of Science: The Rockefeller Foundation and Latin America*. Bloomington: Indiana University Press.

Curti, Merle and Kendall Birr. 1954. *Prelude to Point Four. American Technical Missions Overseas (1838–1938)*. Madison, Wisconsin: The University of Wisconsin Press.

Dalrymple, Martha. 1968. *The AIA Story: Two Decades of International Cooperation*. New York: AIA.

Dean, Warren. 1997. *With Broadax and Firebrand. The Destruction of the Brazilian Atlantic Forest*. Oakland, CA: University of California Press.

Delgado, Ignácio. 1995. 'Independência econômica de Minas Gerais: Imagens do Discurso do Empresariado Mineiro nos anos 40 e 50'. *Revista Locus – Revista de História* 1 (1). Juiz de Fora: EDUFJF.

Dicionário Histórico Biográfico Brasileiro pós-1930. 2001. 2nd ed. Rio de Janeiro: Editora da Fundação Getúlio Vargas (FGV).

Dulci, Otávio Soares. 1999. *Política e recuperação econômica em Minas Gerais*. Belo Horizonte: UFMG.

Engerman, David, Nils Gilman, Mark Haefele and Michael Latham (eds). 2003. *Staging Growth. Modernization, Development, and the Global Cold War*. Amherst: University of Massachusetts Press.

Escobar, Arturo. 1995. *Encountering Development. The Making and Unmaking of the Third World*. Princeton, New Jersey: Princeton University Press.

Evangelista, Ana Maria da Costa and Dalva Carolina de Menezes Yazbeck. 2008. 'Serviço de alimentação da previdência social (SAPS)'. *Revista Virtú*, Juiz de Fora: Universidade Federal de Juiz de Fora.

Fitzgerald, Deborah. 1986. 'Exporting American agriculture: The Rockefeller Foundation in Mexico, 1943–53'. *Social Studies of Science* 16 (3): 457–83.

Fitzgerald, Deborah. 2003. *Every Farm a Factory. The Industrial Ideal in American Agriculture*. New Haven: Yale University Press.

da Fonseca, Maria Rachel Fróes et al. Escola Superior de Agricultura e Veterinária. In *Dicionário Histórico-Biográfico das Ciências da Saúde no Brasil (1832–1930)*. Rio de Janeiro: Casa de Oswaldo Cruz/Fiocruz – http://www.dichistoriasaude.coc.fiocruz.br.

de Freitas, Luís Martins, Andrew Colin McClung and Wreal Lott. 1960. *Field Studies on Fertility Problems of Two Campos Cerrados, 1958–1959*. New York: Ibec Research Institute.

Galeano, Eduardo. 1997. *Open Veins of Latin America: Five Centuries of the Pillage of a Continent*. New York: Monthly Review Press.

Garfield, Seth. 2010. 'The environment of wartime migration: Labor transfers from the Brazilian Northeast to the Amazon during World War II'. *Journal of Social History* 43.

Garfield, Seth. 2020. 'A Amazônia no imaginário norte-americano em tempo de guerra'. In Magali Romero Sá, Dominichi Miranda de Sá and André Felipe Cândido da Silva (eds), *As Ciências na História das Relações Brasil-EUA*. Rio de Janeiro: Mauad X.

Haag, Carlos. 2009. 'O capitalista missionário: a aventura brasileira de Nelson Rockefeller', *Revista Pesquisa Fapesp*, São Paulo, n. 157.

Hamilton, Shane. 2018. *Supermarket USA. Food and Power in the Cold War Farms Race*. New Haven and London: Yale University Press.

Hamilton, Shane. 2019. 'Distributing legitimacy: the politics of milk in post-World War II Venezuela'. *History of Retailing and Consumption* 5 (1)

Harrington, Jerome and Bill Sorenson. 2004. *O desenvolvimento das terras de cerrado do Brasil: a experiência do IRI.* São Paulo: Agronômica Ceres/Instituto de Pesquisas IRI.

Heale, Michael. 2004. *Twentieth-Century America: Politics and Power in the United States, 1900–2000.* London: Arnold-Hodder Headline Group.

Immerwahr, Daniel. 2015. *Thinking Small. The United States and the Lure of Community Development.* Cambridge, Massachusetts; London: Harvard University Press.

Krug, Carlos Arnaldo et al. 1952. 'Melhoramento do cafeeiro. IV - Café Mundo Novo'. *Bragantia* 12 (4–6): 97–129.

Latham, Michael. 2000. *Modernization as Ideology. American Social Sciences and the 'Nation Building' in the Kennedy Era.* Chapel Hill: The University of North Carolina Press.

Latham, Michael. 2003. 'Introduction: modernization, international history, and the Cold War World'. In David Engerman, Nils Gilman, Mark Haefele and Michael Latham (eds). *Staging Growth. Modernization, Development, and the Global Cold War.* Amherst: University of Massachusetts Press.

Lopes, Alfredo Scheide and Luiz Roberto Guimarães Guilherme. 2007. 'Fertilidade do solo e produtividade agrícola'. In Roberto Ferreira Novaes et al. *Fertilidade do solo.* Viçosa: Sociedade Brasileira de Ciência do Solo.

López, J.J. Rojas. 2016. *Del agrarismo histórico a los desafíos del desarrollo territorial em Venezuela.* Caracas.

Loureiro, Felipe. 2020. *A Aliança para o Progresso e o governo João Goulart (1961–1964). Ajuda econômica norte-americana a estados brasileiros e a desestabilização da democracia no Brasil pós-guerra.* São Paulo: Editora da UNESP.

Maddox, James and Howard Tolley. 1956. *Case Studies of Training Through Technical Cooperation.* NPA.

Marinho, Maria Gabriela. 2001. *Norte-americanos no Brasil. Uma história da Fundação Rockefeller na Universidade de São Paulo (1934–1952).* Campinas: Autores Associados; São Paulo: Universidade São Francisco.

Martin, Roscoe. 1952. 'Technical assistance: The problem of implementation', *Public Administration Review* 12 (4).

McCann, Jr, Frank. 1973. *The Brazilian-American Alliance, 1937–1945.* Princeton University Press.

McClung, Andrew Colin, Luis Martins de Freitas, D.S. Mikkelsen and Wreal Lott. 1961. *Cotton Fertilization in Campo Cerrado Soils of the State of São Paulo, Brazil.* New York, IBEC Research Institute).

McCook, Stuart. 2000. *States of Nature: Science, Agriculture and Environment in the Spanish Caribbean (1760–1940).* Austin: Texas University Press.

McCook, Stuart. 2019. *Coffee is Not Forever. A Global History of the Coffee Leaf Rust.* Athens, Ohio: Ohio University Press.

McDonald, Bryan. 2017. *Food Power. The Rise and Fall of the Postwar American Food System.* New York: Oxford University Press.

de Mendonça, Sonia Regina. 1998. 'Agricultura, Poder e Estado no Brasil: um projeto contra-hegemônico na Primeira República'. In Sonia Regina Mendonça and Márcia Motta (eds). *Nação e Poder: As Dimensões da História*. Niterói: EDUFF. v. 1.

de Mendonça, Sonia Regina. 1998. *Agronomia e poder no Brasil.* Rio de Janeiro: Vício de Leitura.

Oberg, Kalervo. 1966. 'Community center project at Chonin, Brazil'. In Arthur Niehof (ed.) *A Casebook of Social Change*. Chicago: Aldine Publishing Company.

Olinger, Glauco. 1996. *Ascensão e decadência da Extensão Rural no Brasil.* Florianópolis: EPAGRI.

Palmer, Steven. 1998. 'Central American encounters with Rockefeller public health, 1914–1921'. In Gilbert Joseph, Catherine Legrand and Ricardo Salvatore (eds). *Close Encounters of Empire: Writing the Cultural History of U.S.-Latin America Relations*. Durham: Duke University Press.

Prutsch, Ursula. 2010. 'Americanization of Brazil or a pragmatic wartime alliance? The politics of Nelson Rockefeller's Office of Inter-American Affairs in Brazil during World War II'. *Passagens. Revista Internacional de História Política e Cultura Jurídica* 2 (4). Rio de Janeiro.

Reich, Cary. 1996. *The Life of Nelson A. Rockefeller: Worlds to Conquer (1908–1958)*. New York: Doubleday.

Rockefeller, David. 2003. *Memoirs*. New York: Random House Trade.

Ribeiro, Leonardo Gomes. 2013. '*Progredir sempre*'. *Os jovens rurais mineiros nos Clubes 4-S. Saber, Sentir, Servir, Saúde*. M.A. Dissertation in Education, Universidade Federal de Minas Gerais.

Ribeiro, José Paulo. 2000. *A Saga da Extensão Rural em Minas Gerais*. São Paulo: Annablume; Minas Gerais: CPP/Emater.

Ribeiro, José Paulo and Geraldo Machado. 1964. *A situação atual da extensão no Brasil.* Rio de Janeiro: Fundação Antunes.

Rivas, Darlene. 2002. *Missionary Capitalist: Nelson Rockefeller in Venezuela.* Chapel Hill, North Carolina: University of North Carolina Press.

Saath, Reni. 2007. *Microscopia eletrônica de varredura do endosperma do café (Coffea arábica L.) durante o processo de secagem*. M.A. Dissertation in Agricultural Engineering, Universidade Federal de Lavras (state of Minas Gerais).

Saloutos, Theodore. 1982. *The American Farmer and the New Deal.* Ames: The Iowa University Press.

Sanchez, P.A. and S.W. Buol. 1980. *Trip Report to Indonesia and Sri Lanka by Soil Management CRSP Planning Team*. Bogor, Indonesia.

Saraiva, Tiago. 2018. 'Anthropophagy and sadness: cloning citrus in São Paulo in the Plantationocene era'. *History and Technology* **34** (1): 89–99.

Scott, James. 1999. *Seeing Like a State: How Certain Schemes to Improve the Human Condition Have Failed.* New Haven, CT: Yale University Press.

da Silva, Claiton Marcio. 2013. 'Uma contribuição para o desenvolvimento de sua comunidade e da Pátria: juventude rural e Clubes 4-S durante a ditadura militar na região oeste de Santa Catarina (1970–1985)'. *Cadernos do Ceom* **23** (33).

da Silva, Claiton Marcio. 2015. *De agricultor a farmer. Nelson Rockefeller e a moderniza- ção da agricultura no Brasil.* Guarapuava/Curitiba: Unicentro/UFPR.

da Silva, Claiton Marcio and Claudio de Majo. 2020. 'The making of a pastureland biome: American scientists, miracle grasses and the transformation of the Brazilian *Cerrado*'. *Environment and History* **29**(2): 185–210.

Siqueira, Jack. 2001. *Planejamento e desenvolvimento em Minas.* Belo Horizonte: Armazém de Ideias.

Sternsher, Bernard. 1964. *Rexford Tugwell and the New Deal.* New Brunswick: Rutgers University Press.

Tota, Antônio Pedro. 2014. *O Amigo Americano. Nelson Rockefeller e o Brasil.* São Paulo: Companhia das Letras.

Tota, Antônio Pedro. 2000. *O imperialismo sedutor: a americanização do Brasil na época da Segunda Guerra.* São Paulo: Companhia das Letras.

Turner, Frederick Jackson. 'The significance of the frontier in American History, 1893'. In John Mack Faragher (ed.) *Rereading Frederick Jackson Turner.* New York: Holt, 1994. pp. 31–60.

United States Agency for International Development Mission to El Salvador. Action Memorandum for the Mission Director. *Project Assistance Completion Report of the 'Coffee Technology Transfer' Project n. 519-0362*, 16 October 1998.

Vieira, Luiz Goes. 1988. *Extensão rural. Origem, evolução, conceituação, filosofia, princípios.* Recife: Universidade Federal de Pernambuco.

Viscardi, Claudia Maria Ribeiro. 2004. 'Mutualismo e filantropia'. *Locus. Revista de História* **10** (1). Juiz de Fora.

Wagley, Charles. 1963. *An Introduction to Brazil.* New York: Columbia University Press.

Wade, Michael K. et al. 1988. 'Overcoming soil fertility constraints in a transmigration area of Indonesia'. *TropSoils Bulletin* **88** (1).Raleigh, North Carolina State University.

Went, Fritz. 1957. *The Experimental Control of Plant Growth. With Special Reference to the Earhart Plant Research Laboratory at the California Institute of Technology.* With contributions by W.C. Ashby. New York: Ronald Press Co.

Archival Sources

(a) Correspondence and memoranda (Rockefeller Archive Center)

From Kenneth J. Kadow to Nelson A. Rockefeller. 7 December 1945. Collection: Family, Record Group: III 4B, Box: 01, Folder: AIA – Bolivar Foundation.

From Nelson A. Rockefeller to Mr. John D. Rokefeller, Jr. Subject: Proposed American International Association. 27 April 1946. Collection: Family; Record Group: III 4B; Box: 11, Folder: 104.

From Robert Hudgens to Chester C. Davis. 12 January 1951. Collection: Family, Record Group: III 4B, Box: 03, Folder 23 AIA – Ford Foundation. p. 09.

From Walter L. Crawford to the Board of Directors of AIA. Subject: Grant to AIA from Rockefeller Brothers Fund for Brazil Program. 6 January 1956. Collection: Family; Record Group: III 4B; Box: 01; Folder: 7B, AIA Brazil.

From Kenneth Kadow to Nelson A. Rockefeller and John Lockwood. Memorandum (no date). Collection: Family. Record Group: III 4 B. Box 01, Folder AIA – Simon Bolivar Foundation.

From Nelson A. Rockefeller to Mr. John D. Rokefeller, Jr. Subject: Proposed American International Association. 27 April 1946. Collection: Family; Record Group: III 4B; Box: 11, Folder: 104.

From Joan to Mr. Nelson [Rockefeller]. Memorandum. Subject: General objectives of the American International Association for Economic and Social Development. Collection: [Family], Record Group: III 4B, Folder: AIA General 1946-1958, n. 02.

From Nelson A. Rockefeller to Frank P. Corrigan. 26 September 1945. Collection: Family, Record Group: III 4B, Box: 01, Folder: AIA – Bolivar Foundation.

From Kenneth Kadow to Nelson A. Rockefeller. Re: Personnel. Newark, Delaware, 29 December 1945. Collection: Family. Record Group: III 4 B. Box 01, Folder AIA – Simon Bolivar Foundation.

From Kenneth Kadow to Nelson A. Rockefeller. Re: Board of Trustees. Newark, Delaware, 29 December 1945. Collection: Family. Record Group: III 4 B. Box 01, Folder AIA – Simon Bolivar Foundation.

From Nelson Rockefeller to Robert J. Kleberg Jr. 21 February 1946. Collection: Family, Record Group: III 4B, Box: 01, Folder: AIA – Bolivar Foundation.

From Kenneth J. Kadow to Nelson A. Rockefeller. 7 December 1945. Collection: Family, Record Group: III 4B, Box: 01, Folder: AIA – Bolivar Foundation

From Robert Kleberg Jr to Nelson A. Rockefeller. Kingsville, Texas. 5 May 1946. Collection: Family. Record Group: III 4 B. Box 01, Folder AIA – Simon Bolivar Foundation.

From Nelson A. Rockefeller to Rafael Oreamuno. 2 April 1946. Collection: Family. Record Group: III 4 B. Box 01, Folder AIA – Simon Bolivar Foundation.

From Kadow to Nelson A. Rockefeller. 26 February 1946. Collection: Family. Record Group: III 4 B. Box 01, Folder AIA – Simon Bolivar Foundation.

From Nelson A. Rockefeller to Mr. Romulo Betancourt. English translation. 19 June 1947. Collection: Family; Record Group: III 4B; Box: 27; Folder: 269.

From Frank P. Corrigan to Nelson A. Rockefeller. Personal and confidential. Caracas, Venezuela, 21 November 1944. Collection: Family. Record Group: III 4 B. Box 01, Folder AIA – Simon Bolivar Foundation.

From Frank P. Corrigan to Nelson A. Rockefeller. Personal. 21 July 1945. Collection: Family. Record Group: III 4 B. Box 01, Folder AIA – Simon Bolivar Foundation.

From Nelson A. Rockefeller to Gene Holman. 14 November 1945. Collection: Family, Record Group: III 4B, Box: 01, Folder: AIA – Bolivar Foundation.

From Frank Corrigan to Nelson Rockefeller, Caracas, Venezuela, 6 November 1945. Collection: Family. Record Group: III 4 B. Box 01, Folder AIA – Simon Bolivar Foundation.

From John E. Lockwood to Nelson A. Rockefeller. American International Association. Program for Brazil. 21 May 1946. Collection: Family. Record Group: III 4 B. Box 01, Folder AIA – Simon Bolivar Foundation.

From Valentim F. Bouças to Nelson A. Rockefeller. Rio de Janeiro, 9 May 1947. Family. Record Group: III 4 B. Box 13, Folder 134.

From Kenneth Kadow to Morrison G. Tucker. Memorandum. Subject: Fertilizers. Rio de Janeiro, 21 May 1947. Family. Record Group: III 4 B. Box 13, Folder 134.

From Lawrence H. Levy to Executive Committee of the AIA. Memorandum. Fertilizer Experiments in Brazil. 15 October 1947. Family. Record Group: III 4 B. Box 13, Folder 134.

From AIA – Rio de Janeiro to AIA – New York. Memorandum. Subject: AIA Program n. Brazil 01. Rio de Janeiro, 25 July 1947.

From Dee Jackson to Berent Friele. Rio de Janeiro, 3 October 1947. Family. Record Group: III 4 B. Box 13, Folder 135.

From Kenneth Kadow to AIA. Brazil Project n. 1, Home Demonstration Service. 20 August 1948. Family. Record Group: III 4 B. Box 13, Folder 135.

From Morrison G. Tucker to Berent Friele and Dee Jackson. AIA project – number 01 – Brazil Nutrition and Home Demonstration Program. Family. Record Group: III 4 B. Box 13, Folder 135.

From Willian A. Alton to Nelson Rockefeller. Memorandum. Report on visit to Venezuela and Brasil. Personal and confidential. 11 November 1947. Collection: Family. Record Group: III 4 B. Box 01, Folder: Alton, W. H.

From Eurico G. Dutra to Valentim Fernandes Bouças. Rio de Janeiro, 10 April 1947. Family. Record Group: III 4 B. Box 13, Folder 134.

From Henry Bagley to Martha Dalrymple. Subject: Recollections of AIA in Brazil. 5 October 1967. Collection: AIA, Record Group IV IIIB, Box 02, Folder 19.

From Henry Bagley to Dionysio Guedes Barreto. 3 August1956. Collection: AIA (closed section), Box 01, Folder: General AIA (including some India papers).

From Walter Crawford to Wallace Harrison. Subject: Renewal and extension of the AIA São Paulo agreement. 27 May 1954. Collection: Family, Record Group: III 4B, Box 01, Folder 7, AIA Brazil.

From Henry Bagley to Dick Greenebaum. Subject: AIA in state of São Paulo. 28 January 1955. Collection: Family, Record Group: III 4B, Box: 01, Folder 07, AIA Brazil.

From Walter L. Crawford to The Board of Directors of AIA. Subject: Grant to AIA from Rockefeller Brothers Fund for Brazil Program. 6 January 1956. Collection: Family; Record Group: III 4B; Box: 01; Folder: 7B, AIA Brazil.

From Henry Bagley to Francis Jamieson. São Paulo, 17 April 1953. AIA Correspondence. Memorandum (misc.) 1948-1959, 1966. Box 02, folder 14.

From Lawrence H. Levy to Robert Hudgens and Stacy May. Memorandum. Subject: AIA – Fourth Point of President Truman's Program. 7 March 1949.

From Nelson A. Rockefeller to T. Quartim Barbosa. Confidential. 27 July 1949. Collection: Family; Record Group: III 4B; Box 01; Folder: 06 AIA – Barbosa, T. Q.

From Robert Hudgens to Chester C. Davis. 12 January 1951. Collection: Family, Record Group: III 4B, Box: 03, Folder 23 AIA – Ford Foundation.

From Robert Hudgens to Haldore Hanson. 9 August 1950. Collection: AIA (closed section); Box: 02.

From Walter Crawford to Louise A. Boyer. Confidential. Brazil Program. 8 August 1958. Collection: Family, Record Group: III 4B, Box: 29, Folder 283.

Excerpts from letter of 20 October 1955 from Harry W. Bagley, AIA representative in Brazil. Collection: Family, Record Group: III 4B, Box 01, Folder 07 AIA – Brazil.

From Henry Bagley to Francis A. Jamieson. Collection: Family. Record Group: III 4 B. Box 01, Folder AIA – General 1946–1958 2(A).

From [Harry Bagley] to Walter Crawford. 12 October 1956.

From Walter Crawford to Louise A. Boyer. Rio de Janeiro, 9 March 1956. Collection: Family, Record Group: III 4B, Box: 01, Folder 07 B, AIA – Brazil.

From Santiago Apodaca to Walter Crawford. 4 October 1955. Collection: Family, Record Group: III 4B, Box 01, Folder 07 AIA – Brazil.

Excerpt – Letter 15 May 1956 from Santiago D. Apodaca to Walter L. Crawford. Collection: Family, Record Group: III 4B, Box: 01, Folder 07 B, AIA – Brazil.

From Henry Bagley to Walter Crawford. Bahia, 15 May 1956. Collection: Family, Record Group: III 4B, Box: 01, Folder 07 B, AIA – Brazil.

From Henry Bagley to Francis A. Jamieson. Confidential. 29 February 1956. Collection: Family, Record Group: III 4B, Box: 01, Folder 07 B, AIA – Brazil.

Translation of letter, which accompanied draft of national ACAR statutes. Collection: Family, Record Group: III 4B, Box; 01, Folder 07 AIA – Brazil.

From Walter Lion Crawford to Lawrence Levy. 10 February 1957. Collection: AIA, Box 01, Folder 14.

From Walter L. Crawford to Louise Boyer, Berent Friele and Lawrence H. Levy. Memorandum. Subject: Report on Brazil program. 13 September 1959. Collection: Family, Record Group: III 4B, Box: 29, Folder: 283.

From John B. Griffing to Paulo César de Azevedo Antunes. 30 March 1953. Collection: AIA (closed section), Box 01, Folder: operations.

H.F. Prioleau. Memorandum. Proposed Latin American Foundation. 28 September 1945. Collection: Family, Record Group: III 4B, Box: 01, Folder: AIA – Bolivar Foundation.

Dee Jackson. Memorandum for Project n. 1 (SAPS). 13 February 1947. Family. Record Group: III 4 B. Box 13, Folder 135.

Nelson Rockefeller papers. Bolivar Foundation papers. AIA-IBEC Box 1 RAC.

(b) Projects and reports

The Bolivar Foundation. Attached to From Kenneth J. Kadow to Nelson A. Rockefeller. 7 December 1945. Collection: Family, Record Group: III 4B, Box: 01, Folder: AIA – Bolivar Foundation.

The American International Association for Economic and Social Development. An explanation of its objectives and method of operation by Kenneth J. Kadow for Nelson A. Rockefeller. 19 February 1946. Collection: Family. Record Group: III 4 B. Box 01, Folder AIA – Simon Bolivar Foundation.

AIA. The first three years. Collection: Family, Record Group: II 4B, Box: 01, Folder AIA General 1946–1958, n. 02(a).

American International Association for Economic and Social Development. Project n. Brazil 1 – Revised. Title: Home Demonstration Service. Collection: Family, Record Group III 4B, Box 13, Folder 135. [1947]

American International Association for Economic and Social Development. Fertilizer experiments in Brazil. Project n. AIA – 5 – Brazil. Proposed by Dee Jackson. 1 December 1947. Family. Record Group: III 4 B. Box 13, Folder 134.

International Basic Economy Corporation. Legal report on status of corporation. 10 January 1947. Family. Record Group: III 4 B. Box 01, Folder AIA – Simon Bolivar Foundation.

Recommendations for a nutrition program in Brazil. [By Louise Stanley] Collection: Family, Record Group III 4B, Box 13, Folder 135. p. 01. [1947]

American International Association for Economic and Social Development. A statement of organization, activities and objectives. January 1949. Collection AIA, Box 10, Folder 85.

IBEC Research Inc. (IRI) Report. RAC. AIA documents.

American International Association for Economic and Social Development. Collection: Family, Record Group III 4B, Box 01, Folder: AIA – Bolivar Foundation.

Third quarterly report to the Board of Directors. (July–Sept. 1953). Collection: AIA, Record Group IV 3B, Box 15, Folder 132.

AIA Highlights. 24 June, 7 July 1954. Collection: AIA. Box 02, Folder 17.

American International Association for Economic and Social Development. Fourth quarterly report to the Board of Director. (Oct.-Nov.-Dec. 1953). Collection: AIA, Record Group IV 3B, Box 15, Folder 132.

Five-year program proposal for Brazil, Peru, and one country in the Middle East. Collection: Family, Record Group: III 4B, Box: 01, Folder 07 AIA – Brazil.

Notes on a formation of an ACAR do Brasil. Collection: Family, Record Group: III 4B, Box: 01, Folder: 07 AIA – Brazil. p. 03.

Study of the possibilities of the creation in the State of São Paulo of a program of technical assistance and supervised credit. Collection: Family, Record Group: III 4B, Box: 01, Folder 07 AIA – Brazil.

American International Association for Economic and Social Development. Condensed progress report. July–September 1960. Collection: AIA, Record Group: IV 3B, Box 15, Folder 134.

Memorandum. Re: Increase in scope of Ibec Research Institute Activities. Collection: IRI RESEACH INSTITUTE, Record Group: 3.1, Box 475. Folder: 2891.

Memo of Conversations. Ford Foundation on Wednesday evening, May 16th. New York, 21 May 1951. Collection Family, Record Group III 4B, Box 3, Folder 23 – AIA Ford Foundation.

A Few Comments on Communist Party Strategy in Kerala. Collection Family, Box 1, Folder General. F. W. Went. IRI Coffee studies at California Institute of Technology. Part I. Report on coffee Research in Earhart carried out for Ibec Research Institute. October 1954. Rockefeller Archive Center. Collection IRI, Record Group 3.1, Box 476, Folder 2898.

IRI Minutes of the Board of Trustees Meeting. 15 January 1953. Rockefeller Archive Center, Collection IRI, Record Group 3.1, Box 475, Folder 2893.

IBEC Research Institute, *IRI-Brazil. Progress Report to Trustees*, December 1958. Rockefeller Archive Center. Collection IRI, Record Group 3.1, Box 477, Folder 2904.

IBEC Research Institute, *Report to the Trustees, 1956–1957*. Rockefeller Archive Center. Collection: IRI. Record Group: 3.1 Box: 477 Folder: 2903 November 1950 to December 1956 IBEC Research Institute Report November 1950 to December 1956.

From Sherman Leonard to Jerome Harrington. São Paulo, 2 May 1955. Rockefeller Archive Center, Collection IRI, Record Group 3.1, Box 476, Folder 2899.

Excerpts from letter of 20 October 1955 from Harry W. Bagley, AIA representative in Brazil. Collection: Family, Record Group: III 4B, Box 01, Folder 07 AIA – Brazil.

(c) Scientific papers

Griffing, John B. 1953. Air view of the forest. Collection AIA, Record Group IV 3B, Box 02, Folder 12.

Griffing, John B. 1953. Theory and practice in rural improvement. Collection: AIA (closed section), Box 01, Folder: operations.

From Robert Russell. IBEC Research Institute. Fund-raising activities by Robert P. Russell. [New York], 19 October1956. Rockefeller Archive Center, Collection IRI, Record Group 3.1, Box 477, Folder 2902.

Development of methods to improve and to exploit improved moisture relationships. Rockefeller Archive Center, Collection IRI, Record Group 3.1, Box 475, Folder 2894.

Teeter, Paul and Paul Leonard. 1955. Coffee Processing Research for 1955. IBEC Research Institute: Matão. Rockefeller Archive Center. Collection IRI, Record Group 3.1, Box 476, Folder 2900.

Foote, H. Elliott. 1954. A study of the drying of coffee on the terreiro. São Paulo: IRI. Rockefeller Archive Center, Collection IRI, Record Group 3.1, Box 476, Folder 2897.

Bibliography

ACAR (Emater Minas Gerais)

(a) Newspaper clippings

Eis o discurso do Dr. Afonso Paulino. São João Nepumoceno, MG, 19 August 1956. [Newspaper clipping from EMATER Collection]

Jornal O Paraguassú. Paraguassú, Minas Gerais, 2 August 1959.

(b) Book of minutes and reports:

ACAR. Associação de Crédito e Assistência Rural. Relatório do diretor para membros da Junta Administrativa – 1949 a 1953 [Report of Director to the Junta Administrativa da ACAR]. Belo Horizonte: ACAR, 1953.

MINAS GERAIS. ACAR. Report 1956/57. Belo Horizonte [1957].

MINAS GERAIS. ACAR 1959. Dez anos a serviço do povo rural mineiro. Belo Horizonte, 1959.

MINAS GERAIS. ACAR. Programa para o ano agrícola 1959/60. Belo Horizonte, 1962.

(c) Projeto Memória (typewritten or handwritten memoirs of ACAR agronomists and home economists)

Paula, José Alfredo Amaral de. Fatos históricos da ACAR, pesquisados pelo Eng. Agr. José Alfredo Amaral de Paula, Coordenador do Projeto Memória da Emater-MG. Belo Horizonte: EMATER [s.d].

PROJETO MEMÓRIA. 40 anos de extensão rural em Poté. Município: Poté, Minas Gerais.

PROJETO MEMÓRIA. Escritório Local. Candeias.

PROJETO MEMÓRIA. Escritório de Santa Luzia.

PROJETO MEMÓRIA. Fatos pitorescos sobre a ACAR em Lagoa da Prata.

PROJETO MEMÓRIA. 40 anos de extensão rural em Poté. Município: Poté, Minas Gerais.

PROJETO MEMÓRIA. Do: ESLOC/UBÁ Para: ESREG/VIÇOSA. N. 262. DATA: 20-11-91.

(d) Interviews and correspondence

Andrade, João Napoleão de. Entrevista concedida à Romeu Padilha de Figueiredo. Belo Horizonte, 11 November 1981. (Projeto 'Registro da Memória Histórica e Técnica da Extensão Rural no Brasil', da Emater-MG).

Crawford, Walter. Entrevista concedida a Euclides Martins. Belo Horizonte: EMATER, 10 December 1981.

From Walter Crawford and Eugene P. Campbell to Ari Torres and Melvin Dohan. 9 October 1951. (EMATER; Pr. 08, Cx. 55, Doc.14)

From Juscelino Kubitschek to Ari Torres. Belo Horizonte, 22 August 1951. (EMATER; Pr. 08, Cx. 55, Doc.14).

From Ivan T. Cajueiro to Walter Crawford. Belo Horizonte, 25 February 1953.

Livro de Atas da Junta Administrativa da ACAR 1959–1970. Belo Horizonte, 1970.

(e) Other sources and collections

Oliveira, Juscelino Kubitschek de. Mensagem ao Congresso Nacional. Rio de Janeiro, 1956.

Oliveira, Juscelino Kubitschek de. Mensagem ao Congresso Nacional. Rio de Janeiro, 1957.

Oral history interview with Christine Hardy Little. Arlington, Virginia (United States), 23 February 1973. Available in http://www.trumanlibrary.org/oralhist/littlech.htm. Accessed 19 May 2009.

Revista Veja, Os olhos de Washington, São Paulo, n.41, 18 June 1969.

José Calil. Rockefeller e o desenvolvimento da agricultura brasileira, INFORMAÇÕES AGRONÔMICAS Nº 88 – December 1999.

INDEX

J

K

L

M

N

O

P

R

Index

www.ingramcontent.com/pod-product-compliance
Lightning Source LLC
LaVergne TN
LVHW101501200926
848483LV00001B/193